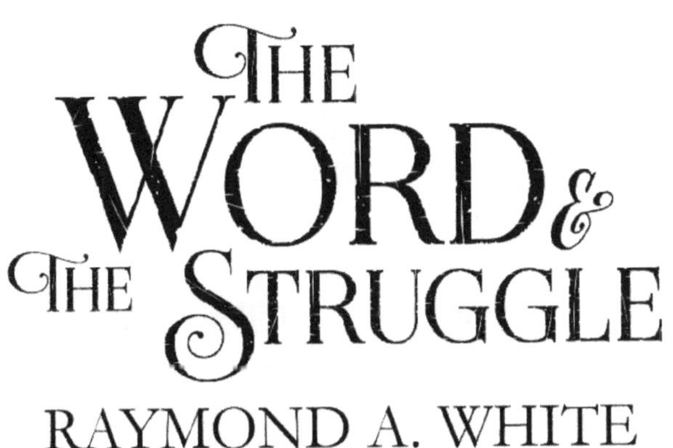

RAYMOND A. WHITE

VOLUME III: THE CHARACTER OF MAN

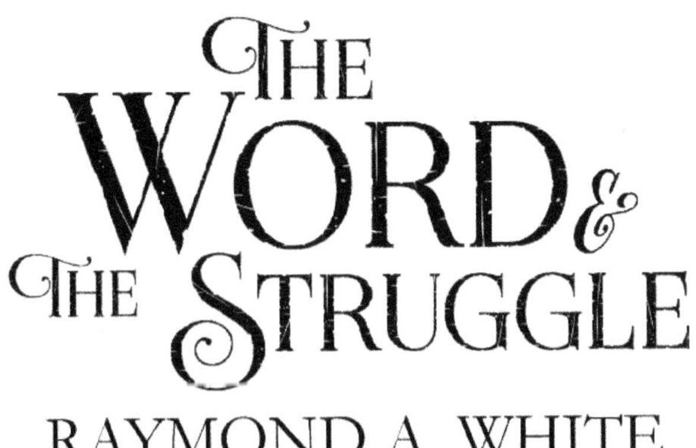

RAYMOND A. WHITE

VOLUME III: THE CHARACTER OF MAN

SKYROCKET PRESS
Santa Clarita, CA

Skyrocket Press
28020 Newbird Drive
Santa Clarita, CA 91350
www.SkyrocketPress.com

Cover design by Emma Michaels & Rebeccacovers
Interior design by Laurisa Reyes

ISBN: 978-1-947394-11-7

Note: Unless otherwise noted, all scriptural references herein are from The King James Version of the Bible (KJV).

Table of Contents

Preface

I am writing this introduction to my father's third volume of essays on Christmas morning 2024. I've read through this collection now several times and am still learning new things with each visit. I think of my dad as a contemporary St. Augustine, both in wisdom and prolificacy. Dad began writing essays about the Bible more than four decades ago and claims I inspired him to do so. Not sure how true that is, but whatever his motivation, I'm so glad he did it.

Dad has always been a deep thinker and not afraid to wrestle with God and other men about his questions. My uncle Cliff reminded me that the name Israel means to wrestle with God. The Old Testament prophet Jacob (whom God named Israel) wrestled physically with the Lord over a desire for a blessing. My father has spent a lifetime wrestling with the Lord over His word.

In my own lifetime, I've come to realize that the majority of people in my church, and possibly all Christians, accept what they are told without question, whether it be about the politics they watch on the news, traditions and assumptions passed down from their parents or culture, or beliefs they've been taught at church. This first became apparent years ago when I wrote political commentaries for several Southern California newspapers and later when I ran a Facebook page. Each election, I'd receive dozens of phone calls and messages from people asking me who they should vote for instead of doing their own research. As years went on, I observed that members of my church often held views that seemed, to me, off the mark, ideas that could be clarified with just a little bit of study beyond the typical "reading the scriptures" we tend to do. How quickly people parrot phrases or ideas they hear in a sermon, as if they had always been their own. I won't spend time here expounding on the specifics of my observations, but I've taken comfort in knowing my parents were not among the sheep, meaning they did not follow politics or religion blindly. They taught me to think for myself, to study and research and come to my own conclusions.

God's word is a complex compilation of letters, history, and documents written by dozens of different men from different eras and cultures and circumstances. These prophets have a lot to say, and not all their messages neatly align with each other. That's what prompted the title of Dad's collection: *The Word and the Struggle.* To really delve into God's word requires one to struggle, or wrestle, with it. Sometimes God's messages to us are conflicting, sometimes critical, sometimes harsh. To trust God means we accept all of it, positive and negative, and that is not always easy to do.

I appreciate how my dad's love of God is not swayed by other people's opinions. He has engaged in countless debates over his lifetime about his views, but he never argues or even defends. He simply lays out the word of God and allows it alone to persuade.

This particular volume of his essays explores God's expectations for all of us, His children. As Christians, what does God want us to do? How does He want us to live? We may not like or agree with everything the Bible has to say on that topic, but it says what it says, and if we profess to be believers, then that means we accept it. Struggle or no struggle.

I hope, as you read, that perhaps Dad's insights will allow you to think outside the box so many of us find ourselves in. Don't worry about what you think you already know. Be open-minded, and you might be surprised by how God speaks to you.

Laurisa White Reyes
December 25, 2024

Abortion and Other Crimes Against Children

Exodus 21:22

Of all moral issues, abortion is the most divisive. People and politics are so polarized that it's hard to imagine how there can be a meeting of the minds to even discuss the issue civilly. I certainly cannot settle the dispute to everyone's satisfaction. No one can, but what I can do and intend to do is to document what the Bible says about the subject so that the Bible's argument becomes compelling.

[1] THE LAW AND KILLING

The Ten Commandments are the foundation of the Torah, much like the Constitution and the Bill of Rights are the foundation of America's legal system.

A particularly important commandment is commandment number 6.

Exodus 20:13 *Thou shalt not kill.*

The commandment seems clear enough, but it invites us to ask, thou shalt not kill *what*? Don't kill animals? No. The Torah demands lots of animal sacrifices. Don't kill murderers? No. The Torah demands executing murderers and other criminals. Don't wage war? No. The Torah is filled with Israel's wars against the Amorites and other nations that offended God.

Then what does "Thou shalt not kill" mean? The Hebrew verb, *ratsach*, which the King James Bible translates to kill, really means murder. The commandment is "Thou shalt not murder," which is how it appears in many other versions, such as the NIV and NASB.

The next question is: What is murder? The Torah helps us answer that by prescribing the death penalty for a list of crimes. Much of that discussion immediately follows in the very next chapter, ***Exodus 21***. Here is an example:

> ***Exodus 21:28*** *If an ox gore a man or a woman, that they die: then the ox shall be surely stoned, and his flesh shall not be eaten; but the owner of the ox shall be quit.* ***:29*** *But if the ox were wont to push with his horn in time past, and it hath been testified to his owner, and he hath not kept him in, but that he hath killed a man or a woman; the ox shall be stoned, and his owner also shall be put to death.*

In other words, if your animal kills someone, that might be a capital crime or it might not. If you knew your animal was dangerous, and you did not restrain it, and it killed someone [a modern comparison might be violent dogs], then that's a capital crime, and you must die. But if the animal's violence is as much a surprise to you as the victim, then it is not a capital crime, and only the animal must die. And so, God distinguishes between what is and is not a capital crime.

[2] The Law and the Unborn

Also in the chapter that immediately follows the Ten Commandments is the critical verse that answers our critical question: What does God think about abortion?

We might first ask ourselves, can the Bible even answer such a question? Since there was no abortion in those days, could the Bible authors have even conceived of the question in order to answer it? Actually, yes, sort of. The question the Torah answers for us is not "What does God think about abortion?" but rather "What does God think about life in the womb, and does God's law protect it?" That question the Bible answers precisely. Here is the text:

> ***Exodus 21:22*** *If men strive, and hurt a woman with child, so that her fruit depart from her, and yet no mischief follow: he shall be surely punished, according as the woman's husband will lay upon him; and he shall pay as the judges determine.* ***:23*** *And if any mischief follow, then thou shalt give life for life.*

So, how important is the life of an unborn child? It is as important as anyone else's. Important enough so that killing an unborn child is a capital crime, punishable by death.

Here is what the verse is about. Two men have a brawl, and a pregnant woman gets dragged into it somehow. As a result, she delivers early because of stress or injury, "her fruit depart from her."

Now, if the mother and the baby are okay, then it's not a big deal. The father can sue the combatants and collect costs, but that's as far as it goes.

But if "any mischief follows" (NIV: "any harm"), then this is a very big deal. A capital crime has occurred, and someone is going to pay with his life.

The word "any" is plural. Therefore, this can only mean if *either* the mother *or* the baby dies. In other words, the unborn baby is a human being whose life deserves to be protected the same as anyone else's. That is one of the law's many duties, to protect the lives of unborn babies. In the American Constitution, Amendment 14 calls this equal protection: "No state shall…deny any person within its jurisdiction the equal protection of the law." So, is a pre-born baby a person? Well, Exodus is defending the pre-born's life with equal protection, so he or she must be a person in the eyes of God.

To be thorough, there is a counterargument against this meaning, which hinges on the Hebrew verb *yasa*, which is translated here as "fruit depart" or "so that her fruit depart from her." The New American Standard Bible (NASB) translates it as "so that she has a miscarriage." If that is correct, that would be a very big deal because the English word miscarriage implies born dead. And if that is true, then a dead baby is not a capital crime, only a dead mother.

But that's not what *yasa* means, and the NASB is wrong. *Yasa* occurs 1,061 times throughout the Old Testament, and it does not mean miscarry. Here's a small sampling:

> ***Genesis 15:4*** *This man shall not be your heir, but one who shall* **come forth from** *your own body.*

> ***Genesis 25:25*** *Now the first* **came forth** *red, all over like a hairy garment, and they named him Esau.* ***:26*** *And afterwards his brother* **came forth** *with his hand holding on to Esau's heel, so his name was called Jacob.*

> ***1 Kings 8:19*** *Nevertheless you shall not build the house, but your son who shall be* **born** *to you, he shall build the house for my name.*

> ***Jeremiah 1:5*** *Before I formed you in the womb I knew you, and before you were* **born** *I consecrated you, I have appointed you a prophet to the nation.*

Since *yasa* is used throughout the Bible to convey birth, it therefore does not mean miscarriage, and the King James "fruit depart" conveys that correct meaning: birth. The context means "born early" or "premature". Therefore, the Hebrew *yasa* does not disclose whether the baby is born alive or dead. For that, we must read the rest of the verse. The words "no mischief" or "any mischief" mean "harm" and are translated harm in other versions (NIV). If there is no harm to the baby or the mother, the father can levy a fine against the combatants, and that's all. But if there is harm to either the baby or the mother, then the penalty is "life for a life"; that is, if either the baby or the mother dies, then a capital crime has occurred, and some combatant will pay with his life. That is the value of an unborn life. It has equal protection under the law.

Now, roll the calendar forward a few thousand years. In America, we kill, on average, a million babies a year in abortion clinics, and our laws do nothing to protect them. In fact, our laws demand that the genocide be permitted. It's on a par with ancient Roman law that permitted throwing Christians to lions or Rome's "patria potestas" laws, which allowed a father to kill his children. But abortion is worse because babies are completely helpless and completely innocent.

So now, answer the question yourself: What does God think of abortion? Well, if God's law kills or executes people who kill unborn babies, in other words, if God considers abortion a capital crime, then you have your answer.

[3] The Unborn In General

For any moral question dealing with life and death, here is the best answer:

> ***Deuteronomy 30:15*** *See, I have set before thee this day life and good, and death and evil.* ***:19*** *I call heaven and earth to record this day against you, that I have set before you life and death, blessing and cursing: therefore* <u>*choose life*</u>*, that both thou and thy seed may live.*

This is excellent advice for anyone considering abortion, or euthanasia, or suicide, or looking for any justification for death. This verse gives excellent philosophy. Choose life, and live. L 'chayim! To Life! We ought not to be surprised that the God of the Bible is pro-life.

How does the Bible view life in the womb? Here's King David's opinion:

> ***Psalms 139:14*** *I will praise thee; for I am fearfully and wonderfully made: marvellous are thy works; and that my soul knoweth right well.* ***:15*** *My substance was not hid from thee, when I was made in secret, and curiously wrought in the lowest parts of the earth.* ***:16*** *Thine eyes did see my substance, yet being unperfect; and in thy book all my members were written, which in continuance were fashioned, when as yet there was none of them.*

David is saying that before God had finished making me in my mother's womb, it was me! In other words, you are you from conception. How then can anyone imagine an unborn baby to be just a "blob of protoplasm" worthy of nothing more than to be flushed down a sink?

So, is life in the womb a baby or not? Not to trivialize it, but if it acts like a duck and quacks like a duck, then it's a duck. Apply that logic to pre-borns, and you'll have the right idea. If she acts like a baby, sucks her thumb like a baby (fetuses do), cries like a baby (fetuses do), and screams in agony when she is cut to pieces (fetuses do that too), then it's a baby, and killing her is murder.

[4] Violence Against Children

Now, about babies in general. Since a baby in the womb is a baby, the broader question is this: Do babies, all babies, deserve to be protected by law? Or are babies non-contributing and therefore non-essential, and therefore dispensable, and therefore disposable?

I want God's opinion. And he has declared his opinion on that issue loud and clear.

Ancient Israel was guilty of many sins, which the Bible carefully documents. The number one sin at the top of that list was their failure to protect babies. Here then is my list of verses that deal with violence against children and God's insistence that we not turn a blind eye to it. Note that the idiom "innocent blood" or "blood of innocents" refers broadly to any innocent person who is murdered, but more specifically, it means children ***(Psalms 106:38)***.

> ***2 Kings 24:3*** *Surely at the commandment of the* LORD *came this upon Judah, to remove them out of his sight, for the sins of Manasseh, according to all that he did.* ***:4*** *And also for the innocent blood that he shed: for he filled Jerusalem with innocent blood; which the* LORD *would not pardon.*

> ***Psalms 106:36*** *And they served their idols: which were a snare unto them.* ***:37*** *Yea, they sacrificed their sons and their daughters unto devils.* ***:38*** *And shed innocent blood, even the blood of their sons and of their daughters, whom they sacrificed unto the idols of Canaan: and the land was polluted with blood.*

> ***Psalms 94:6*** *They slay the widow and the stranger, and murder the fatherless.* That is, they kill orphans.

Proverbs 21:3 *To do justice and judgment is more acceptable to the* L*ORD than sacrifice.* Your justice system is more important than your religion.

Proverbs 24:11 *If thou forbear to deliver them that are drawn unto death and those that are ready to be slain,* **:12** *If thou sayest, Behold, we knew it not; doth not he that pondereth the heart consider it? And he that keepeth thy soul, doth not he know it? And shall not he render to every man according to his works?* "I don't want to get involved" is no excuse. God sees that you are ignoring injustice.

Proverbs 31:8 *Open thy mouth for the dumb in the cause of all such as are appointed to destruction.* Speak out. We pro-lifers could use your help.

Isaiah 1:15 *...when ye make many prayers, I will not hear: your hands are full of blood.* **:21** *How is the faithful city become an harlot! It was full of judgment; righteousness lodged in it; but now murderers.*

Isaiah 26:21 *For, behold, the* L*ORD cometh out of his place to punish the inhabitants of the earth for their iniquity: the earth also shall disclose her blood, and shall no more cover her slain.*

Isaiah 33:14 *The sinners in Zion are afraid...* **:15** *He that...stoppeth his ears from hearing of blood, and shutteth his eyes from seeing evil.* Yes evildoers are guilty, but so are those who permit it.

Isaiah 57:4 *...are ye not children of transgression, a seed of falsehood,* **:5** *Enflaming yourselves with idols under every green tree, slaying the children in the valleys under the clifts of the rocks?*

Isaiah 59:3 *For your hands are defiled with blood, and your fingers with iniquity…* ***:4*** *None calleth for justice, nor any pleadeth for truth…* ***:6*** *…the act of violence is in their hands.* ***:7*** *they make haste to shed innocent blood…*

Jeremiah 2:34 *Also in thy skirts is found the blood of the souls of the poor innocents: I have not found it by secret search, but upon all these.* In other words, you're not even concerned enough to hide your guilt; the blood of innocents is all over your clothes. "Innocent" here has a broad meaning, such as convicting innocent people of crimes they didn't commit. But it could as well mean children. And, since children were being routinely sacrificed by worshippers of Baal and other idols, the "innocent" must include children. After all, who is more innocent than children?

Jeremiah 7:6 *If ye…shed not innocent blood in this place…* ***:7*** *Then will I cause you to dwell in this place.*

Jeremiah 7:31 *And they have built the high places of Tophet, which is in the valley of the son of Hinnom, to <u>burn their sons and their daughters</u> in the fire; which I commanded them not, neither came it into my heart.*

Jeremiah 19:2 *And go forth unto the valley of the son of Hinnom, which is by the entry of the east gate, and proclaim there the words that I shall tell thee.* ***:3*** *…Behold, I will bring evil upon this place…* ***:4*** *Because they have…filled this place with the blood of innocents* ***:5*** *They have built also the high places of Baal, to <u>burn their sons</u> with fire for burnt offerings unto Baal, which I commanded not, nor spake it, neither came it into my mind.* The Hebrew word "Hinnom" became the Greek word "Gehenna" and finally the English word "hell." A fitting etymology for a place where such evil things were done.

Jeremiah 32:35 *And they built the high places of Baal, which are in the valley of the son of Hinnom, to cause their sons and their daughters to pass though the fire unto Molech; which I commanded them not, neither came it into my mind, that they should do this abomination, to cause Judah to sin.*

Ezekiel 7:23 *Make a chain: for the land is full of bloody crimes, and the city is full of violence.*

Ezekiel 8:17 *…Is it a light thing to the house of Judah that they commit the abominations which they commit here? For they have filled the land with violence…*

Ezekiel 9:9 *…the land is full of blood, and…they say…the* LORD *seeth not.*

Ezekiel 11:6 *Ye have multiplied your slain in the city, and ye have filled the streets thereof with the slain.*

Ezekiel 13:19 *And will ye pollute me among my people for handfuls of barley and for pieces of bread, to slay the souls that should not die, and to save the souls alive that should not live, by your lying to my people that hear your lies?*

Ezekiel 16:20 *Moreover thou hast taken thy sons and thy daughters, whom thou hast borne unto me, and these hast thou sacrificed unto them to be devoured. Is this of thy whoredoms a small matter* ***:21*** *That thou hast slain my children, and delivered them to cause them to pass through the fire for them.*

Ezekiel 16:38 *And I will judge thee, as women that break wedlock and shed blood are judged.* Women who have babies they don't want (out of marriage) kill them.

Ezekiel 20:26 *And I polluted them in their own gifts, in that they caused to pass through the fire all that openeth the womb*… They killed all their firstborn with fire.

Ezekiel 20:31 *For when ye offer your gifts, when ye make your sons to pass through the fire, ye pollute yourselves with all your idols…*

Ezekiel 22:2 *…wilt thou judge the bloody city?…* ***:3*** *…The city sheddeth blood in the midst of it…* ***:4*** *Thou art become guilty in thy blood that thou hast shed…*

Ezekiel 23:37 *…and have caused their sons, whom they bare unto me, to pass for them through the fire, to devour them.* ***:39*** *For when they had slain their children to their idols…* ***:45*** *…after the manner of women that shed blood; because they are adulteresses, and blood is in their hands.* The way to get rid of unwanted children is to kill them.

Ezekiel 33:5 *…Ye eat with the blood, and lift up your eyes toward your idols, and shed blood: and shall ye possess the land?*

Hosea 6:8 *Gilead is a city of them that work iniquity and is polluted with blood.* ***:9*** *…so the company of priests murder in the way by consent…* By the consent of priests, by their silence, the innocent are murdered. Here is a Latin phrase for you to ponder: *Qui tacet consentire.* It means: "Silence implies consent."

To you priests, pastors, and clergy who believe your silence keeps you guiltless, that your church shouldn't get involved with politics, and that remaining neutral absolves you of accountability, you who believe your silence will be your defense at the Judgment Day—it is your silence that will condemn you.

Joel 3:19 *Egypt shall be a desolation…because they have shed innocent blood in their land.*

Amos 5:15 *Hate the evil, and love good, and establish judgment* [it's the justice system in view here] ***:18*** *Woe unto you that desire the day of the LORD! To what end is it for you? The day of the LORD is darkness, and not light.* ***:21*** *I hate, I despise your feast days, and I will not smell in your solemn assemblies.* [What good is religion?] ***:24*** *But let judgment run down as waters* [It is a just justice system that I want from you, not religion] ***:26*** *But ye have borne the tabernacle of your Moloch and Chiun…* [Moloch is the god who caused babies to be burned alive. That is why I reject your useless religion.] ***:27*** *Therefore will I cause you to go into captivity beyond Damascus…* [Your religion is done].

Micah 3:10 *They built up Zion with blood…* Churches, are you still ignoring abortion?

Micah 5:14 *And I will pluck up thy groves…* The groves were where the Israelites killed their babies.

Micah 6:7 *…shall I give my firstborn for my transgression, the fruit of my body for the sin of my soul?* Babies pay the ultimate price for the sins of their parents.

My point in all this is that infanticide (murdering children) is not a peripheral moral issue. It is not just one more sin in a long list of sins that angered God. Infanticide was *the* sin that so angered God that he finally had no choice but to destroy the Israelites as a nation and remove them from the land. We see from the repetition that infanticide is *the* core issue — God complains about it over and over. Since it is central to God's grievance, it ought also to be central to ours. But, alas, we focus our moral indignation on so many other issues that violence against children, particularly abortion, gets lost in the shuffle. Too many of us think that drinking coffee is a greater sin than abortion. How can that be?

[5] Hell: A Fitting Etymology

Let's revisit one verse and do some etymology, some word study, to see how much mischief can get tangled up with a single word.

> ***Jeremiah 19:2*** *...go forth unto the valley of the son of Hinnom...they have...filled this place with the blood of innocents* ***:5*** *They have built also the high places of Baal, to* *burn their sons* *with fire for burnt offerings unto Baal...*

Where did most of this horrible stuff happen, this practice of burning children alive? It probably happened all over, but there was one place that history makes special note of, and that place is the Hinnom Valley, which was just outside Jerusalem's wall.

Hinnom was a family name from very ancient times.

> ***Joshua 15:8*** *And the border went up by the valley of the son of Hinnom unto the south side of the Jebusite; the same is Jerusalem: and the border went up to the top of the mountain that lieth before the valley of Hinnom westward, which is at the end of the valley of the giants northward.*

It was just a place, like your local park, until one Jewish king used the place for monstrous evil.

> ***2 Chronicles 28:3*** *Moreover he* [King Ahaz] *burnt incense in the valley of the son of Hinnom, and burnt his children in the fire, after the*

abomination of the heathen whom the L*ORD had cast out before the children of Israel.*

And that evil continued until King Josiah ended it four generations later.

2 Kings 23:10 *And he* [Josiah] *defiled Topeth, which is in the valley of the children of Hinnom, that no man might make his son or his daughter to pass through the fire to Molech.*

But the practice picked up again after Josiah, and for God, that was the last straw.

Jeremiah 19:6 *Therefore, behold the days come, saith the* L*ORD, that this place shall no more be called Topeth, nor the valley of the son of Hinnom, but the valley of Slaughter.*

Judah had three more kings after Josiah, all bad, so the Babylonians swept in and removed the Jews from the land, and thus began their seventy years of captivity, the Diaspora.

When they returned, they had learned their lesson. From that time, the time of Ezra, no Jew would ever again even think of sacrificing a child or any person. It was a lesson bitterly learned.

So, what happened to Hinnom? It was still there — you can't throw away a valley. So, what did they do with the place?

Well, the Hinnom Valley had such an evil history that they did the only thing that seemed fitting: they used it as a land fill, it was their dump site. Over the following centuries, the trash of Jerusalem was hauled out of the city to Hinnom and burned. Since it was a 24/7 operation, on any given night, if they looked in that direction, the people of Jerusalem could see the burning fires of Hinnom.

Then, one day, came a Rabbi of Nazareth named Jesus who preached a sermon on a mountainside. He called them to perfection and gave them some stern warnings. And in that sermon, he drew an image from those constantly burning fires of the Hinnom trash dump. In the Bible, the Hebrew *Hinnom* became the Greek *Gehenna,* which finally became the English *Hell.*

> ***Matthew 5:22*** *whosoever shall say, Thou fool, shall be in danger of hell fire.* [Gr: Gehenna; Heb: Hinnom]

Now you know what the word "hell" means and how it came to mean what it means: that place of continual burning where children once died by the hands of their own parents. So, if you care to imagine a people most fit for "hell," how about people who kill children? It is because of them that the notion of hell exists at all.

Now, there is another word for hell, *Hades*, which has a different meaning. But let's leave that alone and stick with *Gehenna.*

Jesus continued to use this word, *Gehenna* —

> ***Matthew 5:29*** *...whole body should be cast into hell.*
> ***Matthew 10:28*** *...destroy both soul and body in hell.*
> ***Matthew 18:9*** *...rather than ... be cast into hell fire.*
> ***Matthew 23:15*** *ye make him twofold more the child of hell.*
> ***Matthew 23:33*** *how can ye escape the damnation of hell?*
> (Also: ***Mark 9:43,45,47; Luke 12:5; James 3:6***)

I'm not making a case for either a literal or a figurative hell — that's another subject for another time. My point here is that, however evil the sins were that drew Jesus' ire and caused him to threaten them with such a fiery image, the worst sin has to be the one that created the image in the first place. And that sin was, and is, killing babies.

So, for the baby killers out there — yes, pro-choicers, that means you — you're worse than merely *going* to hell, you *created* hell. How will you escape that fate which you yourselves have made?

[6] Church and State

Many believe that religion has no business interfering with law. "Separation of church and state" is the mantra that pro-choicers chant. But let's ask this question: What is the purpose of law? If we dissolved our entire legal system and started over with only one single law, what would that law be? What is the point of law?

I claim (and I hope you will agree) that the first duty of law (God's law, American law, whatever law), and its only duty if it has no other, is to protect innocent people from violent thugs. Surely you must agree with that. Law's first duty then is to enforce "Thou Shalt Not Kill." And that is why our Declaration of Independence insists that among our unalienable rights is our right to "life, liberty, and the pursuit of happiness," the first being "life."

Question: Who should we not kill? Answer: all innocent people, including and especially the most defenseless among us, namely, children, babies, and those not yet born who are as sentient and subject to the horrors of torturous pain as any of the rest of us.

That is the primary duty of civil law. Should abortion then be illegal? Of course!

Are Christian churches then responsible to oppose abortion? Let's review this verse:

Proverbs 21:3 *To do justice and judgment is more acceptable to the LORD than sacrifice.*

This verse is saying that God pays more attention to your justice than to your religion. Too many Christians think it's the other way around, that we should just focus on getting to heaven and let God worry about less spiritual things like injustice.

God is greatly concerned with genocide, and mostly concerned with the genocide of children. I am particularly stressed by churches that are silent about abortion. The pulpit often has much to say about tattoos and dress codes and R-rated movies but little to say about abortion. I applaud Catholics (and I am not a Catholic) and their brave struggle against this butchery. If your church is not part of the fray, you should wonder why and think about Jesus saying:

> ***Matthew 23:24*** *Ye blind guide, which strain at a gnat, and swallow a camel.*

Also, consider this:

> ***1 Peter 4:17*** *For the time is come that judgment must begin at the house of God…*

Do you think you will escape God's judgment because you are in the right church or in the right religion? That is the point that John the Baptist made to the Pharisees and Sadducees —

> ***Matthew 3:9*** *…think not to say within yourselves, we have Abraham to our father: for I say unto you, that God is able of these stones to raise up children unto Abraham.*

In other words, "Think not to say within yourselves, 'I am a Christian so God will spare me.'" You may learn the hard way that you are wrong. God can make Christians (even your kind of Christians) out of rocks, so how special do you think you are? That's John's point. Whatever your religion, holding the truth may be as much to your condemnation as to your salvation.

My advice to you is this: You really ought to do something meaningful towards saving the lives of our innocent babies. They are being sacrificed daily on today's altars of Moloch, the gurneys of Planned Parenthood. What will you do about that? Anything? Or nothing?

As for myself? My starting place is this: I vote straight pro-life. That means that in the voting booth, I ignore all other issues and vote only for those candidates who will defend, as best they can, the lives of the unborn. That's little enough to do, but it's a start. And why would you vote for an abortion advocate anyway? What other issues do you think are more important?

Still don't want to get involved? Just remember that God hears your silence. To review:

> **Proverbs 24:12** *If thou sayest, Behold, we knew it not; doth not he that pondereth the heart consider it? And he that keepeth thy soul, doth not he know it? And shall not he render to every man according to his works?*

> **Proverbs 31:8** *Open thy mouth for the dumb in the cause of all such as are appointed to destruction.*

Now, one final warning to pro-choice Christians who still don't get it:

> **Matthew 18:2** *And Jesus called a little child unto him, and set him in the midst of them,* **:3** *And he said, Verily I say unto you, Except ye be converted, and become as little children, ye shall not enter into the kingdom of heaven.* **:6** *But whoso shall offend one of these little ones which believe in me, it were better for him that a millstone were hanged about his neck, and that he were drowned in the depth of the sea.*

Who is Jesus talking about? He's talking about new Christians because they are like children in the gospel.

But is he also talking about actual children? Well, who is *most* like children? The obvious, tautological answer is children. Children are most like children. A is equal to A. Whoever else is like children, Jesus' parable works only if his words apply first to actual children, the most deserving of heaven and the most protected by God's love. Jesus brought a child into their midst and said, "To get to heaven, be like her." Surely that child herself, the object of the parable, must qualify for heaven.

What's the penalty for "offending" a child? Something worse than being drowned in the sea. I would not want to be on that side of God's judgment.

What is "offending" a child? There are lots of ways to offend a child: beat a child, starve a child, tease a child to tears, sexually abuse a child, basically, harm a child in any way. But in my opinion — and I have shown that God agrees — the number one answer is to kill a child. So, for pro-choice Christians who stand with baby killers, remember that God's gun-sights are on you, and one day you will have to explain to God why you allied yourself against his most precious.

But doesn't a woman have a right to do as she chooses with her own body? We're not arguing about her body, we're arguing about someone else's body, her baby's body. Now, science has not yet given us a means to abort a baby without killing it (gestation in an artificial womb). Maybe one day that will happen. But so far, it's science fiction, so far we can't abort without killing.

[7] Mormon Addendum

While most Mormons are pro-life, a substantial minority are pro-choice. I have no statistics, but I do know some pro-choice

Mormons, which I think is odd in a church that teaches that we are pre-existent.

When my two sons returned home from B.Y.U. (decades ago), they both said that a major problem with dating there is that many of the girls are pro-choice, and my boys, heeding their father's instruction, would have nothing to do with them.

The Mormon church is pro-life (I wish a bit more loudly), and the large majority of its members are pro-life. I do not know what the Bishop's Handbook says, and if I did, I wouldn't quote it to you anyway. But my difficulty is that abortion is so rarely discussed that perhaps pro-choice Mormons think it's no big deal. That is troubling to me and to many pro-life Mormons.

Be that as it may, since the Church is big on free agency and free speech, I will presume on both (free agency and free speech) and move beyond the Biblical argument to Christians generally and will now target a pro-life argument to pro-choice Mormons specifically.

The standard pro-choice argument goes like this: Life in the womb is not life at all but just a blob of protoplasm waiting to become life, and thus it is always open season on fetuses.

Mormons know better, or should, believing as they do that spirits are pre-existent. Since that little fetal body is inhabited by a pre-existent spirit, any talk of a blob of protoplasm is nonsensical. But for pro-choice Mormons who insist that "but maybe the spirit isn't in the fetus yet" and are therefore willing to take that risk with someone else's life, I offer this verse –

> ***Doctrine & Covenants 59:6*** *...Thou shalt not...kill, nor do anything like unto it.*

So, if you're on the fence about whether life in the womb is really a baby or not, "anything like unto it" should cover that ambiguity and move you off the fence.

What is this verse saying? It is saying that (I'm about to repeat myself, please forgive) if it acts like a duck and quacks like a duck, then it's a duck. That's what "like unto" means.

On September 23, 1995, the Church published "The Family: A Proclamation to the World". What does it say regarding abortion? Is it pro-life? I argue that it is.

> ***:11*** *We affirm the sanctity of life...*

How can life be sanctified and disposable at the same time? Is life in the womb life, or is it not life? Well, look at the ultrasounds — dang it! You have eyes. You see the baby that's in there. You see the heart beating, the thumb sucking, and the squirming and the kicking. One would have to be blind or in denial to see that baby and say that's not a baby. If it's not a baby, then what is it? For sure, it is living. But a living what? A living duck!? No. It is a living person, and killing it is murder.

> ***:13*** *Parents have a sacred duty to rear their children in love and righteousness...*

You can't rear a child in love and righteousness if you don't rear the child. Do you see any other possibility? That means that every baby has the right to be born.

> ***:17*** *Children are entitled to birth within the bonds of matrimony...*

If a child is entitled to birth within the bonds of matrimony, then she must first be entitled to birth. Do you see any other possibility?

> ***:24*** *We warn that individuals who violate covenants of chastity, who abuse spouse or offspring…*

I've already written that there are many ways to abuse a child, and the number one worst way is to kill a child. And the word here is "offspring," which necessarily includes pre-borns; whether a fetus is a child or not, it is certainly an "offspring."

> ***:26*** *We call upon responsible citizens and officers of government everywhere to promote those measures designed to maintain and strengthen the family as the fundamental unit of society.*

If a thing is evil (meaning that it harms people, I am not talking about victimless crimes), do we have the right to outlaw it? Like, for instance, slavery. This final verse claims that we do have the right to pass laws to prohibit evil. Abortion kills babies. That is evil by any standard, and promoting measures to prohibit abortion is within the scope of this verse.

I do wish that there were stronger, unarguable pro-life wording in the Proclamation. For instance, ***:11*** could say, *We affirm the sanctity of life from conception…* That would be bold indeed. Perhaps the Church will eventually amend the Proclamation with more concrete wording, or maybe not. In any case, the verses I've quoted are pro-life enough, at least as I read them.

One might argue that the Proclamation is not scripture, at least not yet. I'll respond to that with this verse, which *is* scripture —

> ***Doctrine and Covenants 134:2*** *We believe that no government can exist in peace, except such laws are framed and held inviolate as will secure to each individual the free exercise of conscience, the right and control of property, and the protection of life.* ***:7*** *We believe that rulers, states, and governments have the right and are bound to enact laws for the protection of all citizens …*

Of course, we will haggle over the meaning of life that the government ought to protect. My point is that the verse does not quibble over this life or that life but protects life in general, and that necessarily includes life in the womb, I do believe.

Well, now you know what the Bible says, what the Doctrine and Covenants says, and what the Proclamation says. And you're thinking, "But we believe in living prophets. What do *they* say?" Good question. Here's my list:

"In a paradoxical period when violating the sanctity of human life is heralded as a right and chaos is described as liberty, how blessed are we to live in this latter-day dispensation…" (David A. Bednar, "Watchful unto Prayer Continually" - General Conference November 2019)

"Adultery, promiscuity, out-of-wedlock births, and elective abortions are but some of the bitter fruits that grow out of the ongoing sexual revolution." (D. Todd Christofferson, "Sustainable Societies" - General Conference, November 2020)

"One cause of the diminishing birthrate is the practice of abortion. Worldwide, there are estimated to be more than 40 million abortions per year. Many laws permit or even promote abortion, but to us this is a great evil." (Dallin H. Oaks, "Protect the Children" -General Conference, November 2012)

"...mortal life is sacred to us. Our commitment to God's plan requires us to oppose abortion and euthanasia." (Dallin H. Oaks, "Truth and the Plan" - General conference, November 2018)

"Our Father's plan encourages a husband and wife to bring children into the world and obligates us to speak in defense of the unborn." (Neil Anderson, "The Eye of Faith" - General Conference, May 2019)

"Years ago, feeling deep concern for the number of abortions in the world, President Gordon B. Hinckley addressed the women of the Church with words that are relevant for us today. He said: ... What is happening to our appreciation of the sanctity of human life? Abortion is an evil, stark and real and repugnant, which is sweeping over the earth. I plead with the women of this Church to shun it... If an unanticipated child is expected, let us reach out with love, encouragement, and, when needed, financial help, strengthening a mother in allowing her child to be born." (Neil L. Anderson, "The Personal Journey of a Child of God" - General Conference, May 2021)

One final verse, then I'm done.

Doctrine and Covenants 84:87 *Behold, I send you out to reprove the world of all their unrighteous deeds, and to teach them of a judgment which is to come.*

Anger

Proverbs

Proverbs 12:16 *A fool's wrath is presently known: but a prudent man covereth shame.*

When a fool loses his temper, he is proud of it, maybe he even brags about it. When a wise man loses his temper, he is ashamed of it and wants to conceal it. There is this saying: "A wise man is twice angry, the second time with himself." If you must get angry, at least have the sense to understand how foolish you were and apologize to everyone who was unfortunate to overhear your tirade. A fool doesn't get it.

Proverbs 14:17 *He that is soon angry dealeth foolishly…*

It is not anger per se that God hates, even Jesus got angry, and certainly God gets angry. But it's the quick anger, the short fuse temper, that's generally a bad thing.

Proverbs 14:29 *He that is slow to wrath is of great understanding: but he that is hasty of spirit exalteth folly.*

Again, wrath is justified at times, but it must be slow wrath, thought out to some degree. Before you engage, ask yourself these questions: Is this fight worth picking? Is this the hill you want to die on? It may be, but be sure first.

Proverbs 15:1 *A soft answer turneth away wrath: but grievous words stir up anger.*

The way to start a fight is to say angry words. You can usually avoid a fight with careful words. When angry words are spoken to you, the knee-jerk reaction is to respond in kind, be a mirror, answer anger with anger. But that turns an initial hostility into a full-blown fight. But if you instead answer that initial hostility with calm words (okay, you talk, I'll listen), inquiring words (so I'll understand, what exactly are you angry about?), maybe even confessing words (yes, I used your pliers and forgot to put them back, sorry), usually that will calm the other person down and restore peace.

It's all in the tone. Anything you have to say can be better said in a soft tone. Even things that are deadly serious and laced with rage, like "I want a divorce," can be said civilly. Whatever the issue, however negative, it can be better dealt with without the shouting.

Proverbs 15:17 *Better is a dinner of herbs where love is, than a stalled ox and hatred therewith.*

I love a rich man's prime rib (stalled ox) more than a poor man's diet of broccoli. But if the broccoli is served in a home of love while the beef in a home of anger, I'll take the broccoli.

Proverbs 15:18 *A wrathful man stirreth up strife: but he that is slow to anger appeaseth strife.*

Sometimes, to avoid a fight, you need to just slow down a bit. Just don't act from reflex. Pause. The delay of even a few seconds can often give you control of your temper.

Proverbs 16:32 *He that is slow to anger is better than the mighty; and he that ruleth his spirit than he that taketh a city.*

Anger is not just about families; sometimes it is political. Nations go to war because someone is angry with someone else. If you must go to war, of course, you must win. But isn't it better to avoid the conflict by staying calm and seeing if everyone can be made happy with a compromise?

Proverbs 19:19 *A man of great wrath shall suffer punishment; for if thou deliver him, yet thou must do it again.*

Uncontrolled anger must be met with a negative response of some kind. If it is not, then the anger will be repeated again and again. Uncontrolled anger should not be treated with impunity, otherwise the angry person will become an incorrigible sociopath.

Proverbs 25:28 *He that hath no rule over his own spirit is like a city that is broken down, and without walls.*

This is a man with an uncontrolled temper. But not just a temper, "no rule over his own spirit" refers to any kind of compulsive behavior that he indulges without restraint. Anger is one such behavior to be sure. Promiscuous sexual indulgence is another. Drug addiction, gambling, too much television, too much food, too much sleep, too much whatever — all such uncontrolled behaviors are destructive and are like a city *without walls*; in other words, he has no defense, he is vulnerable to the inevitable consequences.

Proverbs 26:21 *As coals are to burning coals, and wood to fire; so is a contentious man to kindle strife.*

Generally, a fight begins because someone just likes to argue, or, as my dad used to say, someone has a "contrary nature." Or we might say that such a person just has a bad attitude or is always trying to assert control, trying to get others to submit.

Proverbs 29:22 *An angry man stirreth up strife…*

What would be amusing, if it weren't so maddening, is how surprised angry people are when their unrestrained anger causes others to be angry with them. What do they expect to happen? Surrender? Anger causes anger. How do you get that simple idea into the head of perpetual troublemakers? It must eventually dawn on them that *they* are the cause of the incoming anger, and *they* could have prevented it by not being angry in the first place. The anger directed at them is just a reflection of their own anger.

Proverbs 30:33 *Surely the churning of milk bringeth forth butter, and the wringing of the nose bringeth forth blood: so the forcing of wrath bringeth forth strife.*

You think that your verbal shot will be the last word, but it won't be. Instead of being the last word, your angry shot will only escalate the battle. You need to understand that the other person will respond to every verbal abuse, and there will be no *last word.*

Ecclesiastes 3:8 *…a time to hate…*

It's tempting to think that there's never a right time to hate. This verse says otherwise. When is it right to hate? I'm sure that if I had discovered the Auschwitz concentration camp in 1945, I would have hated the Nazis as much as any other Allied soldiers. And I do not feel inclined to forgive Muslim suicide bombers who specialize in blowing up children. I'm just pointing out that there are times when hatred is appropriate.

How about Jesus? Did he ever hate anyone? If not quite hate, he was certainly angry with false religionists who used their privileged position to enrich themselves at everyone else's expense and called that "service to God." That's why Jesus cleansed the temple. And if you think he regretted doing it, then why did he do it twice?

> ***Ecclesiastes 7:9*** *Be not hasty in thy spirit to be angry: for anger resteth in the bosom of fools.*

The advice is not don't ever get angry, but don't get angry quickly or easily. When a person is quick to get angry, it's because anger *resteth in the bosom*, anger is in his or her heart, and such people are fools. A peaceful person, who does not bear anger in the heart, might still get angry, but if so, the anger has been thought out and is justified.

COMPROMISE: WHERE DO YOU DRAW THE LINE?

Daniel 1:1-8

The world asks much of us, and God asks much of us, and the two conflict when the world wants something from us that God insists we cannot give.

Knowing where to draw the line is not always as easy as it sounds. Of course, when God gives a clear commandment, there is a clear line which we must not cross. The problem is that not every situation is a "letter of the law" situation. There are many "spirit of the law" situations where God's word can apply or might not, depending on how much you're willing to infer.

Truth is, you can tie yourself up in knots trying to obey all sorts of "spiritual laws" — (or "higher laws" as I heard a bishop call them who thought God should have forbidden some things in marriage that he didn't). Jesus warned against just such pickiness in our striving for perfection. ***Matthew 23:24*** *Ye blind guides, which strain at the gnat, and swallow a camel.*

There is a saying that gets to the heart of this matter: "Many people feel guilty about things they shouldn't feel guilty about, in order to shut out feelings of guilt about things they should feel guilty about" (Sydney J. Harris). Mr. Harris is exactly right, and that leaves us having to fend for ourselves in many ethically gray areas.

In the opening verses of the book of Daniel, we find an excellent example of ethical haggling to help us set our moral compass. In 605 B.C., certain young men were taken from Jerusalem to Babylon as sort of exchange students, but really they were hostages, an encouragement for the Jews to behave. They were young Jewish scholars sent to learn in Babylon.

> ***Daniel 1:6*** *...among them were...Daniel, Hananiah, Mishael, and Azariah.*

Three things were required of these young men, and so they had some decisions to make.

[1] They Had to Receive a Pagan Education

> ***Daniel 1:4*** *...whom they might teach the learning and the tongue of the Caldeans.*

Secular education does pose risks to Christian children. It does seem that some teachers think their life calling is to destroy the faith of young people. But God nowhere forbids secular education, so Daniel and his friends could say with a clear conscience, "Bring it on. We'll attend your university and learn your ways. Our faith will cope, and we might even learn something."

Where you go to school is your business. God has nothing to say about that, really. If my grandkids ask for recommendations, I'll be happy to give my opinion, and give warnings. But to say "God wants you to go here and not there" is sheer nonsense.

[2] They Had to Receive Pagan Names

> ***Daniel 1:7*** *Unto whom the prince of the eunuchs gave names: for he gave unto Daniel the name of Belteshazzar; and to Hananiah, of Shadrack; and to Mishael, of Meshach; and to Azariah, of Abednego.*

To understand the stakes, we should take a moment to understand the names. Daniel, a Hebrew name, means "God is Judge." His new Babylonian name Belteshazzar meant "Baal provides." Hananiah means "The Lord is gracious." His new name Shadrack refered to the Babylonian god Aku. Mishael means "what the Lord is." His new name Meshack meant "what Aku is." Azariah means "the Lord is my helper." His new name Abednego meant "Nebo's servant." (Nebo was another Babylonian god.)

Now, I might have a hissy-fit if my kids came back from abroad with anti-Christian names, but understand that God doesn't forbid it. Pick this name, pick that name, it doesn't matter, but don't drag God into it creating commandments that God never uttered. Daniel and his friends felt comfortable compromising on this issue.

[3] They Had to Eat Pagan Food

Daniel 1:5 *…the king appointed them a daily provision of the king's meat.* ***:8*** *But Daniel purposed in his heart that he would not defile himself with the portion of the king's meat.*

Now they had a problem. God *had* given the Jews a strict dietary law, and there were certain things, non-kosher things, that kosher Jews were simply not permitted to eat. Daniel knew this, and that's where Daniel and his friends drew the line. To set their dietary law aside would be to set God aside, and that they would not do. That was the end of compromise, and they made their stand.

There are two lessons here, maybe three.

First: There are things we can and should compromise on. Paul found it necessary to sometimes be Jewish and other times be gentile: ***1 Corinthians 9:20*** *Unto the Jews I became as a Jew that I might gain the Jews.* Was this hypocritical, to flip-flop between two cultures?

No. It was being practical, and he was violating no commandment doing it.

Second: There are things we should not compromise on. When God draws a line, that is a line we should stand on. ***1 Timothy 5:22*** *Keep thyself pure.*

And perhaps third: If you really can't tell the difference, well, ask God and see what he thinks.

Confession

1 John 1:9, Psalms 32:3-6

Confession is admitting guilt. Why would someone do that? A confessor might confess because he was caught and had no other choice *but* to confess. But we would not consider that genuine, nor would that move us to consider pleas for leniency. What might move us to leniency would be a sincere confession motivated by true contrition and a burdening sense of guilt. And what would evidence that? Spontaneity and submission.

[1] Sincere Confession

Spontaneity means that it comes from the confessor without prior discovery, without being confronted with the truth; that is, the confessor would have gotten away with it, but personal guilt will not tolerate "getting away with it," and so confession drives its way to the surface.

Submission means accepting consequences and penalties and just judgment without conditions or demands for clemency. This is why prayer (which means plea) is offered with bowed head — a bowed head is simply offering one's neck, just as a dog does to end a lost fight by rolling on its back and offering its jugular. Although a confessor does not demand clemency, the confessor may (or may not) plead for clemency, for unearned mercy.

In some extreme situations, the guilt may be so pressing that the confessor begs for the full penalty to be executed, as was the case of Judas who begged to be arrested.

Matthew 27:3 *Then Judas, which had betrayed him, when he saw that he* [Jesus] *was condemned, repented himself, and brought again the thirty pieces of silver to the chief priests and the elders,* ***:4*** *Saying I have sinned in that I have betrayed the innocent blood. And they said, What is that to us? See thou to it.* ***:5*** *And he cast down the pieces of silver in the temple, and departed, and went and hanged himself.*

"I have shed innocent blood" is a confession to a capital crime and a plea to be arrested and executed. But they wouldn't accommodate that ("What is that to us?") because his confession would implicate them, and they couldn't have that. So, at their suggestion, "See thou to it," Judas executed a just penalty against himself, "and went and hanged himself." That's how completely guilt can overwhelm a person. He did not seek or want forgiveness, he wanted justice against himself because his guilt demanded it.

This invites an interesting question: Was Judas's death an act of suicide or an act of justice rightly executed? And is there a difference? If I were Judas's defense attorney at the final judgment, I'd argue the second — that he did indeed pay for his crime and therefore ought to receive some clemency, although Judas would probably reject it.

It occurred to me years ago that perhaps the best plea for forgiveness is not one that requests acquittal but one that requests no consequences to our victims. After all, every sin has a victim, that's why a sin is a sin. What guilt really demands of us is that we hope that the bad thing we've done turns out to have harmed no one. If that is the case, then acquittal becomes a moot point. So, a best prayer for forgiveness might be, "God, I pray that I have harmed no one," rather than, "God acquit me." The first is directed to others while the second is directed to self.

That is not to say that the second is less valid. I am merely saying that when we pray out of concern for ourselves, should we not as well pray out of concern for others, particularly our victims?

[2] EXAMPLES OF CONFESSION

The Bible has many examples of confession — some sincere and some not — and there is much we can learn from them.

> ***Psalms 31:9*** *Have mercy upon me, O LORD, for I am in trouble: mine eye is consumed with grief, yea, my soul and my belly.* ***:10*** *For my life is spent with grief, and my years with sighing: my strength faileth because of mine iniquity, and my bones are consumed.*

The point is: my problems are my own fault. The writer is not blaming God for his miseries, he is blaming himself, and he is begging God for mercy. Please fix my mistakes.

> ***Psalms 32:3*** *When I kept silence, by bones waxed old through all my roaring all the day long.* ***:5*** *I acknowledge my sin unto thee, and my iniquity have I not hid. I said, I will confess my transgressions unto the LORD; and thou forgavest the iniquity of my sin. Selah.* ***:6*** *For this shall every one that is godly pray unto thee in a time when thou mayest be found…*

This text is David's confession over Uriah and Bathsheba.

One might ask, why did David receive forgiveness when his predecessor, Saul, did not? The answer may be that David felt tremendous guilt, and Saul never did. Saul blamed God while David blamed himself.

Everyone sins. So, what's the difference between a good man and a bad man? A good man knows what sin is, he acknowledges it in himself, and his guilt eats at him until the fear of punishment is dwarfed by the need to be free of the guilt. "I did this, so forgive me or punish me, but I have to get this out." That's the road to forgiveness.

Whenever we're asked to forgive someone, our natural impulse is to wonder if that someone is being sufficiently punished by his or her own guilt. If yes, we're more inclined to forgive. If no, then we're disinclined to forgive. At the very least, we want to see some real sorrow, not sorrow for getting caught, but sorrow for guilt. When someone says, "I'm sorry," we want to know, do they really mean it? If so, then we're inclined to say, "It was nothing, don't worry about it." Well, God feels the same way.

> ***2 Corinthians 7:9*** *Now I rejoice, not that you were made sorry, but that ye sorrowed to repentance: for ye were made sorry after a godly manner, that ye might receive damage by us in nothing.* ***:10*** *For godly sorrow worketh repentance to salvation not to be repented of: but the sorrow of the world worketh death.*

"Sorrow of the world" means sorry for getting caught while "Sorry after a godly manner" means sorrow from guilt, and there is all the difference in the world.

> ***Psalms 38:4*** *For mine iniquities are gone over mine head as an heavy burden they are too heavy for me* ***:18*** *For I will declare mine iniquity; I will be sorry for my sin.*

This author feels that the only way to get out from under the burden of sin is to confess and submit.

[3] Good Men

But now this question: What about really good men? What do they have to confess? For in instance, Isaiah. How did he feel about himself?

Isaiah 6:5 *Then said I, Woe is me!* [Cursed am I] *for I am undone; because I am a man of unclean lips, and I dwell in the midst of a people of unclean lips: for mine eyes have seen the king, the* LORD *of hosts.*

Isaiah 59:12 *For our transgressions are multiplied before thee, and our sins testify against us: for our transgressions are with us; and as for our iniquities, we know them.*

Isaiah 64:5 *…we have sinned…* **:6** *But we are all as an unclean thing, and all our righteousnesses are as filthy rags…*

Isaiah feels guilt because he had stood in the presence of the holy God. It is a shared guilt to be sure, "*our* transgressions," but he does not exclude himself, he does not see himself as more innocent than others. All claims he might have to righteousness are "as filthy rags," so how can he or anyone use any such "righteousness" as a defense?

Jeremiah 14:20 *We acknowledge, O* LORD, *our wickedness, and the iniquity of our fathers: for we have sinned against thee.*

Daniel 9:5 *We have sinned, and have committed iniquity, and have done wickedly, and have rebelled, even by departing from thy precepts and from thy judgments.*

Jeremiah and Daniel shared Isaiah's sentiment, I'm not better than anyone else.

I don't know if this is encouraging (that good men are as bad as we are), or discouraging (if good men are so bad, then what chance do we have?). Take your choice.

Luke 5:8 *Depart from me for I am a sinful man.*

And this is Peter. The message is: Be as good as you can be, that's bad enough.

[4] Regular Confession

Also, we should make a habit of confessing. Apology, for instance, is a form of confession, and we now do it so often that it has become a matter of standard courtesy.

One thing that a habit of confession does for you is it puts the brakes on sin and deters you from committing some great sin that you really don't want to have to confess because it will hurt everyone. Here is a life controlling thought: "Whoa! I'd better not do *that* (even though I want to) because I really don't want to have to confess it." That's a good thought and I think what James had in mind.

James 5:16 *Confess your faults one to another…*

[5] Confess For Forgiveness

And finally, of course, confession puts us on the right path to forgiveness. Confessing to be forgiven is not disingenuous, it is what God wants and expects from us. Confession is an essential part of the repentance process, and God really wants us to repent, and he really wants to forgive.

> ***Ezekiel 33:11*** *I take no pleasure in the death of the wicked.*

> ***1 John 1:9*** *If we confess our sins, he is faithful and just to forgive us our sins and to cleanse us from all unrighteousness.*

Contention

Proverbs

It is nothing new to say that contention makes family life miserable. But what causes contention? If we could solve that riddle, that would save lots of families.

We'll get some insight from the Bible, and most often, we'll find, the root cause of contention is pride.

> ***Proverbs 13:10*** *Only by pride cometh contention: but with the well advised is wisdom.*

What contention is usually about is pride, egos in conflict. If we can ever subjugate the ego, make it less important, or at least satisfy its cravings without subjugating our partners, then the contention will cease.

> ***Proverbs 14:1*** *Every wise woman buildeth her house: but the foolish plucketh it down with her hands.*

Some people, women and men, appear to want to destroy their family because picking fights, bickering and complaining about small matters, seem calculated to do just that. Why any person would want to destroy his or her home, seemingly intentionally, is a mystery. But people do that. It is as though somewhere between sane and insane there is a middle place where sane people suspend their sanity and behave, if not quite insanely, then at least *un*-sanely. They are not insane, not crazy, but for some unfathomable reason (unfathomable even to themselves) they choose, at a moment, to act un-sanely in a nearly insane and self-destructive way.

Now the Bible has some things to say about women and some things to say about men. Abuse can come from either direction or both at once. To be fair, let's read a few verses side by side so we don't pick on a gender.

Women	Men
Proverbs 19:13 *…the contentions of a wife are a continual droppings.*	***Proverbs 26:21*** *As coals are to burning coals, and wood to fire; so is a contentious man to kindle strife.*
Proverbs 21:19 *It is better to dwell in the wilderness, than with a contentious and an angry woman.*	***1 Corinthians 11:16*** *But if a man seem to be contentious…* (wanting to argue about trivialities)

Generally, a fight begins when someone wants to pick a fight. Some men are always ready to "kindle strife." They are flammable, with a short fuse. Or, as my dad used to say, they have a "contrary nature," which just means they are ill-tempered.

Usually, this contrary nature is a pride thing. Some people seem to have a need to assert control over others, to make others submit.

I heard a speaker, a marriage counselor, once say that the root cause of contention very often is "unmet expectations." In other words, what you are getting from the marriage is less than what you think you deserve. But it's not just the feeling of being short-changed but also the feeling of disrespect. If couples can get that under control, then pride dissipates and so will the contention.

Here are four magic words that will defuse most fights before they begin: "**You may be right**." Memorize those words and use them often. They will help.

My overall point is this: You cannot always avoid a disagreement. And some disagreements will erupt into an argument. Avoiding all fights is not a reasonable goal. What *is* a reasonable goal is to fight fairly, kindly. Always be aware that there are words the point of which can injure a soul through an entire life. That is what I call hitting below the belt. Never, ever, hit below the belt or you may regret those words through your entire life. Do not use words as a weapon. Always think, "If I say what I'm thinking, will these words injure this person I love?" If yes, control your temper and say something else, something less attacking.

And never yell. Yelling is high disrespect. Anything you have to say can be better said calmly without the demand, without the disrespect, without the yelling. Avoid the yelling and something good happens: communication. And with good communication, both generally get what they want.

Courage: The Crossroads of Destiny

Esther 4:8-15

Heroism is humanity's most admirable virtue. Jesus said it best.

> ***John 15:13*** *Greater love hath no man than this, that a man lay down his life for his friends.*

History does not long remember people who amass great fortunes, but history long remembers those who do great things for others at great cost to themselves. We call such people heroes. Celebrities are eventually forgotten, but heroes remain in our hearts forever.

There are also near-heroes — people who were well-principled and rightly motivated but who didn't quite muster up. What is the difference between near-heroes and real heroes? In a word, courage. At the crossroad of destiny where we finally meet the real danger, the difference between victory and defeat is courage, the will to do the right thing no matter the cost.

The Bible is a catalog of great heroes, and at the top of that list is Esther.

Esther was the Queen of Persia, wife of King Ahasuerus, and unbeknownst to her husband the king, she was a Jew. One day, she received fearful news from her uncle Mordecai of a plot to kill all the Jews. Mordecai said to her,

> ***Esther 4:8*** *…go in unto the king, to make supplication unto him and to make request…*

Well, that's a simple enough request. Just go ask the king to make it right. But there was a problem. Her uncle's request was simple, but it was not at all safe.

> ***Esther 4:11*** *…whosoever…shall come unto the king into the inner court who is not called, there is one law of his to put him* [or her] *to death, except such to whom the king shall hold out the golden scepter, that he may live: but I have not been called to come in unto the king these thirty days.*

In other words, she could die. The danger was real. Not only did the law allow the king to kill her if she caught him on a bad day and he was in no mood for leniency, but he had also shown no interest in her for a month — he did have a harem. And he had recently made it quite clear how he dealt with disrespectful wives — Vashti was now his ex-queen. And further, he was possibly angry that his army had so far failed to defeat the Greeks. This was not a man to cross.

The danger was real enough, and she knew it, and Mordecai knew it. Mordecai had a decision to make. Should he press her to take this life-threatening action or not? Was the issue worth the risk? It was, and he did.

> ***Esther 4:13*** *…Think not with thyself that thou shalt escape in the king's house, more than all the Jews.* ***:14*** *For if thou altogether holdest thy peace at this time, then shall there enlargement and deliverance arise to the Jews from another place; but thou and thy father's house shall be destroyed: and who knoweth whether thou are come to the kingdom for such a time as this?*

In other words: Esther, if you won't do this because you think you and your family are safe in the palace and this edict won't touch you, you're wrong. This evil will reach in and get you too; you're in the same danger as the rest of us.

So, Mordecai lectures his niece about the real danger she faces. But then he quickly adds a more positive message: Esther, this is your moment. This is your destiny. This is why you're here. God made you queen to save us. He has called you to greatness. Now do it! And she did.

Was she swayed by the treat of genocidal death? It certainly got her attention. But we are often more terrorized by imminent dangers than by distant dangers, so I have to believe that what swayed Esther was an inescapable urge to do the right thing, to protect others even at great personal risk. That, plus the tug of destiny, pushed her into harm's way. Esther accepted the danger, put her neck on the block, and took action.

She needed two things. First, she needed faith. She needed to believe that God would bring her safely though this and that this was not a futile effort. And so she asked —

Esther 4:15 *Fast for me.*

She was not blind to the danger. She knew she could die, and she wanted to curry God's favor with a general fast.

A fast is a show of faith, the natural result of worrisome concern. It is a statement to God: "God, we're really worried down here. So much so that we are in no mood to eat." And when we are so concerned, as Esther was, God does act in our behalf. Esther really believed that, and it was her faith that allowed her to move into danger.

But second, beyond faith, she needed courage. Faith is wonderful and motivating. But she was risking her life to do the right thing, and she knew it. Faith notwithstanding, it could all go wrong. To do this thing, she had to be at peace with the worst possible outcome.

Esther 4:15 *So will I go. And if I perish, I perish.*

There may be braver words spoken in the Bible, but I'm sure I don't know what they are. These words of courage and resignation are on a par with the Lord's words: ***Luke 22:42*** *not my will but thine be done.*

Esther saw at that moment the crossroad of her destiny. This was her moment of resolve when courage said *I will do this, whatever the outcome.* "If I die, I die," so be it, but this thing I must do. *That* is courage.

Notice the beautiful and delicate mix of faith and courage. It is no contradiction to believe that God is in control and also to know that he might not intercede. Logic dictates that faith and courage are mutually exclusive: the more faith, the less need for courage. But that reasoning doesn't help in real life. In real life, we need both. We need faith to get us to the danger and courage to engage it.

Esther did what she could to increase her faith. She asked for a general fast because she sincerely believed it mattered — that God would be influenced by her faith and the faith of the nation. But in the end, it was her courage, "if I die, I die," that got her through that door into the perilous presence of the king. Whatever God decides to do, she reasoned, I will do this thing. That's faith *and* courage, and that careful blend lies at the heart of every great destiny.

Debt

Romans 13:8, Nehemiah 5:3-12

Debt is so pernicious that it's challenging to know where to begin a discussion about debt. It's been said that there are two kinds of debt: good debt and bad debt. From my perspective, there is only one kind of debt and that's bad debt.

Rather than unload a lot of my opinions on you, I'll just turn the discussion over to the Bible and let the good book tell you what it thinks about debt.

[1] National Debt

> ***Deuteronomy 15:6*** *thou shalt lend to many nations but thou shalt not borrow.*
>
> ***Deuteronomy 28:12*** *thou shalt lend unto many nations and thou shalt not borrow.*

A healthy nation can afford to be generous and loan or give to other nations, but God forbids Israel to borrow. Taking that cue, America, our national debt should be zero.

God instructs Israel against debt. Debt not only destroys individuals and families but entire nations as well.

[2] Getting Out of Debt

What's good for the nation is certainly good for individuals. Wherever the Bible talks about debt, it is always bad.

2 Kings 4:7 *Then she came and told the man of God. And he* [Elisha] *said, Go, sell the oil, and pay thy debt, and live thou and thy children of the rest.*

Elisha had given this poor woman a miraculous gift from God, an overabundance of oil. But then what? What should she do with it? Elisha's first advice to her was sell the oil and get out of debt. When you're out of debt, even poverty is manageable, but when you're in debt, nothing is manageable.

[3] Borrowing

2 Kings 6:5 *But as one was felling a beam, the axe head fell into the water: and he cried, and said, Alas, master! For it was borrowed.*

The man's concern was not that he lost an axe head but that he lost a *borrowed* axe head. Integrity demands that we have more concern for other people's things in our charge than for our own.

[4] Savings

2 Chronicles 17:12 *And Jehoshaphat waxed great exceedingly; and he built in Judah castles, and cities of store.*

"Cities of store" means reserve. The nation had more produce than it needed, so the king saved the surplus. Those were good times.

A wise government saves instead of squanders. America is in deep trouble financially because the government is spending us into oblivion with trillion dollar deficits rather than storing wealth.

[5] Corrupt Bankers

Next is a story that you are probably not familiar with, but you should be.

When Nehemiah and thousands of Jews returned to Palestine to reestablish their nation, they all came in good faith, wanting to contribute and rebuild the city, seeking the good life in their own new country, Israel. But something got in the way of that dream.

> ***Nehemiah 5:3*** *Some also there were that said, We have mortgaged our lands, vineyards, and houses, that we may buy corn because of the dearth.* ***:4*** *There were also that said, We have borrowed money for the King's tribute* [borrowed to pay taxes] *and that upon our lands and vineyards.* ***:5*** *Yet now our flesh is as the flesh of our brethren* [they own us] *our children as their children: and, lo, we bring into bondage our sons and our daughters to be servants, and some of our daughters are brought into bondage already: neither is it in our power to redeem them; for other men have our lands and our vinyards.* ***:6*** *And I* [Nehemiah] *was very angry when I heard their cry and these words.* ***:7*** *Then I consulted with myself, and I rebuked the nobles, and the rulers, and said unto them, Ye exact usury, every one of his brother. And I set a great assembly against them.* ***:8*** *And I said unto them, We after our ability have redeemed our brethren the Jews, which were sold unto the heathen; and will ye even sell your brethren? Or shall they be sold unto us? Then held they their peace and found nothing to answer.* ***:9*** *And I said, it is not good what ye do: ought ye not to walk in the fear of our God because of the reproach of the heathen our enemies?* ***:10*** *I likewise, and my brethren, and my servants, might exact of them money and corn: I pray you, let us leave off this usury.* ***:11*** Restore, *I pray you, to them, even this day, their lands, their vineyards, their olive yards, and their houses, also the hundredth part of the money, and of the corn, the wine, and the oil, that ye exact from them.* ***:12*** *Then said they, We will restore them, and will require*

nothing of them; so will we do as thou sayest. Then I called the priests, and took an oath of them, that they should do according to this promise.

Here we have the same old story. It seems that the more things change, the more they stay the same. Banks and governments enrich themselves by burdening the ordinary people with taxes and interest.

Jewish workmen were rebuilding the city, and Jewish farmers were supporting them, just everyday working folk trying their best to contribute their time and energy into rebuilding the city and its wall, and wouldn't you know it, as always, scum-sucking politicians and greedy bankers jumped in and took advantage of the situation and bled the people dry by taking their farms and houses and even selling their children into slavery.

How does that happen? The people can't pay their onerous taxes, so they borrow money from the bankers. But the people can't pay back those loans because of the onerous interest, so the banks foreclose and sell the people into slavery.

So, Nehemiah reads the banks and politicans the riot act. But then when they finally acquiesce, Nehemiah doesn't trust them to keep their word, so he makes them take an oath.

Is this any different than America today? Not a bit. Except we don't allow slavery. Oh really? The banks suck away lifetimes of work, and that's not slavery? We, all of us ordinary people, find that by the time we reach retirement age that we've squandered away maybe 80% of our total life's wealth, stolen from us by the government and by the banking system. And how is that not slavery? I recommend that you Google articles about the Federal Reserve Bank and begin to understand why you're still paying that million dollar mortgage debt for that $300,000 house you bought thirty years ago, and why your lifetime of earnings has been sucked away by bank usury.

Here's the short version of how this sucker's game works. You want to buy a house. The accommodating banks loan you money, fiat money which doesn't exist until it is conjured into existence by the Federal Reserve System. So now you can gratefully buy your house and owe your soul to the bank.

But wait a minute. Why did you have to borrow the money? Because houses are so expensive. Why are they so expensive? Why indeed. Because the ever-increasing supply of fiat money that the Federal Reserve System creates out of nothing continually drives up the price of everything. It's called inflation, folks. Whatever the government subsidies, its price goes up. Like heath care. Want to know why the cost of health care keeps going up? Because the government keeps subsidizing it. Real estate behaves just like that.

The upshot is that what you should have been able to buy without debt or low debt, you cannot buy without incurring massive, lifelong debt simply because the banks and government finance it. And they get away with this crime because the money doesn't really exist except as they create it on the fly. And you, poor mortgagee, now owe the bank a lifetime of your work which has been stolen from you by a corrupt bank system. And we don't call that slavery? Why not? Oh, because we have a 13th amendment that says there's no slavery. I see.

All that from Nehemiah? Yes, because that's what our government and our Federal Reserve banking system have been doing to us, robbing us of our wealth.

Psalms 15:1 *LORD, who shall abide in thy tabernacle? who shall abide in thy holy hill?* ***:2*** *He that walketh uprightly, and worketh righteousness…* ***:5*** *He that putteth not out his money to usury.*

Righteous people don't loan with interest. Well, that would be extreme wouldn't it? That would shut down half (or all) the world's commerce. Or would it?

There is something reasonable in this. Why *should* the world's economy be centered around debt, and more to the point, unlimited debt? Debt is unlimited because the currency is unlimited. Increasing currency inflates prices, which increases the velocity of money, which inflates prices even more to where everyone owes money for things purchased at prices higher than their true value.

Banks get rich at everyone else's expense. My own opinion? The world would be better off without banks! Well, I don't mean banks in general, I mean the Federal Reserve banking system. Why should governments and their central banks control economies with their fiat money? That's the fox watching the henhouse. Governments and the FED rob the people blind with taxes and inflation and interest, constantly sucking our GNP into their rat hole spending programs. *We*, the people, create wealth. The government and the FED suck away our wealth with inflation, and they get away with it because they control the currency.

And the president who caused it to happen, Woodrow Wilson, knew it. After the damage was done, he said, "I am a most unhappy man. I have unwittingly ruined my country. A great industrial nation is controlled by its system of credit. Our system of credit is concentrated. The growth of the nation, therefore, and all our activities are in the hands of a few men. We have come to be one of the worst ruled, one of the most completely controlled and dominated governments in the civilized world. No longer a government by free opinion, no longer a government by conviction and the vote of the majority, but a government by the opinion and duress of a small group of dominant men."

Did I get all that out of this one little verse? Actually, yes. All that verse says is, debt is bad. Well, if debt is bad (and it is), then why is our entire economy based on debt? There's only one reason that I can think of: to enrich the banks and the government at the expense of the people. America operates under the notion that the American economy *needs* the Federal Reserve banking system, and that is the big lie. The American economy and American families would do just fine and would be far better off if the FED and its parasite system would just go away.

Thomas Jefferson knew it from the beginning. In 1802 he said, "I believe that banking institutions are more dangerous to our liberties than standing armies. If the American people ever allow private banks to control the issue of their currency, first by inflation, then by deflation, the banks and corporations that will grow up around the banks will deprive the people of all property until their children wake-up homeless on the continent their fathers conquered."

Jefferson was exactly right, and that is exactly what has happened.

What might we do that might actually help? My suggestion: Fire the damned FED and default on the trillions of dollars that the American government and the American people owe to the FED. Almost half (40%) the national debt is owed to the FED. Defaulting on the FED would immediately free up trillions of dollars with the stroke of a pen, money that would fund Social Security, Medicare, and the interest on the national debt. That would give our bond holders (like China for instance) a warm fuzzy feeling that we maybe can manage our financial affairs after all.

But who would print our currency? The U.S. Treasury of course. And they would do so without charging interest — it is after all their job; we pay them to do that with our taxes.

We really should return to the gold standard. That's a harder sell, but it should be done. The point of a gold standard is to prevent the government from robbing us by inflation.

Now here are some outrageous ideas that you haven't heard of. The U.S. Treasury should become a fourth branch of government, not beholden to Congress, with the same veto authority as the Supreme Court. The Supreme Court vetoes laws it determines to be unconstitutional. Fair enough. The Treasury should veto laws that are fiscally unsound; that is, Congress and the President should be forced — and I do mean *forced* with full arresting police powers — to balance each and every budget. Government should not be allowed to overspend, borrow, inflate, co-mingle, or levy taxes without demonstrating reciprocating value. Government must be held fiscally accountable with full disclosure, just as corporations are. The American voters must not be allowed to vote the nation into bankruptcy. And candidates must be *required* to explain how they intend to pay for each campaign promise without overspending the budget, and if they are lying, it is the Treasury's duty to expose such campaign lies. In short, the Treasury's duty should be to maintain a sound economy and to do so without scamming wealth away from the American people.

[5] DEFAULTING

Psalms 37:21 *The wicked borroweth, and payeth not again: but the righteous sheweth mercy, and giveth.*

Being a deadbeat is no different than being a crook. Borrowing and not repaying is just a clever way of stealing. How about borrowing then repaying with devalued dollars? Our government does that all the time. Inflation is a thief that robs us all.

[6] LENDING

Psalms 112:5 *A good man sheweth favour, and lendeth…*

It's tempting to just never lend. As Benjamin Franklin said, "Neither borrower nor lender be." But that overlooks the fact that sometimes poor people get desperate and have no choice but to ask you for a loan. To refuse is unkind. However, when you've loaned to a desperate person, don't demand it back. Doesn't that make it a gift? Well, maybe. It depends on what the desperate person is able or not able to do. There is the parable of the forgiven servant, ***Matthew 18:24-27***. The story goes awry, but ignoring the sad ending, that the master was willing to forgive the debt at all is its own message.

I said above that we'd be better off without banks, now I've retracted it. It's not banks per se that are evil, it is the Federal Banking system where banks loan money that doesn't exist, thus earning interest from nothing, essentially an infinite yield and inflating the economy so that no one can buy what they need without incurring debt. That's theft and that's evil. What banks should do is loan money *that they have*. There are times when people need to borrow, but those should be exceptional circumstances like building a business, and banks should accommodate that. Our problem is that we borrow in *normal* circumstances to constantly keep pace with a FED-induced inflation. Get rid of that, and borrowing and lending can do what it's supposed to do: finance rare ventures.

[7] Surety

> **Proverbs 6:1** *My son, if thou be surety for thy friend, if thou hast stricken thy hand with a stranger* **:2** *Thou art snared with the words of thy mouth.*

> **Proverbs 11:15** *He that is surety for a stranger shall smart for it: and he that hateth suretiship is sure.*

Proverbs 17:18 *A man void of understanding striketh hands, and becometh surety in the presence of his friend.*

Proverbs 22:26 *Be not thou one of them that strike hands, or of them that are sureties for debts.*

It's foolish to get into debt, but to incur someone else's debt, that's even more foolish. Contracts of debt are traps, and especially of other people's debts.

Don't co-sign another's debt. That "friend" of yours will leave you hung out to dry. You'll see how much of a friend he really was when he leaves you on the hook for his debt. Well, sometimes it's worth the price to be rid of such a "friend."

[8] Laziness

Proverbs 12:24 *...the slothful shall be under tribute.*

Lazy people find themselves hopelessly in debt. Not just because they won't work to pay off their debts, but because laziness breeds expensive tastes. When you're not working, you spend excessively.

[9] Rich and Poor

Proverbs 22:7 *The rich ruleth over the poor, and the borrower is servant to the lender.*

Debt abdicates freedom. When you borrow, you make yourself a slave. Debt is like a ball and chain. The more debt you have, the less choices you have.

[10] Debt Free

> ***Romans 13:8*** *Owe no man any thing…*

There's no simpler way to say it, "owe no man anything," live debt free.

> ***1 Corinthians 7:23*** *Ye are bought with a price; be not ye the servants of men.*

Whatever else this verse means, it certainly means don't borrow. Debt makes you a slave to someone else.

[11] Final Advice

I know that many people get rich from so-called "good debt." People like Donald Trump make billions from the leverage of borrowed money invested into big real estate. But I know other people who had millions and lost it all, including profitable businesses, because leverage is a two-edged sword that can tear you apart when things go bad. I've known several millionaires (three off the top of my head), personal friends who lost everything because of heavy debt at exactly the wrong time.

My advice is this: Yes, leverage gives you an advantage, but that increased advantage is balanced by increased risk. And a wise part of investing is knowing when to take money off the table, pare down your risk, and retire debt. Yes, you might enjoy a bigger, nicer house by submitting to a bigger mortgage. But what if you lose your job next year? Isn't it better if you're not teetering on that "what if" precipice?

Debt is like Jesus' second temptation: It's easy to convince yourself that if you jump off the pinnacle that God will catch you. Well, he might, or he might not.

Debt is also like crossing a river one stone at a time. You could jump from stone to stone, even skipping some stones to speed your crossing. That might make sense if a bear is after you. But ordinarily, securing each step before you commit to it makes more sense. It is more comforting, though slower, to make sure that your next step is secure on the next stone before you remove your previous step from the previous stone. You could maybe run across, but chances are you'll fall in the river and get drenched.

When you pay off a debt before moving ahead, you eliminate just one more potential for disaster. And that's a good thing.

Here's a saying to appropriately end this subject: "The man who seeks to be rich in a day will be hung in a year" (Leonardo Da Vinci). Leonardo may have had in mind horse thieves and bank robbers, but I think he could just as well have had in mind America's debt-ridden society.

Distractions

1 Kings 20:39-42

Sometimes the task at hand is not so important, like reading a novel. Sometimes the task at hand is very important, like reading a novel for a term project. Whatever the task, distractions can scuttle our best intended efforts to get important things done and on time.

Distractions can be sneaky. Sometimes we don't even know we're being distracted. And they can be deadly. For instance, talking on a cell phone while driving can get you killed.

[1] The Distracted Soldier

Here is a Bible example of a person who fell into just that sort of trap. Fate caught him talking on his cell while driving (ancient version of course) and it got him killed.

> ***1 Kings 20:39*** *And as the king passed by, he cried unto the king: and he said, Thy servant went out into the midst of the battle; and, behold, a man turned aside, and brought a man unto me, and said, Keep this man: if by any means he be missing, then shall thy life be for his life, or else thou shalt pay a talent of silver.* ***:40*** *And as thy servant was busy here and there, he was gone. And the king of Israel said unto him, So shall thy judgment be; thyself hast decided it.* ***:42*** *And he said unto him, Thus saith the LORD, Because thou hast let go out of thy hand a man whom I appointed to utter destruction, therefore thy life shall go for his life, and thy people for his people.*

This was a good soldier who had risked his life in combat. Now he had one small task: keep a prisoner. Easy. But he failed. While he was distracted, "busy here and there," his prisoner escaped. And the penalty? He paid with his life. A high price for being "busy here and there."

What could that soldier possibly have been doing that was so important to keep him "busy here and there" and let his charge escape, and die for the mistake? I can't imagine.

[2] Your Distractions

What keeps you busy? Television so you can't study? Bowling so you can't be with your family? Computer Solitaire so that you can't write that novel you've been promising yourself you'd write? Recreation is a fine thing, but not when you have something really important to do.

"I'll have time" is the usual justification for goofing off when there is important work to be done. Deadlines, exams, and interviews are missed by leaving them to the last minute. People could go to an interview an hour early but instead suppose that five minutes is sufficient. And it might be, except for that flat tire. And now the missed job interview is somehow the tire's fault.

The amount of attention and preparation you apply to a task must be proportional to the importance of the task. If tomorrow's exam is *really* important, couldn't you have left the television off? And why would you need someone else to tell you, "Shouldn't you be studying?"

I'm sure that dead soldier in the above story would like to have had a do-over. Sorry, life doesn't give do-overs. Do you have a task that is so important that maybe your life depends on it? Then why wouldn't you drop everything else and do just that and nothing else?

Some tasks deserve our 100% attention, like holding onto an important prisoner with a sword at his throat.

Doubt

John 14:2-6

"There lies more faith in honest doubt, believe me, than in half the creeds." — Alfred Tennyson

John 20:27 *Be not faithless but believing*, said Jesus to Thomas. Good advice, and a reasonable commandment.

But faith is a gift, isn't it? (***1 Corinthians 12:8*** *For to one is given…* ***:9*** *…faith…*). So, what if you don't have as much of it as you'd like? If doubts and questions haunt you, does that mean that you are less of a Christian? Maybe you should not ask so many questions but just follow blindly. Some say that. But that can't be right, can it? The purpose of a question is not to get *an* answer but to get the *right* answer. That's where doubt comes in. If it were only about believing, we could just as well worship a rock. There are people who worship rocks. Why don't we worship rocks? Because of doubt, and that's a good thing.

Yes, doubt can keep you from the truth, but it can also keep you from error. There is much to be said for honest doubt. There is one thing worse than unanswered questions, and that is unquestioned answers. When Jesus said, *be believing*, he didn't mean believe any old nonsense that comes along. He meant, "Thomas, believe *this*: that I have risen from the dead." He spoke directly to Thomas because Thomas was having doubts.

How did Jesus deal with doubters? It's important to notice that there were two kinds of doubters: cynical doubters and seeking doubters. Cynical doubters he rejected, ***Matthew 12:39*** *…an evil and* *adulterous generation seeketh after a sign…* They weren't looking for the truth, they were looking for reasons to confirm their rejection.

But that's not all doubters. There are doubters who are truly seeking the truth, seeking doubters, and Jesus did not deal with them harshly. For instance, ***Mark 9:24*** *Lord, I believe; help thou mine unbelief.* This father of a demon-possessed child had a mixture of belief and doubt. Jesus did not penalize him for his doubt, did not say, "Sorry, you're doubting, so I can't help you." What Jesus did was cast out the demon.

The quintessential doubter was Thomas. ***John 20:25*** *Except I shall see…I will not believe.* This was not an altogether unreasonable thing for him to say; after all, everyone else *had* seen. And if you think he should be chided for being short on faith, at least acknowledge that Thomas was long on love: ***John 11:16*** *…Let us also go, that we may die with him.* And he meant it. He believed that if they returned to Jerusalem they would die, but he went anyway

How did Jesus respond to Thomas's doubt? Jesus didn't say, "Thomas, get your attitude right and believe." No, not at all. He said, ***John 20:27*** *…Reach hither thy finger, and behold my hands; and reach hither thy hand, and thrust it into my side: and be not faithless, but believing.*

The idea that Jesus recoiled from doubt is simply not true. He responds to honest doubt, and he answers honest questions. But cynical doubters Jesus had little time for.

It is a true saying that "Stupid questions are better than stupid mistakes." Do you recall when you were a kid in elementary school, and the teacher said something that no one understood? And you weren't brave enough to ask for an explanation, and neither was anyone else? Until, that is, one brave kid raised his hand and said, "Teacher, I don't understand. Will you please explain that again?" Everyone snickered. But the teacher elaborated, and everyone learned, and everyone was grateful to the brave kid who raised his hand and asked the question that everyone was thinking.

That kid was Thomas, doubting Thomas, who questioned everything, and got answers. At the Last Supper, Jesus announced that he was leaving.

> ***John 14:2*** *In my Father's house are many mansions: if it were not so, I would have told you. I go to prepare a place for you.* ***:4*** *And whither I go ye know, and the way ye know.*

He explained that he was going to die, but that was okay because he was going to God and would prepare a place there for them. And don't worry, he added, you'll know how to get there. Then Thomas raised his hand and asked a question.

> ***John 14:5*** *Thomas saith unto him, Lord, we know not whither thou goest; and how can we know the way?*

"No, Jesus," he questions, "we *don't* know the way. What are you talking about?" His question, instead of drawing a rebuke from Jesus, drew an answer, a very important answer.

> ***John 14:6*** *Jesus saith unto him, I am the way, the truth, and the life: no man cometh unto the Father, but by me.*

It's impossible to overstate the majesty and power of these few words. If they had been omitted from the New Testament, we would have lost a lot. "Thomas, you *do* know the way. You know me, and *I* am the way. You don't need a map or a compass or a GPS to get you there; you have me, your personal guide. Trust me. I'll get you there. And not only am I the way, I am the truth that you need to know, and I am the life that you need to have."

Wow! Thank you Thomas for your doubt and for bravely asking the question. Now we all know the answer.

A Good Dream

Genesis 37-50

Proverbs 29:18 *Where there is no vision, the people perish.*

Joseph was a man of vision. It wasn't his doing, he didn't create his dreams, they weren't goals that he wrote on sticky notes and posted on the refrigerator. God gave him his dreams. But Joseph paid attention, believed them, and his dreams were the heart and soul of his life.

His brothers didn't like him much. Truth be told, Joseph was a tattle-tale.

Genesis 37:2 *...and Joseph brought unto his father their evil report.*

Plus the fact that dad liked him best.

Genesis 37:3 *Now Israel loved Joseph more than all his children...*

Plus the fact that Joseph liked to brag.

Genesis 37:5 *And Joseph dreamed a dream, and he told it his brethren...* ***:6*** *And he said unto them, Hear, I pray you, this dream which I have dreamed.* ***:9*** *And he dreamed yet another dream, and told it his brethren, and said, Behold, I have dreamed a dream more; and, behold, the sun and the moon and the eleven stars made obeisance to me.*

All of that made his brothers hate him, really hate him, enough to kill him. But their collective conscience wouldn't go that far, so they sold him as a slave bound for Egypt.

But Joseph's dreams were wonderful dreams. We should all have such dreams.

The problem with his dreams, though, is that God neglected to mention slavery and prison and a broken-hearted father. If Joseph had seen all that, he might have shut up about his dreams. God skipped the bad parts, the nightmares, and showed Joseph only the good parts. God looked at this young, spoiled kid who had an attitude, and God gave him a good dream.

You should focus on your dream, the vision for life that God gives you. It will get you through the tough times. So often God gives people a dream for their life, and they think, "Great. I'll do that." But then stuff happens that they think is too hard, like studying to get through college or staying virtuous so that they can have a marriage that actually works. It's sad when people wimp out and kill their own dream because of weakness before their dream even has a chance to breathe.

Joseph didn't wimp out. He could have. He could have given in to Potiphar's wife, had sex with her, and lived a lie. He could have kept his job as number two man in Potiphar's house. Of course, he would have remained a slave, and he would have been a liar, an adulterer, and a betrayer of his friend. He would have missed out on his dream entirely and been much less than the man God intended him to be.

But Joseph chose the better way. He chose integrity, purity, and, unfortunately, prison.

Why did Joseph do that? How could he fulfill his dream in prison? That wasn't Joseph's concern. Prison or not prison, he had to do what was right.

Jude 11 *Keep yourselves in the love of God.*

That was Joseph's concern, to remain in God's love no matter what. Obey. God will handle the dream.

Then finally, many years later, Joseph's dream was realized. He was second in command over Egypt, he saved Egypt from mass starvation due to famine, and he even saved his own family, those brothers who had sold him into slavery.

Later, when their father Jacob died, Joseph's brothers feared that Joseph would finally take his revenge on them. Nothing could have been further from his mind. Instead, reflecting back on all that had happened, he said this to them –

Genesis 50:20 *But as for you, ye thought evil against me, but God meant it unto good.*

Now that's a good attitude. Trust God, believe the dream that he gives you, and if you live for it and live right, your dream will happen, that or something better.

Romans 8:28 *all things work together for the good to them that love God.*

Employer/Employee Relationships

Ephesians 6:5, Proverbs 27:18

We explore the Bible to learn how to have a right relationship with God, and also our family, and even our neighbors, whoever they might be. But we seldom turn to the Bible for advice on how to have a right relationship with our employer or our employees.

Since so much of our happiness in this life depends on our livelihood (and it's foolish to think otherwise), then we probably should want to see if the Bible has anything to say about work relationships. I've heard the sentiment often enough: "On your deathbed, will you wonder if you spent enough time at the office or with your family?" While I certainly understand and agree with that point, I do wonder if we take it a bit too far, to the point where we think that job and career really don't matter. I think what's really the issue here is that we sometimes use our spirituality (so-called) as an excuse for laziness.

I once heard a pastor say, "Some Christians have their head so much in heaven that they are no earthly good." Taking that as a cue, I'll share some of what the Bible has to say about employment and see if the Bible requires us to be some earthly good after all.

> ***Deuteronomy 22:8*** *When thou buildest a new house, then thou shalt make a battlement for thy roof, that thou bring not blood upon thy house, if any man fall from thence.*

This verse insists that when you are building a new house, that you provide the proper "battlement" (NIV: "parapet", NLT: "railing") around the flat roof so that people don't fall off. If you don't provide such safety, and someone does fall off and dies, then you are judged a murderer because you didn't provide obvious precautions.

In a broader sense, this verse demands common sense and a concern for other people's safety. It doesn't take much to be observant and eliminate obvious hazards by providing railings around roofs, fences around pools, safety sockets for children, and so forth.

There is good reason for OSHA to exist. Employers really are responsible for maintaining a safe work environment for their employees. In the nineteenth century, one of the most dangerous places for a woman to work was in a sewing shop. The inner moving parts of sewing machines were exposed (to save on costs) and women routinely injured their hands. This was so common that you could commonly tell a seamstress by her mangled hands. Finally, common sense and unions prevailed, and employers began providing their factories with covered machines.

Employers, particularly Christian employers, should be mindful of safety issues about the work environment. This is not so much an issue today because of OSHA, and our courts, and our unions demand it. And that's really a good thing.

> ***Job 31:13*** *If I did despise the cause of my manservant or of my maidservant, when they contend with me* ***:14*** *What then shall I do when God riseth up? And when he visiteth, what shall I answer him?* ***:15*** *Did not he that made me in the womb make him? And did not one fashion us in the womb?*

If you are treating your employee unfairly and he has cause to grumble and you are not even listening to his grievance, God will hear him and take his side. After all, God made him as well as you.

This brings to mind the Dickens' classic *A Christmas Story* where Scrooge was so stingy that he wouldn't even burn a fire in the fireplace to keep his bookkeeper warm as he worked, much less provide medical help for his son Tim.

Psalms 101:6 *...he that walketh in a perfect way, he shall serve me.*

You can always teach a new employee the trade, but you cannot teach him integrity. Therefore, when you're hiring, look for integrity first and ability second. For those who are seeking a job, that's a good thing to remember. Above all else, what your prospective employer is looking for is honesty. And if you steal from your boss, or his customers, you needn't be surprised when you get fired.

Proverbs 27:18 *Whoso keepeth the fig tree shall eat the fruit thereof: so he that waiteth on his master shall be honoured.*

Your job is your livelihood. Treat it well, and it will treat you well. If you treat your job with a lack of enthusiasm, don't be surprised when you don't get a raise, don't get promoted, and maybe get fired.

There's a story of two friends who got jobs at the railroad. One was repeatedly promoted until he became the president of the company, the other was never promoted. When asked why the disparity, the lowly employee answered, "I recon it's because I worked for $2 an hour, and he worked for the railroad."

Ecclesiastes 10:20 *Curse not the king, no not in thy thought; and curse not the rich in thy bedchamber: for a bird of the air shall carry the voice, and that which hath wings shall tell the matter.*

This is about loyalty. This is not ethical advice so much as it is practical advice. It's not advice to kiss-up, but it is advice to be loyal. Be loyal to your boss. I'd fire any disloyal employee, wouldn't you? So, why would you bad-mouth the person who signs your paycheck? Doesn't make sense, and it is rightfully risky.

The movie *Transformers* starred Megan Fox. She was also in *Transformers II.* She was not in *Transformers III.* She was fired. Why? Because in an interview, she compared her director Michael Bay to Hitler. When Bay's boss, Stephen Spielberg, heard of it, he had her fired. Well, duh!

Not long ago, a story hit the news of a Coca Cola delivery driver who was fired because he was seen purchasing and drinking a Pepsi from a vending machine. Again, duh! Maybe after being fired from Coke, he sought a job at Pepsi. I doubt that Pepsi would have him.

The point is simple. If you don't appreciate your employer enough to be loyal, why should your employer appreciate you enough to keep you?

> ***Jeremiah 22:13*** *woe unto him that buildeth his house by unrighteousness, and his chambers by wrong; that useth his neighbour's service without wages, and giveth him not for his work.*

There are some people who are always trying to get something for nothing, trying to trick workers into giving them labor and not paying them fairly or paying them at all. Employers have options about many things, like for instance, whether or not to provide health insurance. But there are no options about wages. Minimum wage laws and overtime requirements are mandated by law, and should be.

> ***Malachi 3:5*** *...I will be a swift witness against...those that oppress the hireling in his wages...*

We're living in better times when employees are protected by law against many different kinds of abuse. In times past, an employee (a farm hand for instance) might work four days, get sick, and not be able to show up on Friday, then get fired for his absence. That was abusive enough. But it often would happen that the employer wouldn't pay the sacked employee for the four days he *did* work because he didn't finish the week. That is criminal and an example of "oppressing the hireling in his wages."

> ***Ephesians 6:5*** *Servants, be obedient to them that are your masters…*
> ***:9*** *And ye masters, do the same things unto them, forbearing threatening…*

Here are two rules: #1: The boss is always right. #2: If the boss is wrong, see rule number #1. I heard it said this way: On the job, you have one duty and only one duty. And that is to help your boss do his or her job. That's why you were hired.

And bosses, you have a balancing responsibility to manage a non-hostile work environment. Truth is, your people work better when they are not constantly harassed, so peace is not merely ethical, it is practical; that is, if you are trying to get real work done, keep your employees happy.

> ***Colossians 3:22*** *Servants, obey in all things your masters according to the flesh; not with eyeservice, menpleasers; but in singleness of heart, fearing God.*

Again the advice is that employees do as their employers instruct. But the advice reaches a bit deeper — employees are not to pretend to be doing their job when they really are not, to look like ("eyeservice") they are working when they are not, to curry favor with flattery ("menpleasers", kiss-ups) while doing little actual work.

Colossians 4:1 *Masters, give unto your servants that which is just and equal; knowing that ye also have a Master in heaven.*

Fair pay for fair work. God has blessed you with your business, you should bless your employees in like manner.

1 Timothy 6:1 *Let as many servants as are under the yoke count their own masters worthy of all honour, that the name of God and his doctrine be not blasphemed.*

Employees should appreciate that they have a job at all and appreciate their boss for providing it. Simple gratitude and loyalty and honor not only will keep you employed, but it reflects well on your Christianity. If you dishonor your boss, he may well question your religion. If you can't be respectful to your employer on whom your livelihood depends, you are probably not respectful of anyone else either, and isn't that what Christianity is about? That's a fair question. When you dishonor your boss, that causes him to dishonor your God.

When you honor your boss, we normally take that as treating him with the respect he deserves. But it may mean something else too. It may also mean that when you do your job well, that reflects well on your boss, and he gets credit and honor from other people (*his* boss) because of your fine job. In that sense, honoring your boss means creating honor for him.

Fasting

Isaiah 5:1-9, Zechariah 7:1-10

Food is a gift from God. ***(Genesis 1:30)*** *I have given every green herb for meat.* And it's a good gift. How do we know? Because God made flavors. He could have made everything taste like, well, grass, I suppose. But instead, he made eating pleasurable.

Well, if food is so good, then why should we ever fast? Why not just eat, eat, eat? If some is good, more is better. Right? Wrong! Excess makes good things bad. Money is good ***(Deuteronomy 8:18)***. A wife is good ***(Proverbs 18:22)***. But too much money and too many wives (ask Solomon) is a bad thing ***(Deuteronomy 18:18)***. Food is like that. Moderation is good, gluttony is bad.

But beyond moderate eating, there is non-eating, or fasting. Why do people fast? The Bible indicates that people fast in response to situations. The meaning of a fast, then, is derived, not from a formality, a ritual, but from a reality.

What is the point of fasting? Is it an ordinance? Maybe. But if so, then why? Do we fast to impress God with our willingness to go without food? If that's the point, doesn't that seem rather silly? Why would God care?

The point of fasting is not to impress God with our going hungry but that *we* are impressed and angry and frightened and despairing about things that trouble us. The point is, when we're upset, we're in no mood to eat. When we're dealing with upsetting things, food is the last thing on our minds. Problems make us lose our appetite.

But we do fast as an ordinance. Well, if it is an ordinance then it's fair to ask: What is an ordinance? And how is an ordinance different from the reality it represents?

Consider the ordinance of a grant deed, or the ordinance of a marriage license. Those essential documents are different from the underlying reality they represent. The deed represents the transfer of property ownership: "it's your property now and not mine." The marriage license documents the actual living together as husband and wife. The paper that documents the action (ordinance) is different than the action (reality).

So, what about fasting? If it is an ordinance (and it is), we ought to ask ourselves, an ordinance representing what? Here is a list of biblical fasts and the events that prompted them. As you read them, see if you can tell what they all have in common. Something should jump out at you. Here's my short list:

Exodus 34:28 Moses fasted in the presence of God.
Leviticus 16:29 Israel fasted because of their sins.
Joel 1:14 Israel fasted because of a locust plague.
Nehemiah 1:3-4 Nehemiah fasted because of a broken wall.
Psalms 35:13 David fasted because of too many enemies.
2 Samuel 3:35 David fasted for slain Abner.
2 Chronicles 20:3 Israel fasted because they were attacked.
Ezra 8:21 Ezra fasted because they had no army.
Isaiah 585-7 God said fast for wickedness and hunger.
Matthew 17:21 Jesus said fast when you confront Satan.
Matthew 4:1-2 Jesus fasted when he confronted Satan.
Matthew 9:15 We fast because Jesus is not here.

Notice anything in common yet? Here is my long list:

[1] Old Testament

Judges 20:25 *Benjamin…destroyed 18,000 men* ***:26*** *Israel…wept…and fasted…*

1 Samuel 1:7 *therefore she* [Hannah] *wept and did not eat.*

1 Samuel 7:6 *they fasted and said there, We have sinned against the* LORD.

1 Samuel 14:24 *And the men of Israel were distressed that day: for Saul had adjured the people, saying, Cursed be the man that eateth any food until evening, that I may be avenged on mine enemies. So none of the people tasted any food.*

1 Samuel 31:12 *the valiant men… took the bodies of Saul and his sons* ***:13*** *and buried them and fasted*

2 Samuel 1:11 *Then David* ***:12*** *mourned and wept and fasted until even for Saul*

2 Samuel 3:35 *So do God to me…if I taste bread* [David's grief over Abner's death]

2 Samuel 12:15 *the* LORD *struck the child that Uriah's wife bare* ***:16*** *and David fasted*

2 Samuel 12:22 *While the child was alive I fasted and wept* ***:23*** *but now he is dead, wherefore should I fast? Can I bring him back again?*

1 Kings 21:27 *When Ahab heard* [Elijah's] *words, he rent his clothes…and fasted.*

1 Chronicles 10:12 *the… men took away the body of Saul and buried* [him] *and fasted*

2 Chronicles 20:3 *Jehoshaphat feared…and proclaimed a fast throughout all Judah.*

Ezra 8:22 *I was ashamed to require of the king a band of soldiers* ***:23*** *so we fasted*

Nehemiah 1:3 *the wall of Jerusalem is broken* ***:4*** *I wept and mourned and fasted.*

Nehemiah 9:1 *…assembled with fasting* ***:2*** *confessed their sins and iniquities of their fathers.*

Esther 4:3 *there was great mourning among the Jews, and fasting, and weeping,…*

Esther 4:16 *fast for me…I also and my maidens will fast…and if I perish, I perish.*

Jeremiah 14:12 *When they fast, I will not hear their cry…*

Daniel 10:2 *I Daniel was mourning three full weeks* ***:3*** *I ate no pleasant bread, neither came flesh nor wine in my mouth, neither did I anoint myself…*

Jonah 3:7 *…Let neither man nor beast, herd nor flock, taste any thing…*

Zechariah 7:3 *…Should I weep in the fifth month, separating myself, as I have done…*

What do all the fasts in the *Old Testament* have in common? They were, all of them, reactions to some stressful, negative event — death, or war, or sin, or whatever. Not eating, not being hungry is the body's natural reaction to bad things. So, if you want to show God that you are genuinely concerned about something, don't eat.

[2] New Testament

Matthew 4:1 *Then was Jesus led up of the spirit into the wilderness to be tempted of the devil* ***:2*** *And when he had fasted forty days and forty nights…*

Going into battle, in this case spiritual battle, is serious business.

Luke 2:36 *And there was one Anna a prophetess* ***:37*** *And she was a widow of about fourscore and four years, which departed not from the temple, but served God with fasting and prayers night and day.* ***:38*** *…and spake of him* [Jesus] *to all them that looked for redemption in Jerusalem.*

For a young widow to have to face a long life of aloneness (84 years) is certainly an anguishing experience. What might a person in that situation do with all that time? Anna fasted and prayed and did a lot of temple work. And at the end of that long, lonely, faithful life, she was blessed to see the child messiah and prophecy for him.

Luke 5:34 *…Can ye make the children of the bridechamber fast, while the bridegroom is with them?*

Why would anyone want to fast when Jesus is with them? His presence would be a time of joy not sadness, a time to feast not fast. We fast because we're *not* with the Lord, when he is somewhere else. He's in heaven and we're here. We sorrow that we're not with him.

> ***Acts 13:2, 3*** *As they ministered to the Lord, and fasted, the Holy Ghost said, Separate me Barnabas and Saul for the work whereunto I have called them.*

Why a fast? They fasted because they felt the stress of this heavy ministry responsibility, of doing the job right. Should they set apart Barnabas and Paul or not? This was serious business, not to be dealt with frivolously.

> ***2 Corinthians 6:5*** *In stripes, in imprisonments, in tumults, in labours, in watchings, in fastings.*

Maybe this is an institutional fast that Paul is talking about (fasted and prayed that he wouldn't get beat up anymore), but more likely he is talking about going hungry from the stress of watching out for his own safety and the safety of others.

> ***2 Corinthians 11:27*** *In weariness and painfulness, in watchings often, in hunger and thirst, in fastings often, in cold and nakedness.*

This is a repeat of ***6:5***. Paul's fasts were spans of hunger along with all the other troubles that came his way.

So even in the *New Testament*, all fasting was negative, from sorrow or fear or deep concern for something. Plagues, destroyed cities, invading armies, crime, slain friends, hunger, poverty, sin, Satan — these are the kinds of things that make us fast. In other words, sickening things that make us lose our appetites so that food is the last thing on our minds. Fasting is the natural, physical response to grief, to fear, to stressful things that demand our entire attention. It is the result of concern, the proof that one is not taking a situation lightly.

Positive realities don't make us fast, they make us feast. Negative realities make us fast.

It's also important to notice that fasting was always real; that is, a fast was always about *something* that was actually happening. They never fasted just to have a fast. That makes regular institutional fasting seem rather purposeless, doesn't it? Should we not then try to find purpose in such fasts by focusing our attention on real life problems? Regular fasting then becomes an opportunity for us to take our problems to God and say, "God, *this* is what's upsetting me."

This is not to say that a planned fast is disingenuous. But if a fast never moves beyond its formality, beyond a ritual to some reality, then what is the point? How can a fast draw God's attention to a situation if the faster himself isn't even attentive to the situation?

You want to move God? To do what? If you don't know, how do you expect God to know? If you are not concerned, why do you think God should be?

Fast, yes. The Bible says you should. But, for heaven's sake, fast for *something* — something that actually moves you and causes you concern. That should be easy; there is much in the world to be concerned about.

[3] Is There Ever a Wrong Fast?

God tells Isaiah that, yes indeed, there is such a thing as a wrong fast. That is a fast where the people have missed the point of it.

> ***Isaiah 58:1*** *Show my people their transgression and the house of Jacob their sins.* ***:2*** *Yet they seek me daily, and delight to know my ways, as a*

nation that did righteousness and forsook not the ordinance of their God: they ask of me the ordinances of justice; they take delight in approaching to God. ***:3*** *Wherefore have we fasted, say they, and thou seest not? Wherefore have we afflicted our soul, and thou takest no knowledge?* [God, do you see our fasting? Are you impressed?] *Behold, in the day of your fast ye find pleasure* [You're just having a party], *and exact all your labours* [you oppress your employees]. ***:5*** *Is it such a fast that I have chosen? A day for a man to afflict his soul?* [You think skipping a meal will impress me?]. *Wilt thou call this a fast, and an acceptable day to the* L*ORD?*

Well then, if all of that is a wrong fast, then what is a right fast? God continues and tells us that too.

Isaiah 58:6 *Is not this the fast that I have chosen? To loose the band of wickedness* [fix injustice], *to undo the heavy burdens, and to let the oppressed go free, and that ye break every yoke?* ***:7*** *Is it not to deal thy bread to the hungry, and that thou bring the poor that are cast out to thy house? When thou seest the naked, that thou cover him, and that thou hide not thyself from thine own flesh* [especially help out your family] *?* ***:8*** *Then shall thy light break forth as the morning, and thine health shall spring forth speedily: and thy righteousness shall go before thee; the glory of the* LORD *shall be thy reward.* ***:9*** *Then shalt thou call and the* LORD *shall answer…*

Here are the main points of Isaiah's admonition.

First: Feel genuine sorrow, grief, fear, humiliation, loss for the tragedy that has beset you or someone you care about. Isaiah said, "You're trying to convince me that you're grieving and *ye find pleasure?"* Your fast in a time of pleasure is not convincing Him.

Second: Do something about it. Feed the poor, do justice, and so forth. In other words, work to resolve the problem that you are claiming you are so stressed over. Don't just dump it on God to deal with; *you* deal with it. Try to fix the problem that you claim you're so concerned about.

Third: Feel your grief over the right things. Isaiah gives us a list. There is righteous grief over injustice and poverty. But there is also unrighteous grief, like for example Cain's jealousy of Abel, or David's lust for Bathsheba, or King Ahab's pining for Naboth's vineyard. ***1 Kings 21:4*** *...And he* [Ahab] *laid him down upon his bed...and would eat no bread.* That's fasting (Ahab couldn't eat), but Ahab was fasting for the wrong thing. He was so grieved that he couldn't get someone's else's property that he committed murder. Here's a proper thing to grieve for: How about abortion? We murder over a million babies a year in America. If that doesn't turn your stomach, nothing will.

Fourth: Do all that, and *then* God will take notice of your fasting and will bless you. The ordinance loses it meaning if we don't keep reality in view.

Here is an example of a fast that accomplished nothing good at all. It merely invigorated a wrong thinking people to do a wrong thing.

> ***Jeremiah 36:9*** *...they proclaimed a fast...* ***:10*** *Then read Baruch in the book the words of Jeremiah in the house of the* LORD*...* ***:23*** *...he* [the king] *cut it* [Jeremiah's scroll] *with a pinknife, and cast it into the fire.*

This fast began right, the people heard Jeremiah's words, but ended wrong, they rejected his words, cut them up and burned them. So, the fast proved to be useless.

[4] Do We Need an Institutional Fast?

Before we decide to fast, we should first understand what we are fasting for. If someone asks me to fast, I first ask, "Why?"

When the Jews returned to Judea from their Diaspora, they asked their prophet this very question: Should we continue to fast?

> ***Zechariah 7:1*** *And it came to pass in the fourth year of king Darius, that the word of the LORD came unto Zechariah in the fourth day of the ninth month, even in Chisleu.* [This is a fast for the fall of Jerusalem.] ***:2*** *When they had sent unto the house of God Sherezer and Regemmelech, and their men, to pray before the LORD.* ***:3*** *And to speak unto the priests which were in the house of the LORD of hosts, and to the prophet, saying, Should I weep in the fifth month, separating myself, as I have done these so many years?*

This is a fair question. We mourned and fasted over the destruction of Jerusalem, but now we're back and have rebuilt the city and the temple. Should we continue to fast?

Here's God's answer:

> ***Zechariah 7:4*** *Then came the word of the LORD of hosts unto me, saying,* ***:5*** *Speak unto all the people of the land, and to the priests, saying, When ye fasted and mourned in the fifth and seventh month, even those seventy years, did ye at all fast unto me, even to me?* ***:6*** *And when ye did eat* [had a feast] *and when ye did drink, did not ye eat for yourselves, and drink for yourselves?* ***:7*** *Should ye not hear the words which the LORD hath cried by the former prophets, when Jerusalem was inhabited and in prosperity, and the cities thereof round about her, when men inhabited the south and the plain?* ***:8*** *And the word of the LORD came unto Zechariah saying,* ***:9*** *Thus speaketh the LORD of hosts, saying, Execute true judgment, and shew mercy and compassions every man to his brother:* ***:10***

And oppress not the widow, nor the fatherless, the stranger, nor the poor; and let none of you imagine evil against his brother in your heart.

During the Diaspora, Jews fasted in grief for the loss of their temple. But when the Diaspora was over and the Jews were returning to Jerusalem, they asked Zechariah a fair question: Should we still keep that fast?

God first answered the question with a question: "Did you ever fast for me or were you fasting for yourselves? Did you ever feast for me or were you feasting for yourselves?" In other words, if you think that maybe a fast or a feast is appropriate, examine the motive. If you have a fast, or a feast, are you having it for the right reasons?

And that brings us to this question: Why an ordinance? We have a regular institutional fast because we need to be continually reminded that things are bad even when things are good. Why? Because when life is good we tend to forget God. There is this saying: "Success doesn't change people, it unmasks them."

So, we have a fast to remind us. But if we forget what the fast is about, then it doesn't mean much. We need an institutional fast, yes, but we need to keep it right, to keep us in continual reminder of our fragility and constant dependence on God.

And by the way, God did finally answer their question —

Zechariah 8:19 *...The fast of the fourth month...shall be...cheerful feasts...*

God did change this fast into a feast. Things had improved for them.

Here are other institutional fasts in the Bible.

Leviticus 23:27 *tenth day of seventh month...day of atonement...ye shall afflict your souls.*

"Afflict your souls" probably meant fast.

Esther 9:29 *And Esther the Queen wrote* ***:31*** *to confirm the days of Purim … as they had decreed for themselves and for their seed, the matters of the fastings and their cry.*

Purim is the day of fasting to remember when the Jews almost lost everything.

Jeremiah 36:6 *Therefore go thou, and read…in the ears of the people in the LORD's house upon the fasting day.*

The Jews had a fasting day, and that was the day that Jeremiah went to the temple to read God's word to them. Their fasting accomplished something anyway, they were in a mood to listen to him.

[5] The Power of Fasting

Matthew 17:19 *Then came the disciples to Jesus apart, and said, Why could not we cast him out?* ***:21*** *This kind goeth not out but by prayer and fasting.*

You want to do battle with evil? Then be sincere about it. And one good way to cement your sincerity is to not eat. Fasting focuses your attention, if you let it.

[6] Testimonies

What about testimonies? What's that all about? When we are fasting, is it important to stand up and tell others why we are fasting?

***Deuteronomy 26:2** Thou shalt take of the first of all the fruit of the earth… **:3** And thou shalt go unto the priest… **:4** And the priest shall take the basket out of thine hand… **:5** And thou shalt speak and say before the LORD thy God, A Syrian ready to perish was my father, and he went down into Egypt, and sojourned there with a few, and became there a nation, great, mighty, and populous **:6** And the Egyptians evil entreated us, and afflicted us, and laid upon us hard bondage **:7** And when we cried unto the LORD God of our fathers, the LORD heard our voice, and looked on our affliction, and our labour, and our oppression **:8** And the LORD brought us forth out of Egypt with a mighty hand, and with an outstretched arm, and with great terribleness, and with signs, and with wonders **:9** And he hath brought us into this place, and hath give us this land, even a land that floweth with milk and honey.*

This is so much like a Fast and Testimony Meeting. *First:* We give our tithes and offerings. *Second:* We declare publicly that we remember the problems that we used to have. And *third:* We declare publicly that we remember that God has delivered us from those problems and has blessed us with good things.

A testimony connected with a fast is either a declaration of a problem (God, I need your help), or of a problem that God has resolved for you (God, thank you). But always it has a negative root. That's why it's a fast.

[7] The Opposite of Fast is Feast

You don't fast for positive things, you feast — like at a wedding. You would never fast at a wedding, unless you despise your new son-in-law, *then* you might fast and hope your precious daughter comes to her senses before the I-do's.

After all the fasting we've talked about, we should now talk about some feasting. What do we feast for?

2 Chronicles 7:8 *Also at the same time Solomon kept the feast seven days and all Israel with him…* ***:10*** *…glad and merry in heart…*

This was because of their joy of the newly built and newly dedicated temple that God had conspicuously accepted.

Esther 9:17 *made it a day of feasting and gladness.*

When it was all over, when Esther had her victory and saved the Jews from her husband's rash decree, they had a feast. Of course. It was time to celebrate and be happy.

Jeremiah 16:8 *Thou shalt not also go into the house of feasting, to sit with them to eat and to drink.*

A feast would be a fine thing to have. Let's celebrate and have a party and be happy. That would be nice, but not when a great disaster is coming. They were in a party mood because they didn't know a great disaster was coming. Jeremiah was telling them, but they weren't listening, they were too busy partying.

[8] So, Why Are *You* Fasting?

Are you fasting because you want to impress God? I don't think that impresses God. Are you fasting because your church says you should? I don't think that impresses God either. Maybe this is why you should fast: because you actually feel a strong negative passion — sorrow, grief, fear, etc. — about something.

What *something*? Well, *you'd* better know. If you don't know what you feel sorrow, grief, fear, etc. for, how do you expect God to know? Want to impress God with your problems? Maybe you'd better impress yourself first. Maybe at least think about them and allow yourself to feel the emotion that you should be feeling about your problems and other people's problems. Then maybe God will pay attention to them, if you've paid attention to them first.

Writing down your issues can help. Then at least you know what they are.

There's a device that I use, my own contrivance. In my church, we make our donations with a donation slip, and we keep a carbon copy for ourselves. On the back of that carbon copy I write down the things that I am concerned about. One of the things I believe about God is that he can read. And if I am attentive to my own problems enough to write them down, I believe God is attentive enough to read them, if not from the piece of paper, then from my heart.

Fear

Psalms 56:3-11, Matthew 26:39

The Bible says in many places (particularly in Psalms) fear not, don't fear, don't be afraid. How literally are we to take that?

> ***Psalms 56:3*** *What time I am afraid, I will trust in thee.* ***:4*** *In God I will praise his word, in God I have put my trust; I will not fear what flesh can do unto me.* ***:11*** *In God have I put my trust: I will not be afraid what man can do unto me.*

If we take this literally, then it's a contradiction: "I am afraid" versus "I will not fear." Clearly, it is optimistic exaggeration. The truth is, we all fear what "flesh can do" to us. I fear loss of income, sickness, criminals, government, lawsuits, and a host of lesser threats. I don't live in constant terror of those things because they haven't happened. But if one of them did happen, for instance, if I were kidnapped by terrorists and threatened with torture, of course I'd be afraid. Even Jesus was afraid. That's why he prayed in despair, "let this cup pass from me."

Let's take this verse as it was intended: The more we trust God, the more able we are to manage our fear. But even if we trust absolutely, as did the prophets, we still fear.

God's servants are not fearless, they are just driven. That's important to know lest we leave the scarier tasks to those we think braver than ourselves. Great people have great fears. Their greatness lies not in fearlessness but in bravely facing what they are afraid of. That is the virtue we call courage.

Let's start with Moses. Moses tried everything he could think of to get out of the job that God was calling him to. Each time Moses threw up an obstacle, God responded by giving Moses something to overcome that obstacle.

Exodus 3:11 *Who am I that I should go unto Pharaoh?* In other words, I'm a nobody.
Exodus 3:12 *I will be with you.* I don't care that you are a nobody, I'm on your side.

Exodus 4:1 *But, behold, they will not believe me…*
Exodus 4:3 God replied by turning Moses' rod into a serpent. That, they would believe.

Exodus 4:10 *I am not eloquent…I am slow of speech…* I'm no speaker, get someone else.
Exodus 4:14 *Aaron…cometh forth to meet thee.*

So, whatever problem Moses had that he was afraid of that made him cower away from the task at hand, God resolved that problem. And finally, Moses accepted the assignment.

Now, some more prophets.

1 Kings 19:3 *And when* [Elijah] *saw that* [Jezebel was after him] *he arose, and went for his life.* ***:4*** *…and requested for himself that he might die…*

Job 42:6 *Wherefore I* [Job] *abhor myself…*

Isaiah 6:5 *Woe is me for I am undone because I am a man of unclean lips…and my eyes have seen the Kimg, the* L*ORD* *of hosts..*

Isaiah 64:6 *All our righteousness is as filthy rags.*

Jeremiah 20:9 *I will not make mention of him, nor speak any more in his name.* [Jeremiah resigns] *But his word was in mine heart as a burning fire shut up in my bones, and I was wary with forbearing, and I could not stay.* [But God wouldn't accept the resignation.]

Daniel 10:8 *My comeliness was turned into corruption.*

Jonah 4:2 *I knew that thou art a gracious God and merciful,* ***:3*** *Therefore, O LORD, take my life from me.*

Habakkuk 3:2 *I have heard thy speech and was afraid.*

Luke 5:8 *Peter…fell down at Jesus knees saying, Depart from me for I am a sinful man.*

Matthew 26:39 *O my Father, if it be possible, let this cup pass from me.*

So, there's the list of great people who were afraid. Isaiah, Habakkuk, Job, and Daniel were afraid of God. Elijah was afraid of Jezebel. Moses was afraid of Pharaoh. Jeremiah was afraid of the Jews. Peter was afraid of Jesus, and Jesus was afraid of the cross (he was not a masochist). And Jonah, if you can imagine it, was afraid of succeeding. He would rather die (he said so) than to convert those undeserving Ninevites.

They were each afraid of something, but they each got the job done anyway.

Everyone is afraid of something. You are afraid of something. Just remember that great people are not great because they have no fear but because they do what they have to do in spite of their fear. That is what we call courage.

Sometimes fear is justified, but sometimes fear is not at all justified, as when the angel Gabriel appeared to Mary and said, "Fear not." He meant it. That was no exaggeration. Seeing an angel is frightening, but this angel was Mary's friend and ally and nothing for Mary to be afraid of. And so he calmed her down and reassured her and said wonderful things to her.

"Fear not" can mean either of two things. It can mean that there really is nothing to fear, or it can mean don't worry *so* much about your current peril, manage your fear because God is in control and, even if the worst happens, when this is all over you'll be okay.

Forgiveness

Matthew 6:12-15, Matthew 9:2-8, Isaiah 1:18

What people desperately want is to be innocent, to be free of guilt. Some people pursue that by convincing themselves that they were never guilty in the first place. Others know better and turn to God, the only hope of forgiveness in the universe.

[1] Forgiveness In General

1 Kings 8:30 *And hearken thou to the supplication of thy servant, and of thy people Israel, when they shall pray toward this place: and hear thou in heaven thy dwelling place: and when thou hearest, forgive.*

Israel's prayers were offered with one intention, that God would forgive. That's what the temple was about and the sacrificial system.

Job 9:15 *Whom, though I were righteous, yet would I not answer, but I would make supplication to my judge.*

Even if you really are innocent, you'd do better to plead for forgiveness anyway.

Psalms 51:1 *Have mercy upon me, O God, according to thy lovingkindness: according unto the multitude of thy tender mercies blot out my transgressions.*

Blot out means to erase, or cover up like white out, or strike through. God has recorded my sins in a ledger, and I want him to delete his record of them.

Psalms 99:8 *...thou wast a God that forgavest them, though thou tookest vengeance of their inventions.*

This is interesting. God forgives *and* takes vengeance. Aren't the two mutually exclusive? Apparently not. "I forgive you, but I will punish you anyway." Christians who want to acquit murderers in the name of forgiveness should pay attention to this verse.

Psalms 103:3 *Who forgiveth all thine iniquities...*

Ezekiel 18:21 *But if the wicked will turn from all his sins that he hath committed, and keep all my statutes, and do that which is lawful and right, he shall surely live, he shall not die.* ***:22*** *All his transgressions that he hath committed, they shall not be mentioned unto him: in his righteousness that he hath done he shall live.*

[2] Forgiveness: Availability And Limits

Numbers 35:31 *Moreover ye shall take no satisfaction for the life of a murderer, which is guilty of death; but he shall be surely put to death.*

The object of Israel's sacrificial system was forgiveness. But not for murderers. That crime was just so heinous that there could be "no satisfaction" for it, no way to make it right other than to execute the murderer.

Psalms 68:21 *But God shall wound the head of his enemies, and the hairy scalp of such an one as goeth on still in his trespasses.*

If God judges harshly those who *persist* in their trespasses, then by inference he does *not* judge harshly those who do *not* persist in their trespasses. In other words, God forgives repented sins but does not forgive unrepented sins.

> ***Proverbs 1:28*** *Then shall they call upon me, but I will not answer; they shall seek me early, but they shall not find me.*

> ***Isaiah 1:18*** *Come now, and let us reason together, saith the* LORD: *though your sins be as scarlet, they shall be as white as snow; though they be red like crimson, they shall be as wool.*

These two verses seem to be at odds with each other. In the first, God has dug in his heels and will not forgive no matter how much they plead for it. In the second, God forgives everything. It seems to depend on what mood God is in at the moment.

> ***Matthew 12:32*** *And whosoever speaketh a word against the Son of man, it shall be forgiven him: but whosoever speaketh against the Holy Ghost, it shall not be forgiven him…*

There is a lot of confusion about this verse, and there shouldn't be. It's really very simple. All it is saying is: "You hear my words, and you see my miracles. If you doubt my words, fine, talk is cheap, anybody can say anything. But if you doubt my miracles, then you're lost because that's God's best shot. There's nothing left that God can do to persuade you." My point being that the miracles *are* the testimony of the Holy Ghost that's *why* the "sin against the Holy Ghost" is unforgivable, not because it deserves a stronger punishment but because after witnessing the miracles, there is nothing left to persuade the determined hardened heart of the truth that Jesus is who he says he is, the son of God. That the point of "sin against the Holy Ghost," willful denial in spite of the obvious evidence.

[3] Reasons Why We Should Forgive

Proverbs 19:11 *…it is his glory to pass over a transgression.*

It's to a man's credit to forgive. People notice.

Proverbs 24:17 *Rejoice not when thine enemy falleth, and let not thine heart be glad when he stumbleth:* ***:18*** *Lest the LORD see it, and it displease him, and he turn away his wrath from him.*

The logic here is interesting. If you're glad when your enemy falls, God may actually take *his* side against *you*!

This is highly practical. At the end of World War I, England and France punished Germany so severely with war reparations that the fed-up Germans finally turned their government over to Hitler which brought on World War II. But at the end of World War II, America handled things differently. Instead of punishing former enemies, America's Marshall Plan reconstructed Germany along with much of Europe, and also Japan. Thus, America's former enemies became friends and allies.

How you treat your enemies after a war will largely determine whether or not there will be a next war.

Proverbs 24:29 *Say not, I will do so to him as he hath done to me: I will render to the man according to his work.*

One very good reason to forgive is simply that God says we should.

Matthew 6:12 *And forgive our debt, as we forgive our debtors.* ***:14*** *For if ye forgive men their trespasses, your Heavenly Father will also forgive you.* ***:15*** *But if ye forgive not men their trespasses, neither will your father forgive your trespasses.*

In other words, what goes around comes around. That this thought begins in the Lord's Prayer indicates that reciprocal forgiveness is a reasonable thing to ask of God. We want and expect God to forgive us as we forgive others.

[4] Examples of Forgiveness

Luke 23:34 *Then said Jesus, Father, forgive them; for they know not what they do…*

This, of course, is the quintessential forgiveness text, Jesus forgiving the very people who are crucifying him. That raises the bar very high. But even here there seems to be a condition: "for they know not what they do." In other words, even Jesus doesn't give blanket forgiveness.

Acts 7:60 *And he kneeled down, and cried with a loud voice, Lord, lay not this sin to their charge. And when he had said this, he fell asleep.*

It's been said that the Church owes Paul to the prayer of Stephen. Stephen did not have to forgive; he could have cursed them as he died and would have been within his rights to do so. Had he though, Saul of Tarsus would never have become Paul, and the Church would have lost a lot.

[5] Did God Forgive David?

Many people, including myself, are concerned for David's soul. It's a natural concern because we hate to see a good man destroyed because of a single mistake. But maybe our real concern is not so much for David as it is for ourselves. For if David — that great man who did everything for Israel and for God — could fall and not be forgiven, then what chance do we ordinary people have?

My first answer to the disturbing dilemma is to note that God did forgive him.

> ***2 Samuel 12:13*** *And David said unto Nathan, I have sinned against the* LORD. *And Nathan said unto David, The* LORD *also hath put away thy sin; thou shalt not die.*

But that, on its surface, seems inexplicable because of —

> ***Numbers 35:31*** *Moreover ye shall take no satisfaction for the life of a murderer, which is guilty of death; but he shall be surely put to death.*

Israel's sacrificial system was about forgiving sins, but not murder. Can God violate his own law and forgive murder? I suggest that he cannot.

And that leads me to my second answer to the dilemma which is: maybe David did not commit a murder after all.

Let's explore that possibility, but before we go there, let's first look at God's opinion of David in retrospect. When it was all over, and David was dead, and his descendants inherited his throne in succession, what did God have to say about David? God used David as the high-bar to measure all subsequent kings. Basically, God's message to all the kings of Judah and Israel was: "If you want to be a good king, be like my servant David."

That would be a strange high-bar indeed if David were an unforgiven, damned murderer.

1 Kings 3:14 *And if thou* [Solomon] *wilt walk in my ways, to keep my statutes and my commandments, as thy father David did walk…*

Once again God affirms that he did indeed forgive David's sin with Uriah. The sum of David's life is that he kept God's statutes and commandments.

1 Kings 11:6 *And Solomon did evil in the sight of the* LORD, *and went not fully after the* LORD, *as did David his father.*

It's interesting how fully God yet defends David despite his error with Bathsheba and Uriah.

1 Kings 11:34 *…for David…whom I chose because he kept my commandments and my statutes.*

1 Kings 14:8 *Thou* [Jeroboam] *hast not been as my servant David, who kept my commandments, and who followed me with all his heart, to do that only which was right in mine eyes.*

1 Kings 15:3 *…and his heart was not perfect with the* LORD *his God, as the heart of David his father.*

It is as though David's sin with Bathsheba and Uriah never happened.

1 Kings 15:5 *Because David did that which was right in the eyes of the* LORD, *and turned not aside from any thing that he commanded him all the days of his life, save only in the matter of Uriah the Hittite.*

So, Uriah finally gets at least a footnote, but it's hardly a wipeout of David's career.

Each king, good or bad is compared to David:

1 Kings 15:11 *And Asa did that which was right in the eyes of the* LORD, *as did David his father.*

2 Kings 16:2 *Twenty years old was Ahaz when he began to reign, and reigned sixteen years in Jerusalem, and did not that which was right in the sight of the* LORD *his God, like David his father.*

After all this long string of generations, the author is still comparing kings to David who, in the author's view, did "right in the sight of the *LORD*." And, by the way, this includes the final king of Israel, the eternal king Jesus Christ. That fact is so important that it is the opening verse of the New Testament.

Matthew 1:1 *The book of the generation of Jesus Christ, the son of David…*

All of this is, of course, circumstantial. But still, it is persuasive in that it persuades us to believe that God really did forgive David as he said he did.

But maybe that causes us to wince: Where is the justice for Uriah? How can God forgive so blatant a murder? And if murder is unforgivable, how can God forgive David? Doesn't the law demand the life of the murderer?

These are fair questions. I will now take those questions head on. I have written about this in my *Volume 1: The Old Testament*, and I know I'm taking a literary liberty by repeating myself, but it's important enough to include in this chapter of forgiveness.

I want you to imagine for the moment that I am David's defense attorney, standing before God the judge, and you are the jurors. Here's my case for David:

Your Honor, and ladies and gentlemen of the jury, I claim that David never committed a murder at all. Oh, he *intended* to all right, and *tried* to. But he is not on trial here for *attempted* murder but for *actual* murder, and of that, I claim, he is innocent. The basis of my argument is simple: you cannot murder a corpse.

This idea came to me from a who-done-it movie (I don't recall the name of the movie. Was it an Agatha Christie story? I don't know.) The accused drove a knife through the victim's heart — an act of cold-blooded murder, surely.

But there was only one problem for the prosecution, and that is this: the victim was already dead and had been dead for an hour before the knife attack. Someone else had poisoned him first.

Of course, the accused didn't know that, and he really did stab the victim through the heart to murder him. But is that a crime? Can you be guilty of murdering a corpse?

So, we are left with this question: What's the penalty for stabbing a corpse? Or, in the worst case, what is the penalty for attempted murder? Attempted murder certainly is a crime, and violating a corpse may be. But surely neither is a *capital* crime. Neither of these crimes is actual murder.

I claim that the death of Uriah is like that. David tried to kill him, plotted to kill him, arranged to kill him, but in fact Uriah died from another cause before the murder could be carried out. Thus God, in fact, protected David from his own evil plan.

Let's look at the facts of the story.

2 Samuel 12:16 *And it came to pass, when Joab observed the city, that he assigned Uriah unto a place where he knew that valiant men were.* ***:17***

And the men of the city went out, and fought with Joab: and there fell some of the people of the servants of David; and Uriah the Hittite died also.

Joab was *intending* to murder Uriah per David's instructions. But before he could pull it off, the Jews lost a tactical skirmish and several men died, including Uriah.

The plan was to advance the troops dangerously close to the wall then quickly retreat leaving Uriah stranded. But that's not what happened. They did advance dangerously close but before Joab could execute David's plan, Uriah and his fellow soldiers were already dead, the archers on the wall did their job well. Uriah died from a tactical blunder. Now, is that murder? Is every general's screw-up murder? I think not.

So, tell me. Just what are we accusing David of? Attempted murder? Certainly. Malicious intent? Of course. Negligence? Yes. Incompetent generaling? I imagine Joab's error was a tactical blunder, maybe even manslaughter. But murder? How? Uriah died gallantly doing his duty with the rest of his fallen comrades, as also the millions of other good soldiers throughout history who died for their good cause.

And what of the generals and kings and presidents who ordered them to it? Patton and Lincoln and Washington? Are they all guilty of murder because they ordered their troops into harm's way? You may argue: But David's intent was malicious murder! I argue back, Yeah? So what? He didn't pull the trigger! Fate denied him, or God spared him. Uriah died in battle. So, I ask you, just what are you accusing David of?

To David's credit, although he could have pled innocent (as Saul did), he nowhere does. He instead pleads guilty as charged.

Psalms 51:3 *For I acknowledge my transgression: and my sin is ever before me.* ***:4*** *Against thee, thee only, have I sinned, and done this evil in* *thy sight: that thou mightest be justified when thou speakest, and be clear when thou judgest.*

David never looked for an out but felt tremendous guilt, as well he should. But to those of you who want to lock him away forever without access to forgiveness and use the technicality that "murder is unforgivable," well, I just beat you back with another technicality: *he didn't do it!* God, or fate, or just plain good luck protected him from that guilt.

But in any case, whatever David was guilty of, God forgave. And that's good news to me because I really like being forgiven of my foibles. If God forgave David, I trust that he'll forgive me which is what Jesus Christ is all about.

[6] ACCEPTING FORGIVENESS

Matthew 9:2 *Jesus…said unto the sick of the palsy…Son, be of good cheer; thy sins are forgiven.* ***:3*** *And, behold, certain of the scribes said within themselves, This man blasphemeth.*

Here's the bad news: we are all sinners in need of forgiveness. ***Romans 3:10*** *There is none righteous, no, not one.* Here's the good news: Jesus forgives. Isn't that great news? Well, the scribes didn't think so. Forgiveness is also an accusation which can be insulting — to those who choose to be insulted. There's a marvelous saying: "A fool takes offense when none is intended."

When someone says to us, "I forgive you," our kneejerk response is, "For What? I didn't do anything!" To accept forgiveness, we must first admit guilt. And the scribes wanted no part of that. Then Jesus said —

Matthew 9:4 *Wherefore think ye evil in your hearts?*

They thought they didn't need forgiveness and that Jesus was being outrageous, even blasphemous, to offer it.

That's evil thinking. His forgiveness is not an insult, it is God's gift to mankind. And they needed to know that. So, he showed them as plainly as he possibly could.

> ***Matthew 9:5*** *For whether is easier, to say, Thy sins be forgiven thee; or to say, Arise and walk?*

A fair question, particularly since they couldn't do either. But upstaging them, embarrassing them in public was not what Jesus was about. He really wanted the best for them. He wanted to forgive them. But to do that he had to get them to a place where they could be forgiven. They need to believe. And so —

> ***Matthew 9:6*** *But that ye may know* [he did it for the scribes] *that the Son of man hath power on earth to forgive sins, (then sayeth he to the sick of the palsy,) Arise, take up thy bed, and go unto thine house.* ***:7*** *And he arose, and departed to his house.*

His visible miracle revealed his invisible miracle. You'd think they'd line up to get forgiveness. "My gosh. This guy forgives sins and just proved it. I gotta get some of that." But no. While God forgives, the world denies. Blind to its guilt, the world continues to declare its innocence. But still, although many deny, many do believe.

> ***Matthew 9:8*** *But when the multitudes saw it, they marveled, and glorified God, which had given such power unto men.*

Each person there had a choice to make, as do each of us.

The Lure of Slavery, the Cost of Freedom

1 Samuel 8:1-9

Numbers 14:4 *And they said one to another, Let us make a captain, and let us return into Egypt.*

Until now, Israel had only grumbled about the hard life that their new freedom had brought. But now, they actually planned to abandon freedom and willingly return to lives of slavery. People are at times so fearful that they will gladly give up their freedoms, preferring instead the security (as they imagine it) of entitlements. Grumbling is dangerous, and stupid talk eventually leads to stupid action.

[1] Gideon

On one occasion, just after winning a battle, Israel wanted their general to become their king. Fortunately for Israel, the general wasn't interested.

Judges 8:22 *Then the men of Israel said unto Gideon, Rule thou over us, both thou, and thy son, and thy son's son also: for thou hast delivered us from the hand of Midian.* ***:23*** *And Gideon said unto them, I will not rule over you, neither shall my son rule over you; the LORD shall rule over you.*

Eventually, every nation will be tempted to trade its freedom for entitlements. What such nations need at that moment of bad judgment is a Gideon to say no to the tempting offer and remind them just how important and precious and rare their liberty is.

Few leaders are able to resist such an offer. Gideon was one such leader, and George Washington was another. Each, in his time, walked away from such "glory" when it was offered.

The irony of history is that those men, Gideon and Washington, history rewards with a greater glory *because* they did not seek to be king, while other men who grab glory are forgotten, or remembered as villains. When Washington was offered the crown he said, "I did not defeat George III to become George I." Now that's true greatness. It's no wonder he is remembered as "First in the hearts of his countrymen."

[2] AMIMELECH

Gideon declined the poor glory of kingdom. But unfortunately, his son did not.

> ***Judges 9:2*** *Speak, I* [Amimelech son of Gideon] *pray you, in the ears of all the men of Shechem, Whether is better for you, either that all the sons of Jerubbaal* [Gideon], *which are threescore and ten persons, reign over you or that one reign over you?*

Although Gideon's wisdom delayed tyranny for a generation, the next generation embraced it. Amimelech, Gideon's son, presented himself and offered to be Israel's monarch: "Do you want one ruler or seventy?" meaning his seventy brothers, Gideon's other sons. Unfortunately, Israel accepted Amimelech's offer and made him their ruler.

Amimelech began his reign of terror by killing all his brothers, except one who escaped. Then he launched a series of wars that cost many thousands of lives.

So much for having one man in charge.

We see from this episode how fragile a thing is freedom, and how quickly the destiny of a nation changes when its people decide to follow a tyrant. For all the good that Gideon did, one stroke of a pen and Amimelech undid it all.

Did Israel learn its lesson? For a few generations yes. But eventually the lure of tyranny was too much, and they again wanted a king.

> ***1 Samuel 8:1*** *And it came to pass, when Samuel was old, that he made his sons judges over Israel.* ***8:3*** *And his sons walked not in his ways, but turned aside after lucre, and took bribes, and perverted judgment.* ***8:5*** *And* [Israel] *said unto* [Samuel], *Behold, thou art old, and thy sons walk not in thy ways: now make us a king to judge us like all the nations.*

The people wanted a king. They wanted a solidifying central government. But they already had a solidifying government founded on God and God's law. They just didn't have faith enough to trust it. And with judges like Samuel's corrupt sons, Joel and Abiah, who can blame them for wanting a change? This shows the extent of damage a corrupt government can cause. Not only is the corruption bad and causes injustice, but it also sparks revolution and pushes the people exactly in the wrong direction.

A modern example: Chiang Kai-shek was the corrupt leader of China. He was so corrupt that he executed merchants who refused to accept his valueless currency, and that finally motivated the Communist revolution under Mao Zedong who ultimately murdered 40,000,000 Chinese. Tyranny just leads to more tyranny.

But back to Samuel and his rotten sons. Government (in this case, two corrupt judges) showed itself to be flawed. So how did the people respond? By trading their freedom for tyranny thinking that would solve the problem. They didn't realize that they were throwing out the baby with the bathwater. Freedom is to be cherished, even with bad judges. Submitting to tyranny for *any* reason is a terrible mistake.

[3] Saul

What was their solution to bad leadership? Get a king, a true tyrant that they can't shake off.

> ***1 Samuel 8:7*** *And the* LORD *said unto Samuel, Hearken unto the voice of the people in all that they say unto thee: for they have not rejected thee, but they have rejected me, that I should not reign over them.* ***:9*** *Now therefore hearken unto their voice: howbeit yet protest solemnly unto them, and shew them the manner of the king that shall reign over them.*

You want to sell your freedom away? God will let you do it. God will protest, but in the end, you'll get what you want.

Let's see what they got.

> ***1 Samual 9:2*** *And* [Kisk] *had a son, whose name was Saul, a choice young man, and a goodly: and there was not among the children of Israel a goodlier person than he: from his shoulders and upward he was higher than any of the people.*

Here's the future king: Saul. He was handsome, strong, tall — the local celebrity, the rock star, the football hero, the big screen superstar, every woman's fantasy and every man's wanna-be. And he was a total loser. But that's what the people wanted, so that's what God gave them. You want a celebrity? Here he is, people: Saul. Good luck.

1 Samuel 12:17 *Is it not wheat harvest to day? I will call unto the* LORD, *and he shall send thunder and rain; that ye may perceive and see that your wickedness is great, which ye have done in the sight of the* LORD, *in asking you a king.*

Even though God accommodated their demand for a king, God still considered their demand wickedness. They were a free people. Now they were a monarchy. God is all in favor of government, yes, but government by divinely established laws, a constitution, not a government of tyranny where the leaders can create whatever laws they want to suit themselves.

[4] Kings and Other Tyrants

Proverbs 20:2 *The fear of a king is as the roaring of a lion: whoso provoketh him to anger sinneth against his own soul.*

The point is that governments are here to stay, "resistance is futile." So, learn to live within the system. If you sin against the king, you do so at your peril.

Ecclesiastes 8:4 *Where the word of a king is, there is power: and who may say unto him, What doest thou?*

You can't question the king. You can't say, "What are you doing?" In other words, you can't fight city hall. We give up a lot when we submit ourselves to a central government.

John 6:15 *When Jesus therefore perceived that they would come and take him by force, to make him king…*

It's amazing what people will give up their freedom for. They would have forced Jesus to be king. And for what? Because the night before, he fed 5,000 people. They were willing and anxious to turn themselves over to a king just for free food. How cheaply people hold their liberty.

[5] ZEDEKIAH

Jeremiah 38:5 *Then Zedekiah the king said, Behold, he* [Jeremiah] *is in your hand: for the king is not he that can do any thing against you.*

Zedekiah, for all his faults, at least understood the limits of his power. Ultimately, the people will have their way, good or bad, and there's not much that even the king can do about it.

Jeremiah 34:8 *…king Zedekiah had made a covenant with all the people, which were at Jerusalem, to proclaim liberty unto them.* ***:9*** *That every man should let his maidservant, being an Hebrew or an Hebrewess, go free; that none should serve himself of them, to wit, of a Jew his brother.* ***:11*** *But afterward they turned…*

Now that the people were threatened by Babylon, they yearned for freedom — to the point where it seemed a good idea to free all their slaves. And Zedekiah agreed.

But it was too little and too late. They should have been seeking liberty long before now. But now, they just couldn't give up their spoiled lives. They changed their minds and grabbed their Jewish slaves back. It was a noble effort, freeing their Jewish slaves, but they couldn't stick with it. And when they broke that covenant that they had made with the king and with God, that was the last straw. God brought the Babylonians to conquer them, and they themselves became slaves.

[6] CIVIL RIGHTS

> ***Lamentations 3:35*** *To turn aside the right of a man before the face of the most High.* ***:36*** *To subvert a man in his cause, the* L*ORD approveth not.*

We do have essential civil rights that God has given us. And when tyrants take those rights away from us, God does not approve of that.

America is playing with its own forms of tyranny. When courts legislate from the bench and order legislatures to pass certain laws, that's tyranny. When the President issues executive orders to force the county to obey him, that's tyranny. The temptation to despotic power is just too great for most men to pass up. Lord Acton said it best in 1887: "Power corrupts, and absolute power corrupts absolutely." And America is not immune.

Here is my short list of some of the civil rights which we ought to defend.

[6.1] RIGHT TO ASSEMBLE

> ***Nehemiah 2:20*** *Then answered I them* [Ammonite and Arabian local governors] *and said unto them, The God of heaven, he will prosper us; therefore we his servants will arise and build: but ye have no portion, nor right, nor memorial, in Jerusalem.*

The right to assemble must mean to assemble *exclusively*. If you think you have the right to assemble but the law requires you to admit anyone who asks without discrimination, then you do not have the right to assemble at all. Consider the Boy Scouts. They exclude gays. If we deny them the right to exclude, then we deny them the right to assemble. The right to assemble means *with those you choose,* not with those that the government chooses.

[6.2] Right to Free Speech

Jeremiah 23:28 *The prophet that hath a dream, let him tell a dream; and he that hath my word, let him speak my word faithfully. What is the chaff to the wheat? Saith the LORD.*

God is talking about false prophets. We don't need to shut down false prophets, let them say what they have to say. They have as much right to be heard as anyone else. The lie (chaff) has as much right to be heard as the truth (wheat). You should be able to tell the difference without shutting down free speech.

[6.3] Right to Property

Ezekiel 46:18 *Moreover the prince shall not take of the people's inheritance by oppression, to thrust them out of their possession…my people be not scattered every man from his possession.*

Governments are taking more and more from us. Outrageous taxes, inflation, rent controls, confiscation for invented conservation, oppressive regulations, and eminent domain to take private property to give it to developers — by all these methods and more, government steals from us. And all of that is still not enough to satisfy government's appetite for our stuff, so government runs deficits of trillions of dollars which will likely bankrupt us.

[6.4] Right to Freedom of Religion

Micah 4:4 *...and none shall make them afraid...* ***:5*** *For all people will walk every one in the name of his god, and we will walk in the name of the* LORD *our God for ever and ever.*

We will worship Jehovah, but everyone else will worship whoever they choose. That's the way it should be. Although the God of the Bible often killed people for doing evil, he nowhere killed people for unbelief. It was not the false gods that was the issue but the evil that those false gods caused people to do. Religion (for that matter all beliefs) must be a matter of personal conscience.

The Mormons perhaps say it best with their ***Article of Faith 11:*** *We claim the privilege of worshipping Almighty God according to the dictates of our own conscience, and allow all men the same privilege. Let them worship how, where, or what they may.*

Friendship

Proverbs

Friendship and love are cousin virtues. While not quite the same thing, they do share certain qualities, mostly the quality of caring for another's well-being.

I am not quite sure where friendship leaves off and love begins. They may in fact overlap and entangle. When you love someone, you may consider that you are that person's friend as well, but that's not always the case. Some lovers are enemies. "I love you, but I hate you" is an odd but often true relationship.

On the other side of that coin, just because two people are friends does not mean by any stretch that they also love each other. I have friends that I would never claim to love. To say such a thing as "I love you" to certain friends would be worse than an exaggeration, it might be an uncomfortable presumption with an unclear meaning.

Love is delicate and must never be presumed. But friendship is not delicate and can very often be presumed.

So, love and friendship are alike in some ways and different in other ways. One way that love and friendship are the same is that they are both behaviors, not feelings.

> ***1 Corinthians 13:4*** *Love suffereth long, and is kind* ***:5*** *envieth not…*[etc.]

Nowhere does this text say "love feels…" It instead says, "love does…" The measure of love and the measure of friendship is not how one person feels towards the other but how one person treats the other. The adage "what you do speaks so loudly that I can't hear you" describes precisely this nature of both love and friendship. To claim to love someone or even be friends with someone and yet treat that person badly is pretense.

Jesus described love at its extreme.

> ***John 15:13*** *Greater love hath no man than this, that he lay down his life for his friend.*

Here he mingles together the two notions of love and friendship. Love is doing loving things. Friendship is doing friendly things. And extreme love and extreme friendship are manifested only by extreme sacrifice, sometimes dying.

Now let's explore the Bible and see what else we can learn about friendship.

[1] Advice

> ***Proverbs 15:22*** *Without counsel purposes are disappointed: but in the multitude of counselors they are established.*

One thing friends are really good for is that they give good advice, and without that good advice, what we are trying to do may fail. When you are seeking advice from counselors, you'd better hope that they are trusted friends, people who actually care for your well-being. We often receive advice from counselors who are not our friends but pretend to be. Good examples are salesmen and politicians.

[2] Esteem

Proverbs 16:24 *Pleasant words are as an honeycomb, sweet to the soul, and health to the bones.*

Another thing that friends are good for is that they say things that make us feel good about ourselves. There are times, especially after a failure, when what we need more than just about anything else is a convincing compliment from a true friend, someone who will tell you that you're okay and convince you that it's true.

[3] Adversity

Proverbs 17:17 *A friend loveth at all times, and a brother is born for adversity.*

You've heard of a fair-weather-friend; that is, a friend who is friendly in good times but not in bad. Here's another saying: "A true friend is one you can call at 3:00 A.M."

[4] Reciprocation

Proverbs 18:24 *A man that hath friends must shew himself friendly…*

Friendship must reciprocate with true friendly behavior, or you'll soon be friendless. Do not be so smug in your popularity that you presume on other people's friendships. This is a problem that celebrities have a lot — everyone treats them so friendly that they think they are wonderful and don't need to reciprocate that friendship. There are words that describe such people. One of them is "jerk."

[5] Availability

Proverbs 27:10 *...better is a neighbour that is near than a brother far off.*

A characteristic of friendship is availability. If your best friend is never around but a lesser friend is, then maybe your lesser friend is really your better friend.

[6] Examples

Philippians 2:25 *Yet I supposed it necessary to send to you Epaphroditus...* ***:27*** *For indeed he was sick nigh unto death: but God had mercy on him; and not on him only, but on me also, lest I should have sorrow upon sorrow.*

Had Epaphroditus died, Paul would have missed him greatly. Paul's sorrow would not have been for Epaphroditus' sake, but for his own sake. The personal loss would have been hard to bear. A sign of true friendship is genuinely missing your friend when he is gone.

James 2:23 *And the scripture was fulfilled which saith, Abraham believed God, and it was imputed unto him for righteousness: and he was called the Friend of God.*

Of all the friends you might have, wouldn't it be nice to be God's friend? That God is our friend is clear enough. But are we his friend? What have you done for him lately?

1 Samuel 18:1 *And it came to pass, when he had made an end of speaking unto Saul, that the soul of Jonathan was knit to the soul of David, and Jonathan loved him as his own soul.*

Jonathan, King Saul's son, never resented David's destiny to become king, and David never sought to take the kingdom from Saul's family. That David was destined to be the future king was God's doing, not David's, and however things turned out, these two were friends for life. They would have willingly died for each other.

John 11:16 *Then said Thomas, which is called Didymus, unto his fellow disciples, Let us also go, that we may die with him.*

Jesus was about to place himself in harm's way — again. It would have been easy to say, "If you're going back to Jerusalem, you're going alone." But self-preservation was not on Thomas's mind. For better or worse, he wanted only to be with Jesus, even if it meant dying with him. That's friendship.

[7] LIMITS ON FRIENDSHIP

There's no law that says you have to be friends with every jerk that comes your way. Some people who want to be your "friend" you'd be wise to avoid.

Proverbs 22:10 *Cast out the scorner, and contention shall go out; yea, strife and reproach shall cease.*

Someone who is always critical, always scorning, always dragging you down with his special brand of pessimism, you don't have to keep that person in your circle of friends.

Proverbs 22:24 *Make no friendship with an angry man; and with a furious man thou shalt not go.* ***:25*** *Lest thou learn his ways, and get a snare to thy soul.*

Keep your distance from angry people and criminal types. Not only because their temperament makes for an unhappy environment (and why should you be unhappy?) but also because their temperament will rub off on you. You will become what they are, and that you don't need.

[8] Harsh Friendship

Proverbs 27:6 *Faithful are the wounds of a friend…*

The point of this verse is first, you can trust what your friend says, and second, you can trust that he will say what you need to hear even if you don't want to hear it.

A true friend is one who is more interested in your well-being than he is even in the friendship itself. He may say something that you don't want to hear but that you need to hear, like for example, "Your fly is open." Or for a harsher example which might cost him your friendship, "Your spouse is cheating on you." Neither would likely be reported to you by a non-friend.

Jesus did that a lot. He told people that they needed to repent. That was a very unpopular message that ultimately cost him his life. But he had to say it because it was the truth, and he was the best friend the world ever had.

[9] Sweet Friendship

Proverbs 27:9 *Ointment and perfume rejoice the heart: so doth the sweetness of a man's friend by hearty counsel.*

Besides the good things that friends do for you, they're just nice to have around.

Giving

Proverbs

More words of the Bible are devoted to the subject of money than any other subject. And more than half those verses that deal with money deal specifically with giving. Of all the things that God has commanded us to do or don't do, God seems to be most concerned with how we help chronically poor people, the true have-nots.

[1] The Poor and the Generous

Mark 14:7 *For ye have the poor with you always…*

There is never a time or a society that does not have truly poor people, and God judges every society largely on how it deals with those people.

So, let's explore the Bible now and see what we might learn about how to face the constant poverty that surrounds us.

Deuteronomy 15:7 *thou shalt not harden thine heart, nor shut thine hand from thy poor brother.* ***:8*** *lend him* ***:9*** *Beware that there be not a wicked thought in thy heart, saying, The seventh year, the year of release, is at hand; and thine eye be evil against thy poor brother, and givest him nought.*

Loan to the poor and don't worry that you may never get any of it back.

Israel had not only a Sabbath Day but also a Sabbath Year. In that Sabbath Year, all slaves were released, and all debts were forgiven. What this verse is saying is don't be concerned about the Sabbath Years. If your poor brother needs a loan, you might think about the Sabbath Year coming up soon and you won't get your money back. This verse is saying, don't worry about that, and don't worry that you might not get your money back. If you never get it back, then you are a generous giver.

> ***Deuteronomy 15:10*** *Thou shalt surely give him, and thine heart shall not be grieved when thou givest unto him: because that for this thing the LORD thy God shall bless thee in all thy works, and in all that thou puttest thine hand unto.*

When you give, don't feel bad that now you're out a few bucks. Instead, feel good that you did something good for someone, and besides, God will bless "all thy works," your business, your job, your family, and the causes that you contribute your time and effort to. A generous person seems to be lucky a lot. The fact is, he is blessed and protected.

> ***Job 4:5*** *Offer the sacrifice of righteousness, and put your trust in the LORD.*

When you're giving, you may worry that you'll go broke being generous. That's a reasonable concern, but trust God that you'll be okay.

> ***Psalms 41:1*** *Blessed is he that considereth the poor: the LORD will deliver him in time of trouble.*

> ***Proverbs 3:9*** *Honour the LORD with thy substance, and with the firstfruits of all thine increase.* ***:10*** *So shall thy barns be filled with plenty, and thy presses shall burst out with new wine.*

Proverbs 11:24 *There is that scattereth, and yet increaseth, and there is that withholdeth more than is meet, but it tendeth to poverty.* **:25** *The liberal soul shall be made fat: and he that watereth shall be watered also himself.*

This is an interesting contradiction of money that the generous get richer, where the stingy go broke. Proverbs repeats this theme a lot.

Proverbs 15:6 *In the house of the righteous is much treasure: but in the revenues of the wicked is trouble.*

Proverbs 17:5 *Whoso mocketh the poor reproacheth his Maker: and he that is glad at calamities shall not be unpunished.*

Proverbs 19:17 *He that hath pity upon the poor lendeth unto the* LORD; *and that which he hath given will he pay him again.*

Proverbs 21:13 *Whoso stoppeth his ears at the cry of the poor, he also shall cry himself, but shall not be heard.*

Proverbs 21:26 *He coveteth greedily all the day long: but the righteous giveth and spareth not.*

Proverbs 22:9 *He that hath a bountiful eye shall be blessed; for he giveth of his bread to the poor.* [*Bountiful eye* means to see what someone else *should* have.]

Proverbs 28:27 *He that giveth unto the poor shall not lack: but he that hideth his eyes shall have many a curse.*

Proverbs 29:7 *The righteous considereth the cause of the poor: but the wicked regardeth not to know it.*

Proverbs 31:20 *She* [the virtuous woman] *stretcheth out her hand to the poor; yea, she reacheth forth her hands to the needy.*

Daniel 4:27 *Wherefore, O king, let my counsel be…shewing mercy to the poor…*

Acts 10:31 *…thine alms are had in remembrance in the sight of God.*

2 Corinthians 9:7 *Every man according as he purposeth in his heart, so let him give; not grudgingly, or of necessity: for God loveth a cheerful giver.* ***:9*** *As it is written, He hath dispersed abroad; he hath given to the poor: his righteousness remaineth for ever.*

[2] Limits to Generosity

Generosity is, of course, a good thing. You just read the verses. But is generosity *always* a good thing in every circumstance no matter what? Should there be balance?

In politics there is a perpetual tug-of-war between liberals who are so sympathetic to the poor that they would bleed the rest of us to death with ever increasing taxes to pay our "fair share," and conservatives who try as best they can to say enough is enough, we've paid our fair share many times over.

With this tension always ongoing and with no end in sight, it makes sense to see if the Bible might weigh in on the matter. Are there limits to generosity?

[2.1] A Dishonest Receiver

> ***2 Kings 5:22*** *And he* [Gehazi, Elisha's servant] *said…even now there be come to me from mount Ephraim two young men of the sons of the prophets* [this is a lie]*: give them, I pray thee, a talent of silver, and two changes of garments* [Geharzi's greed overcame him, he just wanted stuff] ***:23*** *And Naaman said, Be content, take two talents.* ***:26*** *And he* [Elisha] *said unto him* [Gehazi]… ***:27*** *The leprosy therefore of Naaman shall cleave unto thee, and unto thy seed for ever. And he went out from his presence a leper as white as snow.*

Naaman was very generous and grateful for the opportunity to repay the kindness that had been given to him — he was cured of leprosy. He had no idea of the damage his generosity was about to cause — his leprosy was about to fall on Elijah's servant.

Sometimes you need to be a bit cautious with your kindness. Sometimes there are unintended consequences, as in this example, Gehazi being stricken with leprosy. And for another example, unlimited welfare to single mothers encourages those mothers to not bother to marry the fathers of their children, which in turn increases the number of fatherless households, which in turn creates a poverty cycle from children growing up in fatherless households. So, this generosity actually causes the problem it's trying to solve.

Today if you perpetually give to someone who constantly abuses the gift, society would call you an "enabler", that is, you enable someone to continue in self-abusive behaviors. Half the trick in stopping the self-abusive behavior is to stop the enabler.

[2.2] The Greedy Poor

> ***Deuteronomy 23:24*** *When thou comest into thy neighbour's vineyard, then thou mayest eat grapes thy fill at thine own pleasure; but thou shalt not put any in thy vessel.* ***:25*** *When thou comest into the standing corn of thy neighbour, then thou mayest pluck the ears with thine hand; but thou shalt not move a sickle unto thy neighbour's standing corn.*

Back then, there were no restaurants, and travelers could only take so much food on a journey, so they needed to find food as they traveled. And, of course, wherever there were farms and orchards, there was food. But did they have a right to take it? They did. But there were limits.

The law allowed anyone to go into a field — it didn't matter who owned the field since it was all a gift from God anyway — and eat what you needed. It was sort of a tax on farmers. The amount of food consumed by a traveler — whether a merchant or a vacationer or an itinerant preacher, as Jesus was *(**Matthew 12:1-8**)*, or just a homeless person — was negligible, so the farmer wasn't giving up much.

What would not have been negligible, however, is if the traveler or poor person took advantage of the situation and filled up a bucket or two or ten with apples or corn or whatever and took it all home. That, the law forbade.

Today, if you go to an all-you-can eat buffet, you really are allowed to eat all-you-can-eat-*here*, at the restaraunt. That does *not* mean all-you-can-carry-home. There is no take-out, no fill your cooler so you can fill your refrigerator at home.

It's the same principle here.

From the liberal viewpoint: The poor need food to live. So eat, at the farmer's expense. Fair enough.

From the conservative viewpoint: What the poor are allowed to take is limited to what they need right now. They are not entitled to take food for later, like tonight's dinner or tomorrow's breakfast. There is no perpetual entitlement to someone else's crops. God does not want starving poor people, but he also does not want starving farmers either. There's a balance.

Also, the text says *standing corn.* The travelers can help themselves to the crop in the field which has not been picked, but not to the harvest in the stacks, or wagons, or barns. If you expect someone else to give you food, all right then, but at least pick and shuck the corn yourself, don't require the farmer to do *that* for you too. The law allows you access, nothing more. You want it? Go get it. Don't expect it to be brought to your door. Poor is one thing, lazy is another.

Today, poor people remain poor because so much is given to them without any effort on their part that they are locked into a cycle of poverty because entitlements make it too comfortable to be poor. They don't have to do anything.

I believe, yes, there should be provision for the poor, but something should be required of the poor to get it. Go sweep the streets, go pick up leaves in the park, go do *some*thing useful, or even something not useful, but something anyway. The government should provide, not dole, but minimal jobs for absolutely anyone who needs money to eat. No resumé required. You want a job? Here's a shovel, go dig. With that arrangement, the poor would soon start improving their lives by moving from job to job, from low responsibility to higher responsibility, and from very low wages (less than the minimum wage) to higher wages.

None of this applies, of course, to the truly invalid, although I would apply it to the partially invalid. A paraplegic with good arms can make license plates. But a quadriplegic can make nothing. And both deserve to not starve. We're all in this life together. You want to eat? Do something useful, if you can.

[2.3] ENTITLEMENTS

Luke 6:30 *Give to every man that asketh of thee…*

Are we really to take this literally? The problem is, when takers find a generous person, the number of takers grows. There were some charities that I used to give to, but then my mailbox started filling up with more and more pleading for contributions from more and more charities until all the crap that landed in my mailbox daily wouldn't even fit in the mailbox. And I couldn't get the post office to stop it. I felt like the Sorcerer's Apprentice (Mickey Mouse) and those water carrying broomsticks that multiplied and kept coming in increasing droves. I only solved the problem by moving and refusing to allow the post office to forward C class mail. That stopped it.

Those charities had abused my generosity. And to any charity who happens to be reading this, I will never again contribute to a charity that does not provide a guarantee of privacy. Or maybe I will send cash, or a money order, but I will not provide my address because I know it will end up on limitless mailing lists.

The most generous person who ever lived was Jesus Christ. Did he have this problem? Yes he did. His generosity drew people like flies — both the worthy needy and the unworthy greedy.

One evening Jesus fed 5,000 people from five loaves and two fish. This great story displays for us his power and his generosity. It also displays their greed. The next morning those same people came back to him looking for breakfast. He told them no and that what they really needed was the bread of life, that is, himself.

John 6:26 *Jesus answered them and said, Verily, verily, I say unto you, Ye seek me, not because ye saw the miracles, but because ye did eat the loaves and were filled.*

In other words, they wanted more free food. And when they realized they weren't going to get a second course, they argued with him and left in a huff.

I understand what Jesus said, "Give to every man who asketh of thee." But even Jesus recognized when people were taking advantage of him, and he didn't like it.

Maybe he also doesn't like it when we take advantage of his grace.

[3] Principles

The following is a list of miscellaneous principles for giving. The Bible bounces around, and we shouldn't want to miss any of it, but we have to make decisions. So here are the ones I've found that seem to belong on my list.

[3.1] Give to God, but also give to the needy

Deuteronomy 16:10 *...give unto the LORD thy God.*
Deuteronomy 15:11 *Open thy hand wide...to thy poor.*

Everyone wants your money, including God. Without generous donations, face it, your church wouldn't exist. The platitude "God doesn't need your money" isn't a fair assessment. If a church's generous givers suddenly decided to stop giving, that church would vanish, the same as any other entity. You need to be generous with God.

However, being generous with God and your church is no excuse for being stingy with the poor, your fellow man. Writing a check to your church does not let you off the hook for helping others who have nothing to do with your church.

Giving to God is simple, even tax deductable. Giving to the beggar whose motive is not clear is not so simple. Or how about the newly widowed young mother around the corner? Or flood victims in Asia? Or drought victims in Africa? Or lepers in Brazil? "Oh, but I give to my church and my church takes care of all that." That's not the directive. God said, "Open *your* hand wide to the poor." God wants *you* involved, he wants to see who *you* care about. Delegating generosity to your church is a pretty good indication that you probably don't much care about anyone.

Think of it this way: What a grand opportunity tactical giving is (that is, to specific people) to let God know, and let yourself know, just who it is you care about. Your attitude should be: "God, I have a great sorrow for *them*, and I have to give." That's a good thing, isn't it, to know that you care — about someone?

[3.2] Sacrificial Giving is Better

> ***2 Samuel 24:24*** *Neither will I offer burnt offerings unto the* LORD *my God of that which doth cost me nothing.*

Here was the situation: David needed God's help and wanted to make a sacrifice. He offered to buy what he needed from Araunah, but Araunah, a generous man and David's friend, basically said, "You don't need to pay me, just take what you need."

We all have friends who are generous with us like that. The problem is, how impressed would God be with your giving if it was just given to you? That's not much of a sacrifice. Well, it would have been a sacrifice alright, but Araunah's sacrifice, and David needed to make his own. And so David said something like, "Thank you friend, but I need to do this. Let me pay for this. Please."

Clearly, giving what you need and find difficult to do without is better than giving what you don't need and wouldn't miss.

> ***Luke 21:3*** *And he* [Jesus] *said of a truth I say unto you, that this poor widow hath cast in more than they all:* ***:4*** *For all these have of their abundance cast in unto the offering of God: but she of her penury hath cast in all the living that she had.*

You'd think it wouldn't matter, a dollar is a dollar, but somehow it does. Sacrifice, and not just giving, brings the blessings. And not just to the receiver, but to the giver as well.

[3.3] GIVE NOW, DON'T WAIT UNTIL YOU ARE RICHER

Hunger won't wait for you to feel more generous, or to make more money.

> ***Luke 16:10*** *He that is faithful in that which is least is faithful also in much.*

Jesus makes the point here that your characteristic of stinginess or generosity has nothing to do with your financial level. If you're stingy when you're poor, you'll be stingy when you're rich. The same with generosity. Character is character, and getting rich does not change your character. Stinginess crosses all class boundaries.

[3.4] GIVE AS YOU DECIDE, NOT AS OTHERS DECIDE FOR YOU

> ***2 Corinthians 9:7*** *Every man according as he purposeth in his heart, so let him give.*

Yes, I know, there is tithing, 10% in my church. But understand that tithing is not a tax. The church does not (as the IRS does) come and take it from you. Whether it is tithing to your church, or a donation to the soup kitchen downtown, or sending medicine to sick people on the other side of the world, giving must be freewill. It must come from your heart, from how you earnestly feel about the sufferings of others. It is your dollar, it is your gift.

Don't let someone else intimidate you into giving. God is giving you the opportunity to be a part of meeting someone else's need. Don't let your joy be corrupted by giving from guilt. Much better is to give from love. Then you can enjoy it, and the gift, I believe, has more power.

[3.5] Be Less Picky

Luke 6:30 *Give to every man that asketh of thee.*

This takes us back to our opening verse. Give when someone needs your help, don't wait until just the right needy person comes along or you're in a mood to give. There are lots of people who need your help, and Jesus wants us to respond to needs as they arise.

Now obviously our resources are limited, and you can't give what you don't have. But still, we should try to respond in some way to each person's need. There's a story (whether true or folklore I don't know) about a billionaire who decided to give everything he owned to everyone on the planet. And when his accountants finished their accounting, the billionaire realized that were he to give everything to everyone, each person on the planet would receive from him one matchstick.

Clearly, you can't be generous with everyone. You don't have the means. But still Jesus did say, "Give to every man that asketh of thee." So somewhere between breaking yourself by trying to give to everyone, and total stinginess, there is a middle ground of sincerely trying to help when help is needed. That is where God wants us to be.

[3.6] GOD BLESSES THE GENEROUS WITH TEMPORAL BLESSINGS

Luke 6:38 *Give and it shall be given unto you; good measure, pressed down, shaken together…*

Is it a sin to want God's blessing? It is a sin to *not* want God's blessing. He wants to give, and he reciprocates to your giving. Believe me, I take all I can get. I have no reluctance at all about asking God for favors.

In old times in Cracker Barrel stores, you'd walk in and buy a sack full of flour. When the shopkeeper fills up the sack, you hope to see him fill it to the top, press it down, and shake it so he can get more in it. That's the good measure of an honest merchant. That's the blessing that God dispenses to generous people.

[3.7] GOD BLESSES THE GENEROUS WITH ETERNAL BLESSINGS

Matthew 25:34 *Come…inherit the kingdom…* ***:35*** *For I was an hungered and ye gave me meat.*

It is no secret that God is looking for generous people to populate heaven with. You should want to be among them.

[4] PERSONAL FAVORITES

I have never been a rich man. And everything I ever gave, I gave from my financial stresses. There are many different charities that I have given to at one time or another, but there are two that I have stuck with me for decades because what those two charities do is where my heart is at. I will share them with you now.

The first is the National Right to Life. If ever there was discrimination against a class of people, it is the world's unborn. Murdered by saline, murdered by scalpel, murdered by whatever clever means abortion "doctors" can devise and get away with, these babies are killed constantly, on average a million a year in this country alone, babies, who will never see the light of day because their mothers and their accommodating "doctors" decided they weren't worthy to live. So, some of my money goes there.

The second is the American Leprosy Mission. It breaks my heart that that most evil of all diseases still has its way in some parts of the world, destroying lives, maiming and disfiguring people, mostly children. This organization sends doctors around the world into isolated regions and looks for and cures this specific disease. May their efforts be blessed, and may that dreaded disease one day be completely eradicated. And so, some of my money goes there.

Of course, there are many, many organizations that help. I have my favorites, you have yours. Let your heart be your guide. Be generous. That God allows you to be generous is itself generous of God. He's letting you on the team, to contribute, to help. Isn't that wonderful?

Greed

Isaiah 5:8-9

Proverbs 22:16 *He that oppresseth the poor to increase his riches, and he that giveth to the rich, shall surely come to want.*

Proverbs 22:22 *Rob not the poor, because he is poor: neither oppress the afflicted in the gate.*

Isaiah 5:8 *Woe unto them that join house to house, that lay field to field, till there be no place, that they may be placed alone in the midst of the earth.* ***:9*** *In mine ears said the* LORD *of hosts, Of a truth many houses shall be desolate, even great and fair, without inhabitant.*

Real estate investors who buy up so many houses, and so much of the land, and hike the prices so high that ordinary people have no place to live, God doesn't like that. All those houses you invest in, they will be vacant.

Isaiah 56:11 *Yea, they are greedy dogs which can never have enough, and they are shepherds that cannot understand: they all look to their own way, every one for his gain, from his quarter.*

Ezekiel 35:2 *Son of man, set thy face against mount Seir, and prophesy against it,* ***:4*** *I will lay thy cities waste…* ***:10*** *Because thou hast said, These two nations and these two countries shall be mine, and we will possess it; whereas the* LORD *was there:*

When Israel and Judea were destroyed, the neighboring nations saw an opportunity to grab all their land and get rich. But the result of that was their own destruction.

Want to get rich by buying stressed real estate? My wife and I tried that. Instead of enriching us, those properties wiped us out financially. Beware of bargains.

> ***Amos 5:11*** *...your treading is upon the poor...* ***:12*** *...they turn aside the poor in the gate from their right.*

> ***Amos 8:4*** *Hear this, O ye that swallow up the needy, even to make the poor of the land to fail*

Any nation that ignores the plight of the poor is a heartless nation and doesn't deserve God's protection.

Guilt

Psalms 32:3, Romans 3:23

Being guilty and feeling guilty are two different things. We are all guilty, and that's bad. And so we feel guilty, and that's good. When we're guilty, we need to feel guilty because that leads us to confession and repentance. Unless of course we feel guilty when there's nothing to feel guilty about, then that's bad.

[1] Feeling Guilty

Job 9:20 *If I justify myself, Mine own mouth shall condemn me: if I say, I am perfect, it shall also prove me perverse.*

When we are guilty, we can't properly defend ourselves, though we may try. If we claim to be innocent when we are in fact guilty, the claim itself makes us even more guilty because it's a lie, and we feel even more guilty for saying we're innocent when we know better.

Psalms 32:3 *When I kept silence, by bones waxed old through all my roaring all the day long.* ***:5*** *I acknowledge my sin unto thee, and my iniquity have I not hid. I said, I will confess my transgressions unto the LORD; and thou forgavest the iniquity of my sin. Selah.* ***:6*** *For this shall every one that is godly pray unto thee in a time when thou mayest be found…*

This psalm was authored by King David. He was feeling really guilty over the matter about Uriah and Bathsheba. Feeling guilt can consume you, and when you are guilty, as David was, it is that feeling of guilt that drives you crazy and finally to confession and submission to whatever penalty is appropriate.

Actually, David didn't confess his sins until he was caught by the prophet Nathan. But when he was caught, it was unburdening that at last he was found out.

> ***Psalms 38:3*** *There is no soundness in my flesh because of thine anger; neither is there any rest in my bones because of my sin.* ***:4*** *For my iniquities are gone over mine head: as an heavy burden they are too heavy for me.*

This author considers that he is physically ill because of his iniquities and God's anger. While it is wrong to ascribe all disease to sin (as Job proves to us), it is certainly true that the stress of guilt can cause illnesses.

A guilty conscience is like drowning, "gone over my head," overwhelming. When someone does something truly evil, if they feel real guilt, then we can feel like there is that justice anyway. But if they feel no guilt, then we feel doubly angry at them, first because of the evil they did, and second because of their lack of conscience, lack of personal grief. I'm betting that God feels like that too and may exact a double penalty against those who feel no guilt and who, in fact, get away with it.

In that regard, Judas Iscariot felt enough guilt to hang himself, which doesn't absolve him of what he did, but at least we feel that some justice was done. Since no one else was willing to punish him, he punished himself. At least he didn't have to also suffer the guilt of having gotten away with it. Punishment, it seems, is merciful in a dark sort of way, and a guilty conscience sometimes longs for judgment.

Psalms 40:12 *For innumerable evils have compassed me about: mine iniquities have taken hold upon me, so that I am not able to look up: they are more than the hairs of mine head: therefore my heart faileth me.*

Feelings of guilt can be so overpowering that one cannot even talk to God about it, "not able to look up." To ask forgiveness can seem inappropriate. This is all the more reason to see this consequence of sin ahead of time, resist it, and avoid all this grief.

Some people think that we should never feel guilty about anything. That's not true. Basically, we should feel guilty about things we are guilty of, but not feel guilty about things that are not our fault. For example, a child may feel guilt about her parents' divorce. That is a terrible unfairness, and it is the obligation of the divorcing parents to make sure that doesn't happen. But it is also the girl's obligation to herself to not blame herself for something she had no control over and could not have prevented.

[2] Claiming Innocence

Proverbs 16:2 *All the ways of a man are clean in his own eyes; but the* LORD *weigheth the spirits.*

However much sin an evil a man commits, he still sees his actions as justified. We tend to excuse ourselves, and we are horrified to have to face up to our own guilt and squirm every which way in our conscience to avoid the confrontation. But it is only when we accept our guilt that we are able to accept Christ's forgiveness.

Proverbs 16:25 *There is a way that seemeth right unto a man, but the end thereof are the ways of death.*

Often that which is wrong seems right at the time, and only afterwards does the folly become obvious. But usually, wrong gives an early warning to our conscience which we really ought to take to heart.

> ***Proverbs 30:20*** *Such is the way of an adulterous woman; she eateth, and wipeth her mouth, and saith, I have done no wickedness.*

Many people have no shame, no feelings of guilt, just a constant assertion of innocence and self-justification. People have a strong need to feel innocent even when they are guilty (especially when they are guilty), and so they deny their guilt with excuses and justifications. That's the inescapable road to hell because there can be no repentance because there is no feeling of the need to repent.

[3] General Guilt

> ***Proverbs 20:9*** *Who can say, I have made my heart clean, I am pure from my sin?*

This is a rhetorical question. The answer, of course, is no one. Even though we all want to be innocent, we all have the nagging suspicion that we are guilty of something.

> ***Romans 3:9*** *What then? Are we better than they? No, in no wise: for we have before proved both Jews and Gentiles, that they are all under sin* ***:10*** *As it is written, There is none righteous, no not one.* ***:19*** *Now we know that what things soever the law saith, it saith to them that are under the law: that every mouth may be stopped, and all the world may become guilty before God.* ***:23*** *For all have sinned, and come short of the glory of God.*

Paul, in order to offer us a general forgiveness in Christ, must first convict us of a general guilt. We are all of us guilty of something, and therefore we all need forgiveness.

There is a problem here, and that is we can become complacent with this feeling of general guilt. In other words, "Of course I'm guilty, we're all guilty. So what?" The problem is that this guilt brushes with so broad a stroke that we are able to trivialize it away. We are confessing *so* much guilt that we are in effect confessing nothing. Thus we hide our real guilt, not with claims of innocence, but by confessing everything. So false guilt then becomes a cloak of concealment for true guilt. There's this saying: "What's harder than finding a needle in a haystack? Finding a needle in a pile of needles."

An illustration: There is a popular radio talk show host, Bill Handel. His show is irreverent about almost everything. He is a centrist who offends conservatives and liberals alike and has found himself having to apologize to one group or another often. So, what he does now is, at the end of each show, he has one of his co-hosts, a lady whose name I don't know, issue a blanket apology to everyone mentioned on the show. She will say something like, "This program apologizes to but is not limited to gays, and Christians, and gun owners, and. … and … and," and in under a minute she will list everyone who could have possibly taken offense by anything said on the show. It's very humorous, and at the same time very serious. But more than anything, it is poking fun at people who take offense so easily. The point is that by apologizing to everybody, Bill Handel is in fact apologizing to nobody, because it's ludicrous.

Too much guilt is like that. If we feel guilty about everything, then we are in fact feeling guilty about nothing. And there are some real things we've done that really do warrant our feeling guilty about. Those are the things we need to find and bring to God, and not to hide them behind a mask of trivial guilt that amounts to nothing.

What Paul really means (in my opinion, and whether he knows it or not) is that we all have true guilt, things that we've done that are non-trivial, that have caused real injury. What Paul is offering us is forgiveness from *those*, not this general and vague feeling of a sinful nature, and a cheap confession which means little.

But, in case you still worry about hidden sins lurking in the shadowy caverns of your sinful nature, sins that you don't know about but you suspect are there, well, Jesus forgives those too. It really is a blanket forgiveness that atones for it all, big and small.

[4] Guilt By Association

> ***Psalms 69:6*** *Let not them that wait on thee, O Lord GOD of hosts, be ashamed for my sake: let not those that seek thee be confounded for my sake, O God of Israel.*

In other words: God, don't blame others for my failings. It's bad enough that I sinned, and worse that I must be punished, but it would be far worse that others should be punished because of me. That's the meaning of this prayer of David's.

Applications are many. An adulterous man seduces a married woman, and so her husband and their children are scarred with a lifetime of consequences. A general recklessly deploys his troops and gets them all killed. A stockbroker makes bad recommendations and loses his client's money. A drunk driver kills a family with children, but he himself survives.

There are countless ways where the consequences of one person's bad judgments become someone else's pain. What makes sin so sinful is the price others have to pay

But this verse has more in view than just the consequences directed to victims. It also speaks to us about guilt by association. Innocent people are often made culpable by another's misdeeds. A husband's gambling addiction loses the house. The wife may plead with the bank, "But I am innocent. Why should I have to lose *my* house?" But her plea will fall on deaf ears. The house, hers and his, is gone. In World War II Japan, American bombs killed as many Japanese children as Japanese combatants. Innocent casualties are called collateral damage and are a particularly ugly way for innocent people to have to pay for the misdeeds of others.

God's judgments are no different. When they fall, they fall on the innocent along with the guilty. We have no idea how many children died in the great flood. Or died in Sodom. Or how many Amorite children died from Israel's invasion.

I do believe that guilty people are not only guilty for the suffering of their victims, but also for the suffering of those who are unable to get out of the way of the incoming judgment. In the story of Jonah, there's this little side drama.

> ***Jonah 1:10*** *Then were the men exceedingly afraid, and said unto him, Why hast thou done this?*

It was clear to everyone on the boat that Jonah was drawing God's judgment like a lightning rod. The problem was that while God's judgment targeted Jonah, the sailors were caught in the crossfire. They were about to die because of Jonah's dispute with God.

Their deaths would have made Jonah's sin doubly sinful, so Jonah told them to throw him overboard. And they did. Why should they have to die as well?

Sometimes we need to act to save the innocent and stop protecting the guilty from the consequences of their own actions. When we try too hard to protect the guilty, very often our efforts cost innocent people their lives. That's why, for example, child protection services often extracts endangered children from the homes of abusive parents. After all, why should a child have to pay for his or her parents' transgressions? Perhaps one day abortionists will finally understand that.

[5] THE UNGODLY

Now we need to ask, who needs salvation? And that brings us first to the ungodly.

> ***Romans 1:18*** *For the wrath of God is revealed from heaven against all ungodliness and unrighteousness of men…* ***:29*** *Being filled with all unrighteousness, fornication, wickedness, covetousness, maliciousness, full of envy, murder, debate, deceit, malignity; whisperers,* ***:30*** *Backbiters, haters, of God,…(etc.)*

No surprise there. The ungodly are guilty, and there's a long list of them. So let's just quickly move on. Anyone else need salvation?

[6] JEWS

> ***Romans 2:1*** *Therefore thou art inexcuseable, O man, whosoever thou art that judgest: for wherein thou judgest another, thou condemnest thyself; for thou that judgest doest the same things.* ***:12*** *…as many as have sinned in the law shall be judged by the law.*

What is in view here is the Jews. The point being, "Ah, but we have the law. Therefore, we are innocent." Paul says, "Not so. It's not having the law that makes you innocent, it's living it, and you don't live it."

Anyone else?

[7] Gentiles

> **Romans 2:12** *For as many as have sinned without law shall also perish without law…* **:14** *For when the Gentiles, which have not the law, do by nature the things contained in the law, these, having not the law, are a law unto themselves:* **:15** *Which shew the work of the law written in their hearts, their conscience also bearing witness, and their thoughts the mean while accusing or else excusing one another.*

Now we see that the gentiles are also condemned. How so? Here's Paul's logic. The gentiles may reason, "Well, the Jews are condemned because they have the law and don't live it. But we don't have the law, so we're innocent by ignorance and can't be condemned by a law that we don't have." Paul says, "Not so. Sometimes you do live the law for conscience sake. And when you live it, you give proof that you really do know right from wrong. You can't escape the law because it's in your hearts. Therefore, when you don't live the law, you're without excuse, and you're guilty."Anyone else?

[8] None Are Righteous

> **Romans 3:9** *What then? Are we better than they? No, in no wise: for we have before proved both Jews and Gentiles, that they are all under sin;* **:10** *As it is written, There is none righteous, no, not one (***Psalms 14:1***)* **:20** *Therefore by the deeds of the law there shall no flesh be justified in his sight: for by the law is the knowledge of sin.* **:23** *For all have sinned, and come short of the glory of God (***Ecclesiastes 7:20***).*

Well, that pretty well covers the ground. Bad people are guilty, the Jews are guilty, the gentiles are guilty, and you and I are guilty.

Does that leave anyone out? Nope. Before God, the whole world is guilty.

[9] Escape

Well then, how can any of us escape condemnation? There is only one way, and that is:

> ***Romans 3:24*** *Being justified freely by his grace through the redemption that is in Christ Jesus.*

> ***Romans 8:1*** *For there is now no condemnation for those who are in Christ Jesus, who walk not after the flesh but after the spirit.*

Honesty

Deuteronomy 25:13-15

The whole notion of honesty seems to be from a bygone era. Today, with chronic cheating in schools at every level, cheating in government, cheating in business and advertizing, cheating in the investment markets, cheating in marriages, cheating everywhere, I have to wonder, why should we even bother to defend honesty? It seems a dead issue.

The number one answer is, of course, that honesty is something that God expects of us. The number two answer is that honesty is the right thing to do. And the number three answer is that sooner or later you get caught, and one way or another you get punished. What goes around comes around.

Here then, for your reading pleasure, is what the Bible has to say about honesty.

[1] Finders Keepers

> ***Deuteronomy 22:1*** *Thou shalt not see thy brother's ox or his sheep go astray, and hide thyself from them: thou shalt in any case bring them again unto thy brother.* ***:2*** *And if thy brother be not nigh unto thee, or if thou know him not, then thou shalt bring it unto thine own house, and it shall be with thee until thy brother seek after it, and thou shalt restore it to him again.*

If you find something that belongs to someone else, return it to him. "Finders Keepers" is not God's way of doing things. Also, if you can't return a found object because of distance or maybe you don't even know whose it is, hold on to it for safe-keeping until it can be returned.

[2] Business

> ***Deuteronomy 25:13*** *Thou shalt not have in thy bag divers weights, a great and a small.* ***:14*** *Thou shalt not have in thine house divers measures, a great and a small.* ***:15*** *But thou shalt have a perfect and just weight, a perfect and just measure shalt thou have: that they days may be lengthened in the land which the* LORD *thy God giveth thee.*

> ***Proverbs 11:1*** *A false balance is abomination to the* LORD*: but a just weight is his delight.*

> ***Proverbs 16:11*** *A just weight and balance are the* LORD*'s: all the weights of the bag are his work.*

This is saying more than be honest, it is saying that honesty is from God. He created money, he created business, and he created honesty.

> ***Proverbs 20:10*** *Divers weight, and divers measures, both of them are alike abomination to the* LORD. ***:23*** *Divers weights are an abomination unto the* LORD*; and a false balance is not good.*

> ***Ezekiel 45:10*** *Ye shall have just balances, and a just ephah, and a just bath.*

An ephah was a dry measure (about 3/5 bushel) and a bath was a liquid measure (about 6 gallons).

Amos 8:5*...making the ephah small, and the shekel great, and falsifying the balances by deceit?* ***:6*** *That we may buy the poor for silver, and the needy for a pair of shoes; yea, and sell the refuse of the wheat?*

They were charging more money (shekel great) for less merchandise (ephah small). Buy cheap and sell shoddy merchandise expensively.

Micah 6:10 *Are there yet the treasures of wickedness in the house of the wicked, and the scant measure that is abominable?* ***:11*** *Shall I count them pure with the wicked balances, and with the bag of deceitful weights?* ***:12*** *For the rich men thereof are full of violence, and the inhabitants thereof have spoken lies, and their tongue is deceitful in their mouth.*

There are many ways to cheat in business. Grocery markets might cheat with dishonest weights to rig the scales. Fabric stores might cheat with dishonest measuring sticks. Governments used to cheat by shaving (clipping) gold or silver off the edges of coins which is why coins today are reeded (the tiny grooves around the edge of a coin) so you can see if it's been shaved.

Honest businesses are places that draw customers. A reputation for honesty is not only good for businesses, but also for communities and the nation. Honesty keeps you in business. Crooks think they are getting away with something, but what they don't understand is word travels fast, and their customer base soon dwindles to nothing.

[3] Borrowing

Psalms 37:21 *The wicked borroweth, and payeth not again: but the righteous sheweth mercy, and giveth.*

To borrow implies a promise to return. But when a borrower never returns a borrowed object, then that amounts to stealing.

[4] INTEGRITY

Proverbs 11:3 *The integrity of the upright shall guide them.*

It is your integrity, or lack of it, that directs your daily decisions about everything. You don't have to decide to do the honest thing, if integrity is your nature you *will* do the honest thing because you can't do otherwise.

[5] CIVILIZATION

Proverbs 11:11 *By the blessing of the upright the city is exalted: but it is overthrown by the mouth of the wicked.*

Civilization prospers when its businesses operate on honesty. When crooks run business and government, the economy falls apart and so does the city. That's why the SEC oversees investment markets, or is supposed to.

[6] VEILED HONESTY

Proverbs 12:22 *Lying lips are abomination to the LORD: but they that deal truly are his delight.* ***:23*** *A prudent man concealeth knowledge*

This might be construed as a contradiction. God loves honesty, but some truths are best left unsaid. There is veiled honesty. For an extreme example, would you ever say to a woman, "You're ugly"? And then defend yourself with, "But it's the truth. I'm just being honest." That's not honesty, that's viciousness cloaked as honesty. So, it's a double sin.

A woman asked her husband, "Do I look fat?" He replied, "Do I look stupid?" There is a place for common sense and good judgment. Some truths ought not to be said.

Jesus taught the people in parables. When asked why, he said that only they who are seeking will find the truth. Jesus was not obliged to spill out all spiritual truth to all antagonists which would only incite even more hostility towards himself, and Jesus said as much —

> ***Matthew 7:6*** *Give not that which is holy unto dogs, neither cast ye your pearls before swine, lest they trample them under their feet, and turn again to rend you.*

Was Jesus promoting dishonesty? No. But he was giving us permission to hold our peace in some situations. We don't need to invite incoming hostility. Judicious selection of what we should and should not disseminate is allowed. As ***:23*** says, *a prudent man concealeth knowledge…* That is permissible and is not dishonest.

[7] Children

> ***Proverbs 20:11*** *Even a child is known by his doings, whether his work be pure, and whether it be right.*

Integrity, or its lack, is conspicuous at even very early ages. It's either there or not. It's hard to learn. Wise employers know to hire integrity and train skills. It's easier to find a skillful employee than an honest one.

[8] Creative Dishonesty

Habakkuk 2:6 ...*Woe to him that increaseth that which is not his!*

There are many ways to acquire things that belong to other people. Robbing banks and stealing cars are only the least complicated. More complicated but just as evil is identity theft, internet fraud, telephone fraud, borrowing and not repaying, selling without disclosing material facts, embezzlement, shop lifting, and so on.

This verse speaks to all of that because it says nothing about how a charlatan transfers money from other people's pockets to his own but only that he does. Whatever that means, it is evil, and this verse pronounces a curse ("woe") on all such.

[9] Conspicuous Honesty

Matthew 5:16 *Let your light so shine before men, that they may see your good works, and glorify your Father which is in heaven.*

Romans 12:17 *Provide things honest in the sight of all men.*

Besides wanting to do the right thing anyway, a second reason to do the right thing is that people are watching. What you do reflects on Christ and Christianity. Be true to what Christianity is, live true to your claim. If you claim to represent Christ, then live accordingly. Be for real. And if others observe it, that's a good thing. It may inspire them.

A father and son went to the movies. The child admission was six years and under. The son was seven. The father asked for two adult tickets. The ticket vendor said, "Why don't you get a child's ticket for your son? You'll save money." The father replied,

"Because he's seven." The vendor replied, "But he looks six. No one will know." The father replied, "*He'll* know."

> ***1 Peter 2:12*** *Having your conversation honest among the Gentiles: that, whereas they speak against you as evildoers, they may by your good works, which they shall behold, glorify God in the day of visitation.*

Your honesty will shut the mouth of critics who judge Jesus Christ by your life. The point of honesty here is to actually be what you claim to be. Don't assert to the world that you belong to Christ then be dishonest. That signals to everyone who knows you that Jesus is useless. Your behavior has to square with your testimony.

[10] When Dishonesty Backfires

> ***2 Samuel 1:10*** *So I* [a young Amalekite] *stood upon him* [Saul] *and slew him, because I was sure that he could not live after that he was fallen: and I took the crown that was upon his head, and the bracelete that was on his arm, and have brought them hither unto my* LORD [David]. ***:14*** *And David said unto him, How wast thou not afraid to stretch forth thine hand to destroy the* LORD*'s anointed?* ***:15*** *And David called one of the young men, and said, Go near, and fall upon him. And he smote him that he died.* ***:16*** *And David said unto him, Thy blood be upon thy head; for thy mouth hath testified against thee, saying, I have slain the* LORD*'s anointed.*

What this young Amalekite said to David was a lie. The truth was ***1 Samuel 31:4*** *Saul took a sword and fell upon it.*

Why did this Amalekite lie and claim that he had himself killed Saul? Because he knew that Saul was David's enemy and he hoped to ingratiate himself to David. Instead, his lie got him killed. He did not expect that although Saul was David's enemy, David was not

Saul's enemy. David had high regard for Saul and reverenced him for what he was: the Lord's anointed.

Since you can never be sure that a lie will improve your situation and it may make things worse, you might as well tell the truth and trust God.

Ezekiel 22:13 *Behold therefore I have smitten mine hand at thy dishonest gain which thou hast made…*

When people make money by dishonest means, God gets angry enough to want to strike them.

[11] Lies In The Bible

It's easy to say that lying is a sin. But in some situations, it seems that some tactical lying is the only reasonable and even moral thing to do. Would you not, for instance, tell a Nazi that there are no Jews hiding in your attic when in fact there are? That's a lie. But what else can you do? Do you really want to argue that it's a sin to save a life with a lie? I wouldn't dare accuse one who is so bold to save a life.

I'm not trying to justify or promote lying, but in all honesty, there does seem to be some situations that defy complete honesty. Here are some examples that the Bible offers.

[11.1] Abraham

Genesis 12:13 [Abraham to Sarai] *Say, I pray thee, thou art my sister: that it may be well we me for thy sake …*

This is the story of Abraham in Egypt. His wife is pretty, and he's worried that some Egyptians might kill him and take Sarai.

Decades later, Abraham has absolute trust in God, but not now. He trusts his lie instead for protection.

As a result, Sarai is taken into a harem and God has to deliver her. Which is maybe part of Abraham's learning experience, that if God is protecting you, you might as well tell the truth.

[11.2] Jacob

Genesis 27:19 *And Jacob said unto his father, I am Esau thy first born*

Jacob takes after his grandfather. This is a bold-faced lie calculated to steal something valuable: his brother's birthright. But on the other hand, Esau sold it willingly. So, was Jacob wrong to lie to get what was rightfully his? Or was it his?

Later, there is a strange story about Jacob wrestling with God, and the Bible offers no explanation what that contest was about. I have a guess. I think they were haggling over the legitimacy of Jacob stealing Esau's birthright. I think Jacob was saying, "It's mine! I bought it." And God was saying, "No, it's not yours. You stole it." And how did it turn out? Jacob won. But God was a sore loser and crippled Jacob, but he let the deal stand. The birthright was Jacob's to keep.

[11.3] Rahab

Joshua 2:4 *And the woman* [Rahab] *took the two men* [Joshua's spies] *and hid them, and said thus* [to their pursuers], *There came men unto me, but I wist not whence they were.* ***:5*** *And it came to pass about the time of the shutting of the gate, when it was dark, that the men went out: whither the men went I wot not: pursue after them quickly; for ye shall overtake them.* ***:6*** *But she had brought them up to the roof of the house, and hid them…*

Rahab told a bold-faced lie. After hiding the spies safely, she told the Jericho soldiers, "They just left. Go quickly. You can catch them."

So, was she a liar? I guess so. Would you have told the same lie under those conditions? I know I would have. Not only did she save the lives of the spies, she saved the lives of her entire family. Is that worth sacrificing a little integrity for? Well, when you're in that situation, you'll have to make that decision.

[11.4] Gibeonites

Joshua 9:3 *And when the inhabitants of Gibeon heard what Joshua had done unto Jericho and to Ai* ***:4*** *They did work wilily* ***:8*** *And Joshua said unto them, Who are ye? and from whence come ye?* ***:9*** *And they said unto him From a very far country thy servants are come* ***:11*** *We are your servants: therefore now make ye a league with us.*

All of this was a lie. The Gibeonites were lying to save themselves from God's wrath. They were on God's hit list, and they knew it. So, they used this lie to extract a promise from Joshua that they would be spared. And because Joshua swore by the God of Israel, he was bound to honor it. Can you blame the Gibeonites for their deceit?

[11.5] Jonathan

1 Samuel 20:27 *And Saul said unto Jonathan his son, Wherefore cometh not the son of Jesse* [David] *to meat, neither yesterday, nor to day?* ***:28*** *And Jonathan answered Saul, David earnestly asked leave of me to go to Bethlehem.*

This was another bold-faced lie. David was hiding because Saul wanted to kill him, and Jonathan was covering for him. Are Jonathan and David guilty of sin because of this contrived deception? That would be a hard case to make. Doesn't saving an innocent person's life justify a lie?

[11.6] DAVID

1 Samuel 21:2 *And David said unto Ahimelech the priest, The king hath commanded me on a business, and hath said unto me, Let no man know any thing of the business…*

Total lie. The king said no such thing. The king is trying to kill David, and David is fleeing. Does that justify lying? — and to a priest? You decide.

[11.7] THE ANGEL

1 Kings 22:23 *Now therefore, behold, the LORD hath put a lying spirit in the mouth of all these thy prophets…*

2 Chronicles 18:19 *And the LORD said, Who shall entice Ahab king of Israel, that he may go up and fall at Ramothgilead? And one spake saying after this manner, and another saying after that manner.* ***:20*** *Then there came out a spirit, and stood before the LORD, and said, I will entice him. And the LORD said unto him, Wherewith?* ***:21*** *And he said, I will go out, and be a lying spirit in the mouth of all his prophets. And the LORD said, Thou shalt entice him, and thou shalt also prevail: go out, and do even so.*

Here's the strangest lie in the Bible. God instructs his angel to communicate lies to King Ahab through prophets so that Ahab will engage in a battle that will get him killed. Does this make God a liar or just the angel? So what's the moral of the story? I'm not quite sure. At the very least it seems to mean that if you're an evil king like Ahab, that you can't count on God to help you.

Hypocrisy

Ezekiel 33:31

Here is a list of Bible verses that pertain to hypocrisy:

> **Proverbs 21:27** *The sacrifice of the wicked is abomination: how much more, when he bringeth it with a wicked mind?*

This verse describes phony religion. Do whatever evil you want, and at the same time think you can make yourself right with God with religion. It doesn't work.

> **Proverbs 26:23** *Burning lips and a wicked heart are like a potsherd covered with silver dross.* **:24** *He that hateth dissembleth with his lips, and layeth up deceit within him* **:25** *When he speaketh fair, believe him not: for there are seven abominations in his heart.* **:26** *Whose hatred is covered by deceit, his wickedness shall be shewed before the whole congregation.*

It's the "covered by deceit" that is the hypocrisy. Honest hatred can at least be defended; it's upfront about its intent. But "speaking fair" when evil is intended, that is a double sin, like Judas' kiss.

> **Proverbs 29:5** *A man that flattereth his neighbour spreadeth a net for his feet.* **:6** *In the transgression of an evil man there is a snare…*

Lying compliments to entrap. Buyer beware. Once you've signed the contract, he's got'cha.

Jeremiah 20:10 *For I heard the defaming of many, fear on every side. Report, say they, and we will report it. All my familiars watched for my halting, saying, Peradventure he will be enticed, and we shall prevail against him, and we shall take our revenge on him.*

When you're important, your enemies scrutinize you very carefully. If you stumble, or show the least bit of hypocrisy, they'll hang you with your slightest misdeed.

Ezekiel 14:7 *For every one of the house of Israel, or of the stranger that sojourneth in Israel, which separateth himself from me, and setteth up his idols in his heart, and putteth the stumblingblock of his iniquity before his face, and cometh to a prophet to enquire of him concerning me; I the LORD will answer him by myself.* ***:8*** *And I will set my face against that man, and will make him a sign and a proverb, and I will cut him off from the midst of my people; and ye shall know that I am the LORD.*

To paraphrase God: "Any man who keeps evil in his heart and keeps his temptations close, then approaches a prophet for an answer from me. He won't need the prophet to give him my answer. I'll tell him myself. Hypocrites won't like the answer they get from me."

Ezekiel 33:31 *...with their mouth they shew much love, but their heart goeth after their covetousness.*

Hypocrisy is showing love but then going after something or someone else. "I love you" are the most pretensive and abused words in the English language.

Joel 2:13 *And rend your heart, and not your garments...*

It's not the show of religiosity that God wants from you but for your hearts to be genuine.

Influences

Genesis 19:14-36, 1 Peter 2:7-8

Lot was a righteous man living in a wicked city.

> ***1 Peter 2:7*** [God] *delivered just Lot, vexed with the filthy conversation of the wicked.* ***:8*** *For that righteous man dwelling among them, in seeing and hearing, vexed his righteous soul from day to day with their unlawful deeds.*

Suddenly, his life fell apart — not because he was unrighteous but because his friends and family had seen too much evil and had been influenced by it. Lot was rich with employees ***(Genesis 13:7*** *herdsmen of Lot's cattle).* When Lot moved to Sodom, they came too. When he left Sodom, they stayed, and died. Evil is addicting. It trapped Lot's friends and his family.

> ***Genesis 19:14*** *And Lot went out, and spake unto his sons in laws, which married his daughters, and said, Up, get you out of this place; for the LORD will destroy this city. But he seemed as one that mocked unto his sons in law.*

When Lot left Sodom, most of his family — his married daughters and their husbands and their children (Lot's grandchildren) — did not leave with him. They stayed, and died.

Who did leave with Lot? Three people only: his wife and two unmarried daughters. But not even all of them made it all the way out.

> ***Genesis 19:26*** *But his wife looked back from behind him, and she became a pillar of salt.*

Who can blame her for looking back? Her daughters were dying, her grandchildren were dying. And so the wrong decision of some family members drew another family member to her death. Lot's wife had good reason to look back, but good reason or not, looking back killed her.

Then, finally, Lot's two young daughters, virgins ***(Genesis 19:8)***, raised in the best home in Sodom, all that he had left in the world, also succumbed to the influence of Sodom.

> ***Genesis 19:33*** *And they made their father drink wine that night: and the firstborn went in, and lay with her father; and he perceived not when she lay down, nor when she arose.* ***:35*** *And they made their father drink wine that night also* [second night]*, and the younger arose, and lay with him; and he perceived not when she lay down, nor when she arose.* ***:36*** *Thus were both the daughters of Lot with child by their father.*

Where did they learn to do such a thing, these two young virgin girls? In Sodom, of course. They heard evil from their friends, just as their father had heard *(**1 Peter 2:8** seeing and hearing)*. They heard it at school, they saw it on television or whatever their local entertainment was in Sodom. They were engulfed by it, till it seemed not so wrong at all.

Lot thought he could keep the influences of Sodom out of his home. He was wrong.

Wouldn't it have been better if they had not gone to Sodom at all? We can't escape the influences of this world, but the next time your kids watch television, or see a movie, or go to a party believing they are immune to surrounding influences, think a bit about Lot and his family.

Jealousy

Exodus 20:17

Jealousy is a nuisance feeling that strips away happiness. More than that, it motivates people to behave in unjust and self-destructive ways. And it is forbidden.

> ***Exodus 20:17*** *Thou shalt not covet thy neighbor's house, thou shalt not covet thy neighbor's wife, nor his manservant, nor his maidservant, nor his ox, nor his ass, nor anything that is thy neighbor's.*

This tenth commandment does not forbid coveting per se – indeed, to not covet, to not want, would make us not human. What this commandment forbids is coveting those things which belong to our neighbor.

We want things. Of course we want things, for ourselves, for our families, and for others. Certainly we want food, and housing, and a decent job, and the necessities of life, and a lot more than that. That is not what the verse is talking about. What the verse *is* talking about is wanting what we cannot have because they belong to someone else. Anything else is fair game.

So, let's discuss jealousy.

[1] Jealousy Harms You

> ***Proverbs 14:30*** *A sound heart is the life of the flesh: but envy the rottenness of the bones.*

Jealousy does that. It rots away your life, your happiness, your joy. It just turns everything into a dark cloud. And it is physically damaging.

[2] People Who Were Jealous

Genesis 4:5 *But unto Cain and unto his offering he* [God] *had not respect. And Cain was very wroth, and his countenance fell.* ***:8*** *…Cain rose up against Abel his brother, and slew him.*

The first documented jealousy was Cain's. God approved of Abel's sacrifice, which was a blood offering, and disapproved of Cain's offering of vegetables. The point seems to be that Abel's offering was a confession of sin while Cain's offering was a denial of sin, "Look at my produce. Aren't they wonderful?"

What makes Cain's violence even more inexcusable was that God had given him a second chance, "Go back and try it again. You'll get it right next time." And Cain might have. But it was the jealousy that proved his undoing and led him to murder. And it was not just murder but murder with a vengeance. In the text, the word "slew" really means "slit his throat." In other words, Cain's violence was a statement, "You want a blood offering? I'll give you a blood offering. Here's Abel. How about that?" That's rage which comes from unbridled jealousy.

Numbers 16:1 *Now Korah, the son of Izhar, the son of Kohath, the son of Levi,* ***:3*** *And they gathered themselves together against Moses and against Aaron, and said unto them, Ye take too much upon you, seeing all the congregation are holy, every one of them, and the* LORD *is among them: wherefore then lift ye up yourselves above the congregation of the* LORD*?* ***:8*** *And Moses said unto Korah, Hear, I pray you, ye sons of Levi:* ***:10*** *…seek ye the priesthood also?*

Korah was a Levite, a man of high station already. But that wasn't good enough. He was jealous of Moses and wanted to be his equal. And his jealousy led not only to his own death but also many of his followers.

> ***1 Samuel 18:7*** *And the women answered one another as they played, and said, Saul hath slain his thousands, and David his ten thousands.* ***:8*** *And Saul was very wroth, and the saying displeased him…*

Saul was jealous of David, so much so that it drove him to madness and to murder. He tried several times to murder David but failed only because David was divinely protected.

> ***Ezra 4:2*** *Then they* [the people of the land] *came to Zerubbabel and to the chief of the fathers and said unto them, Let us build with you: for we seek your God, as ye do; and do sacrifice unto him since the days of Esarhaddon king of Assur which brought us up hither.* ***:3*** *But Zerubbabel and Jeshua and the rest of the chief of the fathers of Israel said unto them, Ye have nothing to do with us to build an house unto our God; but we ourselves together will build unto the* LORD *God of Israel, as king Cyrus the king of Persia hath commanded us.* ***:4*** *Then the people of the land weakened the hands of the people of Judah, and troubled them in building.*

The people of the land sought the God of Israel, and they were snubbed by Zerubbabel. I think that Zerubbabel's action was uncalled for remembering that Solomon hired lots of foreign labor to build his temple, which gave the whole region a sense of pride. But that's another issue.

The issue here is that these foreign people reacted to Zerubbabel's snub with hostility, which reveals that their supposed faith ("we seek your God") was not as sincere as they'd claimed. If you truly love God, you will remain true to him even if he rejects you, as Job said, ***Job 13:15*** "Though he slay me, yet will I trust him."

These people, if they really loved God as they said, would have offered help again and again without condition. "We'll provide material, money, labor, whatever," and eventually this new Jewish influx would have accepted their help, and a strong bond of friendship would have been formed. Instead, they let jealousy make them enemies of God, and they became Samaritans, despising the Jews down to the age of Christ.

> ***Esther 5:11*** *And Haman told them of the glory of his riches, and the multitude of his children, and all the things wherein the king had promoted*

him, and how he had advanced him above the princes and servants of the king ***:13*** *Yet all this availeth me nothing, so long as I see Mordecai the Jew sitting at the king's gate.*

What's doubly sad about jealousy is when it is pointless. Haman had everything a man could want. Why couldn't he have just been content with that? Why did he have this jealous compulsion to destroy Mordecai and all the Jews? When a poor man is jealous, that at least makes sense. But a rich man to be jealous? Why bother?

[3] People Who Were Not Jealous

Moses was not jealous of other prophets.

Numbers 11:27 *And there ran a young man, and told Moses, and said, Elad, and Medad do prophecy in the camp.* ***:28*** *And Joshua the son of Nun, the servant of Moses, one of his young men, answered and said, My lord, forbid them.* ***:29*** *And Moses said unto him, Enviest thou for my sake? Would God that all the LORD's people were prophets, and that the LORD would put his spirit upon them!*

It would never occur to Moses to be jealous of other prophets. Indeed, he at the first tried to decline the job hoping that God would pass it onto someone else.

Jonathan was not jealous of David.

1 Samuel 18:1 *...the soul of Jonathan was knit with the soul of David, and Jonathan loved him as his own soul.*

This in spite of the fact that Samuel had prophesied that David would one day be king and therefore Jonathan, the rightful heir, never would.

David was not jealous of Solomon

1 Chronicles 17:16 *And David the king came and sat before the* LORD*, and said, Who am I, O* LORD *God, and what is mine house, that thou hast brought me hitherto?*

David wanted to build the temple, it would have been his crowning legacy. But God said, no, your son will build it. Now David could have been upset by that, jealous, so to speak, of his own son. But he wasn't. His attitude was: "Hey, the house I'm in, I didn't build it, God, you did. So whatever you want to do is fine with me." All David wanted was for God to be glorified, and he proceeded to make his son's job easier by gathering the materials. He just wanted the job done, he didn't care who did it or who got the credit, as long as God got the glory. ***1 Chronicles 22:8-11***

Hezekiah was not jealous of the priests.

2 Chronicles 29:11 *My sons, be not now negligent: for the* LORD *hath chosen you to stand before him, to serve him, and that ye should minister unto him, and burn incense.*

Hezekiah reminds the priests that they and they alone were chosen to serve God in the temple. This is unlike Uzziah, his grandfather, who usurped the priestly duty and was stricken with leprosy ***(26:19)***. Hezekiah knew better.

John the Baptist was not jealous of Jesus.

John 3:30 *He must increase, but I must decrease.*

It was becoming obvious to everyone that Jesus's following was growing at John's expense, and John's followers knew and were jealous for John. But John knew his place and that he was expendable for a far greater cause. Instead of being upset by that, he gloried in it. He had achieved his goal, he had made Jesus the center of attention.

Martha was not jealous of Mary.

John 11:28 *And when she had so said, she went her way, and called Mary her sister secretly, saying, The Master is come, and calleth for thee.*

Martha was never jealous of Mary although Jesus may have loved Mary more.

When Jesus arrived at the tomb of Lazarus, it was Martha who had come to greet him, not Mary. Mary was too distraught with grief to leave the house. Then, after a conversation with Martha, Jesus asked for Mary.

Some people in that situation might have said something bitter like, "Why do you want her? I'm here." But not Martha. She loved Jesus and Mary too much for pettiness. Martha just wanted to help people, and Jesus in particular. "You want Mary? I'll get her."

Sometimes people want to be jealous for Martha's sake. Don't be. Martha was not jealous for her own sake. Martha wanted only one thing: to give the Lord whatever he wanted. People with that attitude are never jealous.

Jesus was not jealous of others.

Mark 9:38 *And John answered him, saying, Master, we saw one casting out devils in thy name, and he followeth not us: and we forbade him, because he followeth not us.* ***:39*** *But Jesus said, forbid him not: for there is no man which shall do a miracle in my name, that can lightly speak evil of me.* ***:40*** *For he that is not against us is on our part.*

Christianity is very divided. But it is not the division that is so troubling, it is the jealousy — each denomination fretting that some other denomination might be serving God a bit better. "Heretic," "Apostate," "Cult" are all terms that Christians have reserved for each other. Well, at least we've gotten past burning each other at the stake.

Peter was not jealous of Paul.

2 Peter 3:15 *And account that the longsuffering of our Lord is salvation; even as our beloved brother Paul also according to the wisdom given unto him hath written unto you.*

Paul had been, on occasion, angry with Peter ***(Galatians 2:11-14)*** but Peter was never angry with Paul, never annoyed, never jealous. All that Peter ever wanted was that the gospel got preached. And Peter, I'm sure, was grateful that Paul was so good at it.

Paul was not jealous of other preachers.

Philippians 1:15 *Some indeed preach Christ even of envy and strive; and some also of good will;* ***:16*** *The one preach Christ of contention, not sincerely, supposing to add affliction to my bonds.* ***:17*** *But the other of love, knowing that I am set for the defense of the gospel.* ***:18*** *What then? Notwithstanding, every way, whether in pretense, or in truth, Christ is preached; and I therein do rejoice, yea, and will rejoice.*

Paul had competition. It's hard to imagine a missionary being combatively competitive with other missionaries, but so it was. Or maybe it's not so hard to imagine seeing that Christianity is engulfed in just such schisms. But all Paul really cared about was that the message of Christ was successfully being preached.

[4] Does God Forgive Jealousy?

Yes, of course he does.

Luke 15:31 *And he said unto him, Son, thou are ever with me, and all I have is thine.*

Jesus' parable of the prodigal son is rich with meaning. But it's not just about the prodigal son, it's also about the faithful son, and his fit of jealousy, and his father's reassurance to him, "All I have is thine." So, just what is there to be jealous about?

Jealousy is pointless, that's the point. Allow a father to rejoice over the repenting sinner. Be glad *for him* who gives you so much and don't be judgmental of his favoritism. You have everything. Indeed, what in the world do you have to be jealous about?

There's another issue here: Would you let jealous destroy you *while* God is busy forgiving you? Cain fell into just that trap. God was forgiving Cain, and that drove Cain into a deep and murderous rage. The brother of the prodigal did not make Cain's mistake.

[5] DON'T ENVY EVIL PEOPLE

> ***Psalms 37:1*** *Fret not thyself because of evildoers, neither be thou envious against the workers of iniquity.* ***:2*** *For they shall soon be cut down like the grass, and wither as the green herb.*

Justice, the Law, and the Courts

The Bible begins with the Torah which was and is a revealed codified legal system. It was, in fact, the constitution of a new nation, namely, Israel.

Why would God's first revelation be a legal system rather than a promise of heaven? That itself tells us something about God and his will for us. Clearly, God wants us to get along and tries to achieve that by whatever means possible.

But from the Creation on, people have mistreated each other. And so, God created law and made Moses his law-giver.

Since God's judicial system, Torah, is so much at the forefront of God's thinking, it deserves more of our attention than we commonly give it. We should try a bit harder to understand it, and maybe we should use it to evaluate our own legal system to see how our laws measure up. So, let's begin.

[1] Torah

The Torah begins with creation and God's high hopes for man. But things quickly turn ugly. Mankind falls, then there is a murder, then worldwide violence which causes God to regret the whole project, and finally a worldwide flood to eliminate the violence.

Things at that point are looking pretty bleak. But then there is a new hope and a new beginning for mankind. But with that new beginning comes a new and violent commandment —

> ***Genesis 9:6*** *Whoso sheddeth man's blood, by man shall his blood be shed: for in the image of God made he man.*

God had wished better things for humanity, where everybody got along because they simply cared for each other. But that was not to be. So, to make things work better this time, God instituted law. First, this terse directive to Noah, then later, a complete codified legal system to Moses, which we call the Mosaic Law.

Right at the beginning there are two most critical points —

First:

Exodus 20:16 *Thou shalt not bear false witness against thy neighbor.*

This 9th commandment is not simply a commandment against lying, it is a commandment against false accusations. It is the key to making the law, any law, work. Truth in court is the fundamental requirement. Courts have no hope of administering justice if they can't get at the truth first. Perjury must necessarily be the first prohibition in any legal system.

Second:

Deuteronomy 4:2 *Ye shall not add unto the word which I command you, neither shall ye diminish ought from it, that ye may keep the commandments of the LORD your God which I command you.*

The Mosaic Law, in God's mind, was so complete, so done, so correct that it ought never to be tampered with. There was no congress to create new law, they already had law. And judges were to judge only and not legislate from the bench, which today's judges are in the habit of doing.

So, on those two foundational ideas, no perjury and no tampering with the law, we can now proceed to everything else that the law says.

Deuteronomy 16:18 *Judges and officers shalt thou make thee…and they shall judge the people with just judgment.* ***:19*** *Thou shalt not wrest judgment; thou shalt not respect persons, neither take a gift: for a gift doeth blind the eyes of the wise, and pervert the words of the righteous.*

"Don't wrest judgment" means don't twist the law to make it say something different than what it actually says. In modern language, don't legislate from the bench. This is God's demand for (in modern language) "strict constructionist" judges who are content to apply the law and not create law. Activist judges are strictly forbidden. In other words, stay true to the precise wording of the law, their Constitution.

"Don't respect persons" means equal protection; that is, apply the law equally to all. Don't be influenced by wealth or station. It's tempting to acquit a defendant just because he is a black football hero. In many people's opinion, O.J. Simpson was acquitted of two murders simply because we love sports heroes. Such preferences violate God's demand for justice at the core.

"Don't take gifts" means don't accept bribes, don't sell judicial favors. But more than that it means don't accept gifts or favors of any kind from anyone because they make judges evaluate testimonies differently, sometimes without even realizing it.

Deuteronomy 16:20 *That which is altogether just shalt thou follow.*

A judge once said, "This is not a court of justice, sir, this is a court of law." He and the entire legal system seem to have missed the whole point of what law is about. The point of law is not to create a bunch of rules but to administer justice. There is a letter and a spirit, and both matter.

There is a subtle difference between legal and lawful. Legal speaks to the letter of the law, and lawful to the spirit. In Nazi

Germany, it was legal to murder Jews, but it was never lawful. Passing laws may make murder legal, but such laws can never make murder lawful. Legislation does not make an immoral law lawful. In American law, murdering unborn babies is legal, but all the legislation that Congress can ever dream up will never make abortion lawful.

> ***Deuteronomy 17:7*** *At the mouth of two witnesses, or three witnesses, shall he that is worthy of death be put to death; but at the mouth of one witness he shall not be put to death.*

The commonsense-ness of this is obvious. Anybody can fabricate a lie against anybody. But is the accusation true? Remember the 9th commandment, *thou shalt not bear false witness.* How is the judge to know the difference between a valid accusation and a lie? If you have two witnesses, you can interrogate them in two different rooms. If their testimonies agree, they are probably telling the truth. If their testimonies contradict, they are probably lying.

The classic example of this is the apocryphal story of "Susanna and the Elders" which appears in the Catholic Bible. You should read it. It makes the point very well.

But even two witnesses is not fail safe. The court is to use every means possible to ascertain the validity of the witnesses, however many there are. Modern forensic technology goes a long way to helping courts get it right.

[2] Joshua

Eventually Moses died, and it fell to Joshua to actually create the nation that Moses dreamed of and to implement its laws.

One of the things that Joshua set up was a system that today we might call Habeas Corpus, which is Latin for "you have the body" and refers to a writ requiring that a person who is detained be brought before a judge. Habeas Corpus safeguards against unfair imprisonment. It is the essential fairness of American and British law. Basically, this guarantees that the accused will have their day in court, meaning a fair trial.

Israel had a similar thing, a sort of self-imposed protective custody arrangement called cities of refuge. Under Torah law, if you killed someone, whether by accident or self-defense or actual murder, the victim's family had a right to appoint an "avenger of blood" whose job it was to kill you. What *you* had was a right to flee.

> ***Joshua 20:2*** *Appoint out for you cities of refuge* ***:3*** *that the slayer that killeth any person unawares and unwittingly may flee thither: and they shall be your refuge from the avenger of blood* ***:4*** *And when he doth flee unto one of those cities shall stand at the entering of the gate of the city and shall declare his cause in the ears of the elders of that city, they shall take him into the city unto them, that he may dwell among them.* ***:5*** *And if the avenger of blood pursue after him, then they shall not deliver the slayer up into his hand; because he smote his neighbour unwittingly, and hated him not beforetime.* ***:6*** *And he shall dwell in that city, until he stand before the congregation for judgment, and until the death of the high priest that shall be in those days: then shall the slayer return, and come unto his own city, and unto his own house, unto the city from whence he fled.*

The city of refuge was basically protective custody, a self-imposed prison to avoid being killed by the avenger of blood. The city of refuge had a court where the slayer could plead his case. What the slayer is claiming is that, yes, he killed someone and that is why the avenger is after him. But, no, he is not guilty of murder. It was an accident or self-defense or there was some circumstance that made this killing not murder. Basically, the city of refuge is Habeas Corpus, in that the slayer gets his day in court, and protective custody in that it deters retaliation if he can reach the court before the avenger reaches him.

This is high motivation for the slayer to submit himself to the justice system because until he does, it's open season — the avenger has an unlimited hunting license. This transfers the responsibility of arrest from the police to the accused. It's no longer the duty of the cops to find and arrest him. The slayer, on the other hand, is desperate to get to the jailhouse to place himself under their protection away from the gun-sights of the avenger. He is highly motivated to get himself into custody as quickly as possible for his own safety's sake.

(We see hints of this in movies. You know the plot: a mobster is in custody and the police are trying to persuade him to cooperate. What finally elicits his cooperation is their threats to release him — he knows that on the streets he wouldn't last long with the mob after him.)

Once the slayer has arrived at and been accepted by the city of refuge, he is remanded for trial. If he is found innocent of murder (but guilty of manslaughter having caused a death by accident), he remains in the city of refuge until the high priest dies, then he is free to go home, having, in modern terms, paid his debt to society for having accidentally killed someone. But if he is found guilty of murder, he is executed. The city of refuge is not a place for murderers to hide.

This not only protects the innocent slayer (innocent of murder, not innocent of manslaughter) from the avenger, it also protects the avenger in that it recognizes the avenger's right to kill the slayer if the avenger can get to the slayer before the slayer can reach the safety of the city of refuge.

Let's take a not-so-far-fetched example. If a drunk driver kills your wife in an "accident," and in your anger you find him and kill him, under Torah law revenge is your right, the law cannot touch you. But if the drunk is taken into custody, once he's in jail you cannot reach him. He is now in the hands of the court, and what the judge decides is right and just; that decision is the law. If the slayer serves ten years for manslaughter, that's it, he's paid his debt to society and you, the avenger, have no more recourse.

So, if you want to settle the score, you have a right to do that. But you'd better do it quickly. Avenge your wife if you must but do it now; you can't keep revenge in abeyance to be used at a later time.

But to reiterate, none of this offers protection to a murderer. A murderer may find a few more days of life in a city of refuge, but when he is found guilty of murder, he will be executed.

All this makes sense. Today in America, if you kill a killer, you are likely to be arrested, which makes no sense at all. The law, if it cannot protect us, should at least get out of our way and allow us to protect ourselves. The law should be promoting justice, not running interference for felons.

Let's consider some possible changes to our law:

First, any non-felon American citizen should have the right to carry a concealed weapon. Violent crime would immediately fall, along with a few street thugs. Would that be a good thing or not? That's an ongoing debate.

And *second,* how about open season on violent felons? By that I mean, the law should not protect violent felons while in the act of committing a violent or near-violent felony. To say it differently, in my view, a felon abdicates his protection of law from the moment he commits a felony. The result of this would be far-reaching in that the law would be prohibited from acting against any citizen who acts against a violent felon.

The caveat would of course be that the citizen would have to be able to prove that the felon was indeed a felon, otherwise a whole new level of injustice would result, i.e., "I killed him because he was burglarizing my home," when in fact I killed him in his yard and dragged his body into my house to make it look like he was burglarizing my home. The issue is guilt and innocence, not technicality. The problem of course, would open season promote justice or just be another legal hiding place for murderers? Justice is never simple.

American law does provide for something like that under the guise of self-defense. But what exactly is self-defense?

I once had a dispute with a policeman. Our neighborhood had a rash of burglaries and he came to give our Neighborhood Watch advice. I asked him if I could shoot a burglar in my house. He said no, I could not, and instead of confronting the burglar, I should take my family to a safe room to avoid contact. I argued, but what if my kid is in a room on the other side of the house so that I have no idea if the burglar is a danger to my kid. Can I shoot the burglar in that case? The policeman assured me that if I shot the burglar that I would be arrested, unless I *knew* my child was in danger. Well, how on earth am I supposed to know that? The policeman had no idea.

That's the conundrum we get into when we give rights to felons. The Bible, as you just read, has some different ideas.

[3] The Kings

1 Samuel 8:3 *And his sons walked not in his ways, but turned aside after lucre, and took bribes, and perverted judgment.*

That Samuel's sons took bribes was not inconsequential. Their corruption led Israel to demand a king against God's wishes. And thus the nation surrendered a great deal of its freedom because of bad judges.

1 Samuel 12:3 *whose hand have I received any bribe to blind my eyes therewith?*

This is how Samuel defends his life of service: he didn't take bribes. The point is that bribery blinds the judge to the truth. This entire verse is a right standard for public servants. This is additionally interesting because his sons *did* take bribes.

2 Samuel 23:1 *Now these be the last words of David… **:3** The God of Israel said, the Rock of Israel spake to me, He that ruleth over men must be just, ruling in the fear of God.*

A lot of time had passed from Moses to David, about four centuries, but in that time, God had not changed. In God's mind still stirred the notion of justice. Kings are to be, above all, just.

1 Kings 3:27 *Then the king* [Solomon] *answered and said, Give her the living child, and in no wise slay it: she is the mother thereof.*

This story of Solomon and the two mothers points to the responsibility of courts to get it right, by whatever means. Justice and fairness is what the law is all about, but justice is impossible without first getting at the truth.

DNA testing and other forensic advances have been a great leap in this quest for judicial truth. But too often, courts let their political goals interfere. For instance, far too many murderers have escaped justice because of Miranda, which is not a law at all but just a judicial decree. Judges too often lose sight of the intent of their office.

1 Kings 21:8 *So she* [Jezebel] *wrote letters in Ahab's name, and sealed them with his seal, and sent the letters unto the elders and to the nobles that were in his city, dwelling with Naboth. **:9** And she wrote in the letters,* *saying, Proclaim a fast, and set Naboth on high among the people* ***:10*** *And set two men, sons of Belial, before him, to bear witness against him, saying, Thou didst blaspheme God and the king. And then carry him out, and stone him, that he may die.* ***:13*** *...Then they carried him forth out of the city, and stoned him with stones, that he died.*

This murder was carefully arranged and was carried out to the letter. This is a classic example of (as I call it) "murder by false witness." In other words, getting the court to do your dirty work for you, to "frame" your victim. And I note here that just because the court is the unwitting murder instrument doesn't make it any less a murder. If, after the execution, the whole truth comes out, the murderer can't defend himself (or herself) by saying to the court, "Hey. I didn't kill him, *you* killed him." I imagine there are just such examples in American case law.

So, the two witnesses rule, which certainly helped Susanna against the scheming elders, did nothing to help poor Naboth. More was expected of the court.

On the positive side, we notice that there was enough law in Israel that this elaborate charade was necessary to murder Naboth. Jezebel couldn't just go kill him, she had to arrange this legal rouse. So, law works. It just doesn't work all the time.

2 Chronicles 19:5 *And he* [Jehoshaphat] *set judges in the land* ***:6*** *And said to the judges...ye judge not for man but for the* LORD*...* ***:7*** *there is no iniquity with the* LORD *our God, nor respect of persons nor taking of gifts.* ***:9*** *Thus shall ye do in fear of the* LORD*, faithfully, and with a perfect heart.*

King Jehoshaphat understood the responsibility of judges. First, they are themselves to be above reproach. Second, they are not to respect persons, meaning do not give preferential treatment to people of status. And third, judges are not to take bribes.

I will tell you a story of the second emperor of Persia, Cambyses. You will think it's grisly, and it is.

One day, Cambyses appointed a new supreme judge. Cambyses toured the new judge through the justice hall and sat him down behind the bench in the judge's chair.

While the new judge was getting the feel of his new environment, Cambyses said to him, "Just so you know, your predecessor took bribes, and I caught him at it. I had him skinned alive. That chair you're sitting in is upholstered with his skin. When you judge, you will sit in that chair."

That's one judge I bet who never took bribes. Our judges should get a similar message. Legislate from the bench and there will be consequences.

[4] PSALMS

Psalms 94:1 *O LORD God, to whom vengeance belongeth; O God, to whom vengeance belongeth, shew thyself.*

I get so weary of people who insist that justice is good and vengeance is bad when there is no clear distinction between the two. The only difference is political — when we like retribution we call it justice, when we don't like it we call it vengeance. The author of this verse makes no such distinction.

Psalms 94:15 *But judgment shall return unto righteousness…*

Righteousness is what we have a right to expect from our justice system.

Every time a murderer gets off, for whatever reason, the whole court system is blighted by wickedness. Every time an innocent person is convicted, for whatever reason, the whole court system is blighted by wickedness.

There is a legal notion: "I'd rather set free 100 guilty men than to convict one innocent man." That is nonsense and is the court's excuse for dismissing its own failures.

God did not create courts to argue about tedious details of the law. Court's are not paid to acquit murderers to keep their conscience clear of convicting any innocent person. The court's are paid to *get it right* — convict the guilty *and* acquit the innocent. A failure on either side is monumental injustice.

Now, of course that's easier said than done. But technology has come a long way. For example, the discovery of DNA, and the invention of computers. We have those tools and others to determine innocence or guilt, and yet we still rely on juries who care less about the truth and more about legal impediments to justice such as inadmissible evidence, rules of the court, and which side has the best attorney. Juries can be and frequently are manipulated by fast-talking lawyers.

A mother who had murdered her two-year old-daughter was acquitted. The reason for the acquittal, according to the jury, was that the prosecuting attorney didn't do a very good job. How does that have anything to do with innocence or guilt? That jury knew the defendant was guilty, but they acquitted her anyway because they were judging the attorney rather than the facts of the case. One day those jurors will face God, and I believe that child's blood will be on their hands. They will share the mother's guilt.

In my opinion, the jury system should be discarded and replaced with something else, something that assesses facts analytically rather than pitting the personalities and competence of opposing attorneys against each other. Think about it. Why should guilt and innocence have anything to do with the competence of the respective attorneys? Why should the defendant get off because he had a good attorney, or convicted because his attorney was a dufus? That attorneys spend so much time with their strategies of jury selection (slanting the jury to his favor) should by itself tell you that there is something rotten about our jury system.

That's trial by lot, and it has little to do with facts. Our system has more in common with voodoo than with justice. I say let's get argument out of the courts and instead of argument, have some real analysis. God's law is clear enough. He is not concerned with the jots and tittles (as Jesus called it), the minutia of the law. God is interested in innocence and guilt. That's it. That's what the law ought to be focused on, not all this other legal *crap!*

And get the defendant's personality out of the courtroom. An endearing smile, a celebrity status, and a shiny new suit have nothing to do with innocence and guilt. It is to the court's shame that the more likable a defendant, the more likely he will walk. This, more than anything else, is why the stupid jury system must go. Jurors are people, and people buy crap from good salesmen, and attorneys are trained to be good salesmen. And the best of them win. This is no way to run a justice system. That is not justice, and that is not what the law is intended to be. Why should the outcome of any trial, criminal or civil, spin on trivialities like attorney competence, defendant personality, and so-called rules of the court?

We should take the law out of the hands of the attorneys and judges and give it to programmer analysts who can do at least as good a job as the legalists have done, and I believe a whole lot better. Facts are what matter, not debate.

There was a time when debate and testimony was the best we had. But computers and analytical thinking and forensic evidence have since come into being. The world has advanced, but our jurisprudence system has not. It's time for an upgrade.

Psalms 94:21 *...which frameth mischief by a law?*

There are times when the law itself becomes the instrument of crime — murder, theft, and more. The story above about Jezebel and Naboth is a perfect example. It unfortunately happens that a criminal, in order to escape justice, will frame someone else, a fall guy. And sometimes that fall guy will spend years in prison or even be executed for someone else's crime. So now there are three injustices: the actual crime, the fact that the criminal got away with it, and the fact that a fall guy paid the price.

But there are other kinds of "mischief by law." Politics is always hungry for new victims. Rent control eagerly transfers wealth from landlords to tenants. A recent expansion of eminent domain now allows governments to take a person's property and give it to a hotel developer. Those are just two examples of "framing mischief by law."

Psalms 98:9 *...with righteousness shall he judge the world, and the people with equity.*

That's the goal, isn't it? To judge with equity. Equal justice for all, just as God promises he one day will.

Psalms 149:6 *Let the high praises of God be in their mouth, and a two-edged sword in their hand.* ***:7*** *To execute vengeance upon the heathen, and punishments upon the people.* ***:8*** *To bind their kings with chains, and their nobles with fetters of iron.* ***:9*** *To execute upon them the judgment written: this honour have all his saints. Praise ye the LORD.*

The American Congress has a nasty habit of passing laws that apply to all of us but not to themselves. Their privileged position allows them to exempt themselves from their own laws. That is a great failing in our legal system that our law makers are above the law. Our representatives ought to be bound with legal chains, forcing them to be bound by their own laws.

[5] PROVERBS

Proverbs 7:22 *...as a fool to the correction of the stocks.*

Apparently, the Jews used stocks. I guess they did not consider that a cruel and unusual punishment.

I also read this text to mean that the law ought to be binding on the courts and not the other way around. Our courts today ignore the law and do whatever they please, setting aside the law to impose their own political agenda, their tyrannical will, on the people. We are told that we are living in a democracy, but in fact we are living in a judicial tyranny. I would rather that the law bind our judges with chains.

Proverbs 15:27 *He that is greedy of gain troubleth his own house; but he that hateth gifts shall live.*

By *gifts* the author means bribes. To take a bribe in any public office seems here to be a capital offense. This is a warning to any office holder and also a warning to those who vote him in: beware of greedy candidates — they'll serve their own interest and not the public interest. That's the definition of corruption.

Proverbs 17:15 *He that justifieth the wicked, and he that condemneth the just, even they both are abomination to the* LORD.

This is exactly the point: freeing the guilty and convicting the innocent. This is liberal judges who think that abortion doctors who kill babies should be free while pro-lifers who picket their homes should go to jail for invasion of privacy.

> ***Proverbs 17:23*** *A wicked man taketh a gift out of the bosom to pervert the ways of judgment.*

> ***Proverbs 17:26*** *Also to punish the just is not good, nor to strike princes for equity.*

> ***Proverbs 18:5*** *It is not good to accept the person of the wicked, to overthrow the righteous in judgment.*

> ***Proverbs 19:5*** *A false witness shall not be unpunished, and he that speaketh lies shall not escape.*

Perjury is a crime and a serious one. Suppose perjury results in the execution of an innocent person. Then the perjury ought to be a capital crime. Imagine that the court is itself used as a weapon of crime just as surely as a gun.

Liberal courts, the ACLU, and lying attorneys get massive judgments against businesses that do nothing wrong at all, thus using the courts as instruments of extortion to *overthrow the righteous.* That's not what courts are meant for. We should not elect such people, appoint them, or allow them into public office, or to have influence of any kind.

> ***Proverbs 20:8*** *A king that sitteth in the throne of judgment scattereth away all evil with his eyes.*

As much as I detest our legal system (with its corrupt and despotic judges creating their own law), a legal system of judges and police power is inescapably necessary. That's why God gave law, to make criminals afraid of justice. Without courts, anarchy would rule and there'd be no safety anywhere. That we have any civility at all, we owe to the courts. Awful, isn't it?

> ***Proverbs 20:26*** *A wise king scattereth the wicked, and bringeth the wheel over them.*

Good judges punish the wicked. I have fanaticized that probation officers might be personally liable for the evil done by the criminals they release, so that if a child abuser on parole murders a child, then the family can sue the parole officer (and court) who released him.

> ***Proverbs 21:3*** *To do justice and judgment is more acceptable to the LORD than sacrifice.*

This is my favorite verse on the subject of law, and it is really important.

It is saying that your justice system is more important than your religion. How you deal with matters of social justice is more important than going to church. How do you impress God? Help your fellow man with right justice. That's what the verse says.

> ***Proverbs 21:15*** *It is joy to the just to do judgment…*

The nature of just people is not only that they execute justice but that they enjoy it. Don't shun jury duty, seek it. Doing justice is a noble thing to do, and it's a pleasure. And besides, it's sometimes fun to see the bad guy get his comeuppance.

> ***Proverbs 24:15*** *Lay not wait, O wicked man, against the dwelling of the righteous; spoil not his resting place.*

Evil people use any means, including the courts, including the internet, to take from honest people. I'm wondering, if LifeLock is really able to protect people from identity thieves, why is the government, whose job it is to protect us, and its police powers not protecting us?

Proverbs 24:23 *...It is not good to have respect of persons in judgment.*

For instance, judges and jurors like celebrities — like football players, like Senators — and therefore they let football players and Senators get away with murder. That's a really bad thing.

Proverbs 24:28 *Be not a witness against thy neighbour without cause; and deceive not with thy lips.*

Since the courts have so much power, even the power to take life, it is really important to *not bear false witness* (***Exodus 20:17***, the 10th commandment). That's why perjury is a punishable crime because it turns the court into an instrument of injustice.

Proverbs 25:2 *It is the glory of God to conceal a thing: but the honour of kings is to search out a matter.*

God's job is to atone, cover, and forgive sin. But that's not what judges and courts are for. Their job is to do justice. When a judge forgives crime and calls it mercy, that's not mercy at all, that's an aberration of justice, and he should be removed from the bench.

Jesus said, "I have *not* come to destroy the law." We need our law. God is not an anarchist.

Proverbs 28:17 *A man that doeth violence to the blood of any person shall flee to the pit; let no man stay him.*

Let's take this literally. If a murderer wants to commit suicide, let him. In fact, encourage him to. I'll provide the rope. Let's start with Theodore Frank. Why was that monster who tortured a child to death allowed to live for twenty-three years after his conviction?

> ***Proverbs 29:4*** *The king by judgment establisheth the land: but he that receiveth gifts overthroweth it.*

Judges who take bribes do more than just damage the legal system with unfairness, they destroy the law and ultimately the country.

> ***Proverbs 29:14*** *The king that faithfully judgeth the poor, his throne shall be established for ever.*

I wish there were such judges. The truth is, the poor cannot afford justice, and so the rich, who can afford attorney fees, always win because the poor can't survive the cost. And Small Claims doesn't help because that's not where the real battles are fought.

> ***Proverbs 31:8*** *Open thy mouth for the dumb in the cause of all such are appointed to destruction.* ***:9*** *Open thy mouth, judge righteously, and plead the cause of the poor and needy.*

This is an important abortion text. Come to the defense of those who cannot defend themselves. And of course, the most helpless of those who are appointed to destruction are the unborn. You really should be speaking out in defense of the unborn, or at the very least vote pro-life.

[6] Ecclesiastes

Ecclesiastes 3:16 *And moreover I saw under the sun the place of judgment, that wickedness was there; and the place of righteousness, that iniquity was there.*

In the courts, where we expect justice and righteousness to prevail, even there we see wickedness.

Ecclesiastes 7:7 *Surely oppression maketh a wise man mad; and a gift destroyeth the heart.*

Payoff and bribery. The "good ol' boys." Obama paying off the unions and Acorn for getting him elected. It does indeed destroy the heart to see that our government is so controlled by gangsters.

Ecclesiastes 8:11 *Because sentence against an evil work is not executed speedily, therefore the heart of the sons of men is fully set in them to do evil.*

[7] Isaiah

Isaiah 1:21 *How is the faithful city become an harlot! It was full of judgment…but now murderers.* ***:22*** *Thy silver is become dross, thy wine mixed with water.* ***:23*** *Thy princes are rebellious, and companions of thieves every one loveth gifts, and followeth after rewards:* ***26*** *And I will restore thy judges as at the first, and thy counselors as at the beginning…*

Paraphrase: ***:21*** The faithful city used to have judges who defended the innocent, but now the judges are murderers. ***:22*** Justice and crime are now intermingled. ***:23*** Judges are in the pockets of the criminals and take their bribes. ***:26*** God wants to restore judges who judge by the law, and not kings who, like activist judges, change the law to whatever they want it to be.

Isaiah 5:20 *Woe unto them that call evil good, and good evil…* ***:23*** *Which justify the wicked for reward, and take away the righteousness of the righteous from him.*

What are judges willing to do for bribes? Acquit the guilty and convict the innocent.

Isaiah 9:7 *…to establish it with judgment and with justice…*

Always on God's mind is the justice system, not just the courts but the whole of society's sense of fair play.

Isaiah 10:1 *Woe unto them that decree unrighteous decrees, and that write grievousness which they have prescribed.* ***:2*** *To turn aside the needy from judgment, and to take away the right from the poor of my people, that widows may be their prey, and that they may rob the fatherless!*

All these judges and their "opinions," they are all grievous. Judges shouldn't have "opinions," they should just do what the law says. Too many judges have no sense of justice and make the law a sham with their fiat decrees.

Isaiah 16:5 *And in mercy shall the throne be established: and he shall sit upon it in truth in the tabernacles of David, judging, and seeking judgment, and hasting righteousness.*

God's throne is a court of mercy more than judgment, truth (facts) is the goal and righteousness is the objective, unlike today where political agenda is the goal of far too many judges. Our judges don't want truth and justice, they want power and control.

> ***Isaiah 24:5*** *The earth also is defiled under the inhabitants thereof; because they have transgressed the laws, changed the ordinance, broken the everlasting covenant.*

That's what too many judges do: ignore the Constitution and create their own law to suit themselves. They change the ordinance.

> ***Isaiah 26:9*** *...when thy judgments are in the earth, the inhabitants of the world will learn righteousness.*

> ***Isaiah 51:7*** *Hearken unto me, ye that know righteousness, the people in whose heart is my law...*

God defines righteousness as loving the law.

> ***Isaiah 56:1*** *Thus saith the LORD, Keep ye judgment, and do justice: for my salvation is near to come, and my righteousness to be revealed.*

> ***Isaiah 59:4*** *None calleth for justice, nor any pleadeth for truth: they trust in vanity, and speak lies; they conceive mischief, and bring forth iniquity.* ***:9*** *Therefore is judgment far from us, neither doth justice overtake us: we wait for light, but behold obscurity; for brightness, but we walk in darkness.* ***:14*** *And judgment is turned away backward, and justice standeth afar off: for truth is fallen in the street, and equity cannot enter.*

Here is a plea for truth: Abortion tortures to death unborn children. How's that for a chilling truth? How would you like your arms and legs sliced off with a scalpel or sucked off with a vacuum? Or your skin burned off with saline as you silently scream while dying in agony? How about some truth for a change? That would be refreshing.

> ***Isaiah 61:8*** *For I the LORD love judgment, I hate robbery for a burnt offering.*

It is justice that God wants from us, not religiosity, especially religiosity that is a pretext to helping yourself to someone else's stuff.

[8] JEREMIAH

> ***Jeremiah 5:1*** *…see…if there be any that executeth judgment, that seeketh the truth…*

> ***Jeremiah 5:28*** *They are waxen fat, they shine: yea, they overpass the deeds of the wicked: they judge not the cause, the cause of the fatherless, yet they prosper; and the right of the needy do they not judge.*

> ***Jeremiah 7:6*** *If ye oppress not the stranger, the fatherless, and the widow, and shed not innocent blood…*

"Innocent blood" is a euphemism for children. Don't kill children. But in America, killing children is big business and an established right. Even after The Supreme Court overturned Roe vs. Wade, most states still encourage and welcome killing babies. How evil we have become.

> ***Jeremiah 22:3*** *Thus saith the LORD; Execute ye judgment and righteousness, and deliver the spoiled out of the hand of the oppressor: and do no wrong,* do no violence *to the stranger, the fatherless, nor the widow, neither shed innocent blood in this place.*

Jeremiah 22:16 *He judged the cause of the poor and needy; then it was well with him: was not this to know me? Saith the* LORD.

How do you know that you know God? You know that you know God if you are fair and kind to the poor and the needy.

Jeremiah 33:15 *In those days, and at that time, will I cause the Branch of righteousness to grow up unto David; and he shall execute judgment and righteousness in the land.*

Our hope for a Davidic messiah is intertwined with our hope for a fair justice system. Our lamenting over injustice causes us to long for a messiah who we expect will judge fairly.

Lamentations 3:36 *To subvert a man in his cause, the* LORD *approveth not.*

Everyone has a right to plead his cause in court. But in our system, one of the ways to "subvert a man in his cause" is to sue small businesses because they can't afford to defend themselves. And that it costs frivolous plaintiffs nothing to try invites frivolous lawsuits. That is subverting justice.

[9] EZEKIEL

Ezekiel 5:6 *And she hath changed my judgments into wickedness more than the nations, and my statutes more than the countries that are round about her: for they have refused my judgments and my statutes, they have not walked in them.*

This is condemnation on those who change the law. I believe this applies as well to those judges and lawmakers who are destroying our constitution by bending it and twisting to make it say what it does not say. Remember: *the* law was the constitution of Israel and the foundation of their justice system. When you screw up the justice system, you screw up the law. That's exactly God's complaint here.

There are thousands of examples of judicial abuse and abdication of judicial responsibility. Abortion on demand is one, a so-called "right" that the courts invented out of thin air thus destroying our constitutional "right-to-life" established by the first amendment. Another is the so-called "right" to gay marriage handed down by the Supreme Court as new law. Just as God said: You've *changed my judgments into wickedness.*

> ***Ezekiel 18:8*** *He that…executed true judgment between man and man,* ***:9*** *Hath walked in my statutes, and hath kept my judgments, to deal truly, he is just, he shall surely live, saith the Lord GOD.*

> ***Ezekiel 20:11*** *And I gave them my statutes, and shewed them my judgments, which if a man do, he shall even live in them.* ***:13*** *But the house of Israel rebelled against me in the wilderness: they walked not in my statutes, and they despised my judgments…then I said, I would pour out my fury upon them in the wilderness, to consume them.* ***:18*** *But I said unto their children in the wilderness, Walk ye not in the statutes of your fathers, neither observe their judgments…* ***:19*** *I am the LORD your GOD; walk in my statutes, and keep my judgments, and do them.*

Israel's sin was not just sin, it was lawlessness and injustice.

[10] Minor Prophets

Amos 5:12 *…they take a bribe…*

Amos 5:15 *Hate the evil, and love the good, and establish judgment in the gate*

Amos 6:12 *...ye have turned judgment into gall, and the fruit of righteousness into hemlock*

You have turned your justice system into something bad tasting, ugly and awful. By a whole series of bad court decisions, American law has become that: bad tasting.

Micah 3:9 *Hear this, I pray you, ye heads of the house of Jacob, and princes of the house of Israel, that abhor judgment, and pervert all equity.* ***:11*** *The heads thereof judge for reward...*

Micah 3:1 *And I said, Hear, I pray you, O heads of Jacob, and ye princes of the house of Israel; Is it not for you to know judgment?* ***:2*** *Who hate the good, and love the evil; who pluck off their skin from off them, and their flesh from off their bones.* ***:3*** *Who also eat the flesh of my people, and flay their skin from off them; and they break their bones, and chop them in pieces, as for the pot, and as flesh within the caldron.*

It was your job, you government leaders and judges, to understand how to judge justly. Instead of using your office for justice, you use it to skin the people and enrich yourselves. That's high corruption and abuse of power. God paints a pretty vivid picture of judicial corruption.

Micah 6:8 *...what doth the LORD require of thee, but to do justly, and to love mercy, and to walk humbly with thy God.*

We too often think of commandments as spiritual. That's wrong. Commandments are very temporal, they are what the judicial system is made from, how to treat each other by law. God instructs us to "do justly"; that means civil law.

We sometimes see justice and mercy at odds with each other. It depends on who we are showing mercy to. Mercy to criminals is not very merciful to victims, is it?

Micah 7:3 *…the judge asketh for a reward…*

Habakkuk 1:4 *Therefore the law is slacked, and judgment doth never go forth: for the wicked doth compass about the righteous; therefore wrong judgment proceedeth.*

Zephaniah 3:4 *…they have done violence to the law.*

By corrupting the law, they do violence not only to people but to the law itself.

Zechariah 7:9 *…Execute true judgment, and shew mercy…*
Zechariah 8:16 *…execute the judgment of truth and peace in your gates.*
Zechariah 8:17 *…love no false oath.*

Malachi 2:8 *But ye are departed out of the way; ye have caused many to stumble at the law; ye have corrupted the covenant of Levi, saith the LORD of hosts.* **:9** *Therefore have I also made you contemptible and base before all the people, according as ye have not kept my ways, but have been partial in the law.*

[11] EZRA

The Jews were removed from their homeland (Diaspora) and then returned to it (post-Diaspora). When they returned, did their attitude towards their law change? It did.

Ezra 7:26 *And whosoever will not do the law of thy God, and the law of the king, let judgment be executed speedily upon him, whether it be unto death, or to banishment, or to confiscation of goods, or to imprisonment.*

From then on, no Jew would ever bow to an idol or murder a child. They took their law very seriously.

Notice the different penalties for different crimes. Notice that torture and dismemberment are not on Ezra's list. The Jews, like Americans, didn't much care for "cruel and unusual" punishments. Even when they burned someone, they killed them first *then* burned them ***(Joshua 7:25)***.

[12] The Gospels

We Christians somehow have gotten the idea that Jesus' grace dispensed with the law. That is not true. Jesus never had such a thing in mind.

Matthew 5:17 *Think not that I have come to destroy the law, or the prophets: I am not come to destroy, but to fulfill.* ***:18*** *For verily I say unto you, Till heaven and earth pass, one jot or one tittle shall in no wise pass from the law, till all be fulfilled.*

Civilization functions on law. Without law, all societies would disintegrate back to primitive behaviors, and we would once again eat each other.

[13] Acts

Acts 18:12 *And when Gallio was the deputy of Achaia, the Jews made insurrection with one accord against Paul, and brought him to the judgment seat,* ***:13*** *Saying, This fellow persuadeth men to worship God contrary to* *the law.* ***:14*** *And…Gallio said unto the Jews, If it were a matter of wrong or wicked lewdness, O ye Jews, reason would that I should bear with you:* ***:15*** *But if it be a question of words and names, and of your law, look ye to it; for I will be no judge of such matters.* ***:16*** *And he drave them from the judgment seat.*

This Roman judge, Gallio, was a wise man. He understood what courts are for. He's saying, in essence, if you're charging him with a felony (wrong or wicked lewdness), I'll hear your case. But your grievance is a matter of religious interpretation, you deal with it. I'm going to let you drag the court in to your religious dispute. One has to wonder how many people throughout history have been imprisoned or executed because of their religious views.

Acts 19:38 *Wherefore if Demetrius, and the craftsmen which are with him, have a matter against any man, the law is open, and there are deputies: let them implead one another.* ***:39*** *But if ye enquire any thing concerning other matters, it shall be determined in a lawful assembly.*

If you're going to have a lawsuit get all the squabblers together, there are authorities to figure out who is suing whom ("implead" means third party defendants, in this case Paul and his missionary companions). The point is, no mob rule. The defendants deserve a proper trial in a proper court.

Acts 25:16 *To whom I answered, It is not the manner of the Romans to deliver any man to die, before that he which is accused have the accusers face to face, and have license to answer for himself concerning the crime laid against him.*

The mob wanted Paul dead, but the new governor Festus (procurator) understood Roman law well enough to know you don't execute a man without a proper trial where the defendant sees his accuser face to face. So, again Paul's life is saved by the legal system.

[14] PAUL

This next verse is one of the most misunderstood verses in the Bible.

> ***Romans 12:19*** *Dearly beloved, avenge not yourselves, but rather give place unto wrath: for it is written, Vengeance is mine; I will repay, saith the Lord.*

Too many Christians wrongly understand this to mean that we should forgive violent felons and not send them to prison or execution.

The verse doesn't mean that at all. It means, don't be a vigilante, don't avenge yourself because that is what policemen and courts are for. The text continues with –

> ***Romans 13:1*** *Let every soul be subject unto the higher powers. For there is no power but of God; the powers that be are ordained of God.* ***:2*** *Whosoever therefore resisteth the power* [meaning civil authorities] *resisteth the ordinance of God…* ***:4*** *…if thou do that which is evil, be thou afraid; for he beareth not the sword in vain.*

And that is the point. Don't avenge yourselves, it is God's job to do it for you, and he exacts revenge through the judicial system, the police, the courts, the judges, the executioners, and the law. They are all ordained of God.

> ***1 Corinthians 5:3*** *For I…have judged already…*

Paul could shirk from his duty to judge because of past faults, yet here he is, judging. And so must we. When you are on jury duty, if you acquit a defendant just because Jesus said "judge not," then you make yourself guilty alongside the criminal.

Paul was arguably the most forgiven man on the planet. If anyone were inclined to beg off saying, "Hey, I'm not worthy to judge anyone of anything," that would be Paul. But as an apostle, he was required to judge, and that is exactly what he did. Not because he had a mean streak but from love. He genuinely wanted the best for everyone, and often the best that can happen to a sinner is to be fairly judged.

[15] Conclusion

When I was collecting material for this article, I was amazed, not by the severity of the law and its punishments, but by the frequency of its Biblical discussion. What surprised me was just how fixated God is on Israel's judicial system. I suppose, therefore, that he must also pay a great deal of attention to *our* legal system.

That God revealed civil law makes a strong point: God wants us to get along; I mean, he *really* wants us to get along, so much so that his primary revelation is law and the Bible's constant discussion of it.

That should suggest to us that we, all of us, ought to take our politics and our legal system seriously and to understand when our freedoms are being stolen, and that we ought to more assertively challenge government and defend our freedoms. Our liberty was bought with the blood of brave patriots, and it is a sin to allow governments and courts to continually erode our liberty without even a contest.

God's grievance with Israel was that he had given them freedom and they had squandered it. We seem to be repeating their example. It appears that God loves our liberty more than we do.

Laziness

Proverbs

The Bible gives advice not just on spiritual things like how to be good and go to heaven, but also on the practical things like how to make a living and be a contributing, productive member of society.

Someone once said despairingly of Christians, "Their head is so much in heaven that they're no earthly good." While that may be true of some Christians, it is certainly not true of most Christians, and it is certainly not anything like what the Bible says. Indeed, the Bible shares the opposite message, much of which is in Proverbs.

[1] Proverbs

> ***Proverbs 6:4*** *Give not sleep to thine eyes, nor slumber to thine eyelids.* ***:5*** *Deliver thyself as a roe from the hand of the hunter, and as a bird from the hand of the fowler.* ***:6*** *Go to the ant, thou sluggard; consider her ways, and be wise* ***:7*** *Which having no guide, overseer, or ruler,* ***:8*** *Provideth her meat in the summer, and gathereth her food in the harvest.* ***:9*** *How long wilt thou sleep, O sluggard? When wilt thou arise out of thy sleep?* ***:10*** *Yet a little sleep, a little slumber, a little folding of the hands to sleep.* ***:11*** *So shall thy poverty come as one that travelleth, and thy want as an armed man.*

There are people who seem determined to sleep their way through life. What they don't really get is that sleep makes them easy prey as, for instance, the roe is to the hunter and the bird is to the fowler.

The message concludes with this comparison: If you are lazy, you *will* become poor. That is inevitable. Just as if you get pregnant, you *will* go into labor.

Proverbs 10:4 *He becometh poor that dealeth with a slack hand: but the hand of the diligent maketh rich.* ***:5*** *He that gathereth in summer is a wise son: but he that sleepeth in harvest is a son that causeth shame.*

This person is not really interested in getting the job done. *Slack hand* means token effort, and that results in poverty. The opposite is diligence which results in riches.

Also, there is a moment of opportunity called harvest. More than any other time, that is the time to not be sleeping but to be wide awake and reaping.

Proverbs 12:24 *The hand of the diligent shall bear rule: but the slothful shall be under tribute.*

Those who work hard end up running the company. Lazy people end up on the street unemployed and hopelessly in debt.

Proverbs 13:4 *The soul of the sluggard desireth, and hath nothing: but the soul of the diligent shall be made fat.*

Wishing and wanting give you nothing. Doing and achieving provides you with all the things you want.

Proverbs 14:23 *In all labour there is profit: but the talk of the lips tendeth only to penury.*

Can we take this literally? In *all* labor there is profit? Isn't there some labor that accomplishes nothing?

I would argue to take it literally. In every labor, even hobbies and things that seem pointless, something is being accomplished. If nothing else, at least there is the learning experience. So, yes, I would agree, in *all* labor there is at least some profit. Talk, on the other hand, is cheap. Anybody can say anything, and what do words alone accomplish? Not much.

> ***Proverbs 15:19*** *The way of the slothful man is as an hedge of thorns: but the way of the righteous is made plain.*

Two points here:

First, laziness is unrighteous — the two are contrasted so that righteousness, in this text, can only mean diligent work, the opposite of sloth.

Second, the lazy man never gets anywhere. It's as though he is barricaded by a wall of thorn bushes. What he does do seems to be ineffective, he is constantly impeded, and never gets a break. That is because he has no passion for his work, no momentum, everything seems to always be against him. His work is just tokenism so of course it has no real beneficial effect. But the righteous man, the man who works diligently, every success opens up new opportunities, his way is *made plain*, it is obvious to him what to do next.

> ***Proverbs 18:9*** *He also that is slothful in his work is brother to him that is a great waster.*

Laziness has the same effect as throwing your money away. Perhaps it's worse because he not only has nothing, but he squandered his time as well. At least the waster made something to lose, so someone benefited. But the lazy man, no one benefits because he did nothing.

Proverbs 19:15 *Slothfulness casteth into a deep sleep; and an idle soul shall suffer hunger.*

Proverbs 19:24 *A slothful man hideth his hand…*

A lazy man is never around when there's work to be done. Where is he? Oh, he's on break, or at the water-cooler, or he called in sick. Whenever there is something that needs to be done, he is somewhere else.

Proverbs 20:4 *The sluggard will not plow by reason of the cold; therefore shall he beg in harvest, and have nothing.*

Lazy people always have a good reason. It's too cold, or it's too hot, or it's raining, or it's whatever. What lazy people don't get is that a good excuse doesn't change the outcome — not getting the work done results in poverty, however valid the excuse.

There is a window of opportunity to work and produce. Many sluggards will not seize that opportunity because it is inconvenient, or uncomfortable, or they have something better to do, like watching T.V.. Well, those people needn't be surprised when they finally realize that they are broke and destitute later on. When they should have money to live on, they have nothing.

Proverbs 20:13 *Love not sleep, lest thou come to poverty; open thine eyes, and thou shalt be satisfied with bread.*

Proverbs 21:25 *The desire of the slothful killeth him; for his hands refuse to labour.*

Proverbs 22:13 *The slothful man saith, There is a lion without, I shall be slain in the streets.*

The lazy man will use any pretext to get out of work. "I'm sick," "My car broke down," "My dog ate my homework," "Maybe there's a lion out there."

> ***Proverbs 23:21*** *For the drunkard and the glutton shall come to poverty: and drowsiness shall clothe a man with rags.*

Drowsiness is laziness. He spends all his time sleeping and never makes any money. But unbridled passions for booze and food also lead to poverty.

> ***Proverbs 24:30*** *I went by the field of the slothful, and by the vineyard of the man void of understanding.* ***:31*** *And, lo, it was all grown over with thorns, and nettles had covered the face thereof, and the stone wall thereof was broken down.* ***:32*** *Then I saw, and considered it well: I looked upon it, and received instruction.* ***:33*** *Yet a little sleep, a little slumber, a little folding of the hands to sleep.* ***:34*** *So shall thy poverty come as one that travelleth; and thy want as an armed man.*

A sleeping man cannot avoid poverty anymore than a pregnant woman can avoid labor. This is a repeat of ***6:11***.

> ***Proverbs 26:13*** *The slothful man saith, There is a lion in the way; a lion is in the streets.* ***:14*** *As the door turneth upon his hinges, so doth the slothful upon his bed.* ***:15*** *The slothful hideth his hand in his bosom; it grieveth him to bring it again to his mouth.* ***:16*** *The sluggard is wiser in his own conceit than seven men that can render a reason.*

"A lion in the way" is a proverb for any excuse: well, there must be *some*thing dangerous out there, so I'm better off staying home. "He hides his hand" means he doesn't want anyone to know that he might be available to do something useful because someone might actually ask him to do something. And, finally, he is smug in his laziness, he thinks he is smarter than other men and has it all figured out.

Proverbs 28:19 *He that tilleth his land shall have plenty of bread: but he that followeth after vain persons shall have poverty enough.*

Laziness is contagious. One learns laziness by hanging around with lazy people. They reinforce each other, they are co-enablers.

[2] Other Than Proverbs

Ecclesiastes 10:18 *By much slothfulness the building decayeth; and through idleness of the hands the house droppeth through.*

If you are too lazy to take care of your house, it will fall apart. That's also true of businesses, families, health, and life in general.

The ancient authors of the Bible were wise people. But before I end the subject, I'll share with you a few proverbs from more modern philosophers.

- Laziness is nothing more than the habit of resting before you get tired. - Jules Renard
- The day will happen, whether or not you get up. - John Cairdi
- All our dreams can come true if we have the courage to pursue them. - Walt Disney
- The harder you work, the luckier you get. - Gary Player
- The only way to enjoy anything in this life is to earn it first. - Ginger Rogers

- God gives every bird its food, but He does not throw it into the nest. - J.G. Holland
- The best way to make your dreams come true is to wake up. - J.M. Power

Duties of Leadership

Acts 20:28-35

As a Christian, you may find yourself in a leadership capacity. Suddenly, you'll find yourself responsible, not only for your own Christian behavior, but for others as well.

Here is some advice that Paul left with his own disciples at Ephesus, those whom he was certain he would never see again in this life. He was leaving, soon to die, though he didn't know it, and he was off to other mission fields, leaving local leaders in charge of the fledgling church in Ephesus. And the success of that church depended greatly on what they did and how they led.

[1] Leaders Must Be Right With God Themselves

Acts 20:28 *Take heed therefore unto yourselves, and to all the flock…*

Before you take care of the flock, take care of yourselves. A leader must not be trapped into the "do as I say not as I do" sort of thinking. A leader must lead, from the front, pull not push. Alexander the Great was largely victorious because he directed his troops from the front, he led them into battle, taking the same risks as they, and they followed him anywhere. But his Persian counterpart directed his troops from the rear, and when things went badly, he fled, and that demoralized the troops and guaranteed defeat.

Want to lead? Then lead — from the front. Don't ask anyone to do what you are not willing to do.

[2] Teach the Church

Acts 20:28 *...feed the church of God, which he hath purchased with his own blood.*

To lead means to teach — how to live a Christian life, how to share the good news of Christ with others, and how to lead. Jesus was very anxious for his disciples to take on their roles of leadership and made that quite clear to Peter: ***John 21:16*** *...Feed my sheep.* And that is exactly what Peter and the rest did.

[3] Warn the Church

Acts 20:29 *For I know this, that after my departing shall grievous wolves enter in among you, not sparing the flock.* ***:31*** *Therefore watch, and remember, that by the space of three years I ceased not to warn every one night and day with tears.*

The Church had enemies then as it has enemies today. There are people who would like to see the Church cease to exist, and other people who would like to see the Church morph into something more to their own liking, void of Gospel truth, accepting of every sin that God forbids, in short, a country club where people gather to have fun.

The disciples, the true leaders, were very anxious to get the Church right and keep it right, and so they had to not only teach the truth but also warn against those who taught error.

[4] Pray

Acts 20:32 *And now, brethren, I commend you to God...*

In other words, Paul prayed for them, saying to God in essence, "I am recommending these people to you." Paul wanted them to succeed, first as Christians, but second in whatever leadership capacity they had been asked to perform.

[5] Study

Acts 20:32 *. . . and to the word of his grace, which is able to build you up, and to give you an inheritance among all them which are sanctified.*

There is a handbook, and that handbook is the scriptures. The Bible as we know it did not come into being until the 4th century. But whatever documents or letters they had available, they were to study what God had to say to them.

[6] Their Callings Were Not To Be Self-Serving

Acts 20:34 *Yea, ye yourselves know, that these hands have ministered unto my necessities, and to them that were with me.* ***:35*** *I have shewed you all things, how that so laboring ye ought to support the weak, and to remember the words of the Lord Jesus, how he said, it is more blessed to give than to receive.*

Paul was setting an example. His task was not to use his calling to enrich himself — he could have done that, others tried to — but to bring people to Christ and to save souls. The idea that he might profit from that work was not on his mind. He made his own living and financed his own missions and asked nothing for himself other than a listening audience.

Learning

Proverbs

Obviously, you are not averse to learning or you wouldn't be reading this, or the Bible. Just the same, we ought to take some time to find out what the Bible has to say about learning — not learning this or learning that, but learning in general.

As with other subjects, we find the bulk of Hebrew thinking in Proverbs, and so it is that we turn to Proverbs to learn about learning.

> ***Proverbs 15:5*** *A fool despiseth his father's instruction: but he that regardeth reproof is prudent.*

> ***Proverbs 15:32*** *He that refuseth instruction despiseth his own soul: but he that heareth reproof getteth understanding.*

When a teacher instructs a student, whether learning occurs or not depends greatly on the attitude of the student. Does the student see that instruction as instruction or as reproof? If the student senses reproof, the negativity may be a barrier to learning because the student may be more focused on protecting his ego than on getting the information.

But even if the student senses reproof, he still has a choice. He can protect his ego and learn nothing, which is what fools do, or he can accept his proper role as student, accept the reproof, set his ego aside, and learn. That's the prudent thing to do.

Yes, the teacher should try to be a good teacher by stroking the student's ego rather than attacking it, but ultimately the responsibility for learning is the student's. And good students, wise students, will learn even from bad teachers. If you are a wise student, one who is determined to learn no matter what, you must learn to get what you want from even the worst teachers. And rule number one is: don't let your pride get in the way.

Proverbs 16:21 *...the sweetness of the lips increaseth learning.*

"The sweetness of the lips" is more than *what* is said, it is *how* it is said. When we seek learning, we expect to hear more than just the truth, we expect our teacher to speak the truth in an eloquent way so that we actually want to hear it. When a student is impassioned about a subject, then it sticks.

Information is what comes out of the teacher. Learning is what goes into the student. Teaching is more than conveying information, it is also sales. It is convincing students that what the teacher is saying is worth time and effort to learn. Teachers should make a real effort to hone their teaching skills, that is, if they want to actually teach.

Here's a saying of my own, something I've been saying for decades: "A teacher's highest duty is not to teach but to inspire learning."

Proverbs 16:23 *The heart of the wise teacheth his mouth, and addeth learning to his lips.*

It's hard to learn when you feel no passion for the subject. But when your heart is in it, learning just happens. Good instruction begins in the teacher's heart, then moves to the mind, then the mouth. Then to the student's ears, then mind, then heart. When the information has arrived in the student's heart, real teaching has occurred.

Proverbs 17:10 *A reproof entereth more into a wise man than an hundred stripes into a fool.*

A wise man takes to heart even rebuke, but a fool never listens — you can't even beat the truth into him. To learn, a student must set pride aside, even if the student is being ridiculed or yelled at. A real demarcation between wisdom and foolishness is how you react when your boss yells at you. If you accept the incoming with humility and a desire to do better, you will learn and be a better employee and keep your job. But if you meet hostility with hostility, you will learn nothing and probably lose your job.

Proverbs 17:16 *Wherefore is there a price in the hand of a fool to get wisdom, seeing he hath no heart to it?*

A fool has no passion for learning, so he will pay no price to get knowledge — not money, not effort to study, not even getting up on time to show up to class on time. That's a fool. He ignores his opportunities for education because he has other things to do, like computer games.

This is the downside of free education. Since it is free, students place no value on it and see it as a chore rather than an opportunity.

Proverbs 17:24 *Wisdom is before him that hath understanding; but the eyes of a fool are in the ends of the earth.*

A wise man grabs those opportunities that are immediately available. A fool lives in a fantasyland, daydreaming of far places but does nothing to realize his dreams.

Proverbs 18:1 *Through desire a man, having separated himself, seeketh and intermeddleth with all wisdom.*

Wise men separate themselves from all distractions and passionately focus on the task at hand, and tries to get all the information available. With today's internet, it's pretty easy to get any information you want about anything.

> ***Proverbs 23:23*** *Buy the truth, and sell it not; also wisdom, and instruction, and understanding.*

There is great value in good education. Spend your money and your time on knowledge, and you've gotten your money's worth. "Sell it not" implies, I think, that there are some things you really don't want to share with other people, like for instance, your successful way of beating the stock market.

> ***Proverbs 24:3*** *Through wisdom is an house builded; and by understanding it is established.* ***:4*** *And by knowledge shall the chambers be filled with all precious and pleasant riches.* ***:5*** *A wise man is strong; yea, a man of knowledge increaseth strength.*

It is education and knowledge that gets the really important stuff done. If you don't know what you're doing, what you do can be worse than doing nothing at all, like for example, building a house full of mistakes.

> ***Proverbs 29:1*** *He, that being often reproved hardeneth his neck, shall suddenly be destroyed, and that without remedy.*

Stubbornness against learning leads to ignorance, and often to fatal ignorance. For instance, millions of people die each year just because they will not heed the simple warning on cigarette packs: "Warning! Cigarettes can cause fatal lung disease." Smokers are often reminded of that (it's on every pack) but stubbornly reject the truth, and many pay for that stubbornness with their lives.

Ecclesiastes 4:13 *Better is a poor and a wise child than an old and foolish king, who will no more be admonished.*

Many leaders (particularly old leaders who have been in office too long) won't take advice. That's a perilous situation for the king and the country to be in. This is a good argument for term limits. But a child who is "poor and wise" won't be poor for long.

Daniel 12:4 *...the time of the end...knowledge shall be increased.*

This last verse foresees a future age of great knowledge and fast learning. We have arrived at that time.

It's always been true that anyone who doesn't seek knowledge is a fool, but it is truer today than ever. Today there is *so* much knowledge available, and so much of it is free and at our fingertips that anyone who would pass on that would be a very big fool indeed.

Man's Sinful Nature

Isaiah 64:6, Romans 3:9-23

No other book is as pessimistic about human nature as the Bible. And that is a hard sell, when you think about it. If any writer today submitted such a glum book to a publisher for serious consideration, it would be trashed immediately.

We don't want to hear how bad we are but how good we are. We want to be encouraged, have our egos stroked, we want compliments.

But the Bible message is exactly the opposite. Why then is the Bible still the world's number one best-seller since its core message is so condemning? Probably because we know it's true. And guilt-ridden as we are, we want to escape our natures. It simply won't do for a well-intended psychologist to assure us that we're okay when we know better. We don't want approval, we want escape.

But how do we escape? The only escape available anywhere is the escape offered to us from the very book that condemns us. And that is the book's appeal.

Why do we believe the Bible? Because no one would have written such a book to garner popularity. Therefore, it must be true because, from beginning to end, it was written with such reluctance and self-condemnation that it is impossible for anyone to have made it up. That fact alone makes the Bible reek with integrity. There is no other possible reason why it would have been written other than to reluctantly report the truth. And truth, harsh truth, with no ulterior motive in mind, is refreshing.

And so, for your reading pleasure, or pain, I present to you the pessimistic Bible.

[1] General Condemnation

Let's begin with those verses that condemn humanity collectively, the whole human race.

> ***Job 14:4*** *Who can bring a clean thing out of an unclean? Not one.*

> ***1 Kings 8:46*** *If they sin against thee, (for there is no man that sinneth not)...*

> ***2 Chronicles 6:36*** *If they sin against thee, (for there is no man which sinneth not)*

> ***Psalms 14:2*** *The* LORD *looked down from heaven upon the children of men, to see if there were any that did understand, and seek God.* ***:3*** *They are all gone aside, they are all together become filthy: there is none that doeth good, no, not one.*

This verse is very emphatic and very harsh: *no, not one.* This is an intentional condemnation of the whole human race. But then how are we to understand what immediately follows?

> ***Psalms 14:5*** *There were they in great fear: for God is in the generation of the righteous.* ***15:2*** *He that walketh uprightly, and worketh righteousness, and speaketh the truth in his heart.*

What "righteousness" is he talking about? He just said there are *none that doeth good*, so how are there any righteous?

The Bible wants to have it both ways: No one is righteous, but the righteous speak the truth. How can that be? Either we should just accept that the Bible flip-flops and try not to be theological absolutists, or we can try to harmonize the two sides with something like this: People are both good and bad. Every righteous person has an unrighteous streak and draws both God's praise and God's ire at the same time. Sounds like our own kids, doesn't it? And there's this Mother Goose poem: "There was a little girl, and she had a little curl right in the middle of her forehead. When she was good, she was very, very good, but when she was bad she was horrid." That's the whole human race, very good and very bad.

It's the "horrid" part that occupies our attention now. Let's continue.

> ***Psalms 53:1*** *...there is none that doeth good.* ***:2*** *God looked down from heaven upon the children of men, to see if there were any that did understand, that did seek God.* ***:3*** *Every one of them is gone back: they are altogether become filthy; there is none that doeth good, no, not one.*

> ***Ecclesiastes 7:20*** *For there is not a just man upon earth, that doeth good, and sinneth not.*

> ***Ecclesiastes 7:22*** *For oftentimes also thine own heart knoweth that thou thyself likewise hast cursed others.*

Not only are we guilty, but in our heart we know we are guilty. We might as well admit it. So, we are not only guilty but guilt-ridden as well.

> ***Ecclesiastes 9:3*** *...the heart of the sons of men is full of evil...*

> ***Isaiah 64:6*** *But we are all as an unclean thing, and all our righteousnesses are as filthy rags; and we do fade as a leaf; and our iniquities, like the wind, have taken us away.*

It's not that we don't have righteousness, it's that our righteousness, however good and well-intended, is at best suspect. Everything we do that we might call righteous is motivated by some self-serving purpose. That God accepts anything we do we can only attribute to his far-reaching love.

> ***Jeremiah 17:9*** *The heart is deceitful above all things, and desperately wicked: who can know it?*

> ***Daniel 4:35*** *And all the inhabitants of the earth are reputed as nothing.*

Finally, then, Paul takes all this Jewish negativity, rolls it all together into the opening of his Book of Romans, and condemns us all universally. Then, from that basis, he points to Christ as our only hope for escape.

> ***Romans 3:9*** *…we have before proved both Jews and gentiles, that they are under sin.* ***:10*** *As it is written, There is none righteous, no, not one:* ***:11*** *There is none that understandeth, there is none that seeketh after God.* ***:12*** *They are all gone out of the way, they are together become unprofitable; there is none that doeth good, no, not one.* ***:13*** *Their throat is an open sepulcher; with their tongues they have used deceit; their poison of asps is under their lips:* ***:14*** *Whose mouth is full of cursing and bitterness:* ***:15*** *Their feet are swift to shed blood:* ***:16*** *Destruction and misery are in their ways:* ***:17*** *And the way of peace have they not known.* ***:18*** *There is no fear of God before their eyes.* ***:19*** *Now we know that what things soever the law saith, it saith to them who are under the law: that every mouth may be stopped, and all the world may become guilty before God.* ***:20*** *Therefore by the deeds of the law there shall no flesh be justified in his sight…* ***:23*** *For all have sinned, and come short of the glory of God…*

Wow! That's a pretty ugly picture, and it pretty much sums up what we really are. We, the whole human race, are a bad lot.

For my Mormon readers, I'll add these Mormon verses. Everyone else can ignore them, of course. But I need to include them because Mormons have a general dislike of all things negative and tend to accept such things only from their own scriptures.

> ***Mosiah 2:21*** *…if ye should serve him with all your whole souls yet ye would be unprofitable servants.* ***:24*** *…if ye do* [obey him] *he doth immediately bless you; and therefore he hath paid you. And ye are still indebted unto him, and are, and will be, forever and ever; therefore, of what have ye to boast?*

> ***Mosiah 3:19*** *For the natural man is an enemy to God, and has been from the fall of Adam…*

> ***Mosiah 4:5*** *For behold, if the knowledge of the goodness of God at this time has awakened you to a sense of your nothingness, and your worthless and fallen state.*

> ***Moses 1:10*** *…Moses did again receive his natural strength like unto man; and he said unto himself: Now, for this cause I know that man is nothing, which thing I never had supposed.*

[2] Specific Condemnation

We tend to want to distribute everyone into either of two camps: good or bad. And so, when God condemns people, we want to say, "Well, yes. But God means bad people. There are genuinely good people, and he doesn't mean them."

I wish that were true. The problem is that those we think of as righteous have a different opinion of themselves, especially when they find themselves in the presence of the holy God. So, for the record, here are those verses (that I have found) about "good" people, the best that the human race has to offer, and how they feel about themselves. This is the varsity team, and they come up short.

Genesis 32:10 *I* [Jacob] *am not worthy of the least of all mercies…*

Job 42:6 *Wherefore I* [Job] *abhor myself, and repent in dust and ashes.*

Isaiah 6:5 *Then said I* [Isaiah], *Woe is me! For I am undone; because I am a man of unclean lips, and I dwell in the midst of a people of unclean lips: for my mine eyes have seen the King, the* LORD *of hosts.*

Daniel 9:20 *And whiles I* [Daniel] *was speaking, and praying, and confessing my sin…* ***10:8*** *…there remained no strength in me for my comeliness was turned into corruption…*

Luke 5:8 *When Simon Peter saw it, he fell down at Jesus' knees, saying, Depart from me; for I am a sinful man, O Lord.*

Romans 4:2 *For if Abraham were justified by works, he hath whereof to glory; but not before God.* ***:3*** *For what saith the scripture? Abraham believed God, and it was counted unto him for righteousness.* [Abraham's faith, not his works, made him righteous.]

Revelation 1:17 *And when I* [John] *saw him, I fell at his feet as dead.*

And that is how really good men feel about themselves when they have to face God. The best defense then that you offer to God is not, "God, look how good I am," but rather, "God, forgive me."

And that's the way of it, from the very beginning.

Hebrews 11:4 *By faith Abel offered unto God a more excellent sacrifice than Cain, by which he obtained witness that he was righteous…*

Abel offered a sin (blood) offering. Cain offered a boasting (vegetable) offering. And how ironic this switch is: The wicked Cain says, "I'm good," while the righteous Abel says, "I'm wicked and need forgiveness." And it's been so ever since.

[3] POST-CONVERSION

But, you might argue, we used to be bad, but now we are converted Christians. Surely we are good now, aren't we? I hate to disappoint again, but the scriptures never allow us to get comfortable with our present righteousness. And since I want to make the point most strongly to my Mormon readers, I'll offer up the Mormon verses that make just this point.

Mosiah 4:11 *…if ye have…received a remission of your sins…ye should remember and <u>always retain in remembrance</u>, the greatness of God, and <u>your own nothingness</u>, and his goodness and long-suffering towards you, unworthy creatures…*

Alma 38:14 *Do not say: O God, I thank thee that we are better than our brethren; but rather say: O Lord, forgive my unworthiness, and remember my brethren in mercy — yea, <u>acknowledge your unworthiness</u> before God <u>at all times</u>.*

3 Nephi 28:29 *…there was a change wrought upon them* [the Three Nephites] *insomuch that Satan could have no power over them, that he could not tempt them.*

This last verse I've included because it makes a stunning point, namely, these three Nephites, who undoubtedly were the best of the best and that's why they were chosen, where changed so that Satan could have no power over them. Which necessarily means that before they were changed, Satan *did* have power over them. And they were the best. So, what does that say about us?

The upshot of all this is that just because you are a converted Christian and more determined to live a right life doesn't elevate you to a position of thinking that now you are finally a good person. Not before God, you're not.

I know it's a conundrum. But frankly, I wouldn't really feel all that secure if I had to think of myself as "good" in order to think that God will accept me. Because I'm never sure what "good" God has in mind. Which rung of the goodness ladder does God expect us to reach before we can believe that we are good enough? That's the problem. There is no such rung. If absolute perfection is the goal then we've already lost. Not only because we have already sinned, but because we, each of us, already know that perfection is an unachievable goal. That is the very reason we turn to Christ and not to anyone else.

[4] How Do We Escape?

Since getting better and better is not the escape route, there must be another. And there is. Let us begin with my most favorite verse in the Bible. It is my favorite because it unravels a lot of the conundrum.

> ***Romans 8:1*** *There is therefore now no condemnation to them which are in Christ Jesus, who walk not after the flesh, but after the Spirit.*

This verse says a lot. It is the balance between works and grace, and you don't have to think of yourself as a "good" person, whatever that means.

What does it mean to be "in Christ"? That's not really the right question, it's too big a question. The right question is merely, how do you know that you're in Christ? And the answer is if you are walking not after the flesh but after the Spirit. In other words, it is the *holy walk* that matters, *not the holy arrival!* And that is all the difference in the world. I may not be allowed to think of myself as "good," but I can certainly think of myself as "getting better." And that is what "walk after the spirit" means.

Once we understand that, then we can overcome our fear of God and replace it with boldness.

> ***Hebrews 4:16*** *Let us therefore come boldly unto the throne of grace, that we may obtain mercy, and find grace in time of need.* ***10:19*** *Having therefore, brethren, boldness to enter into the holiest by the blood of Jesus*

> ***1 John 4:17*** *Herein is our love made perfect, that we may have boldness in the day of judgment…*

And, after all, isn't that what we want? Boldness? The right and the privilege to believe that God has accepted us even with all our flaws?

[5] But What About Our Righteousness?

Sorry again. Your righteousness won't do. You have to get someone else's righteousness. But fortunately for us, someone else's righteousness is available.

Romans 10:3 *For they being ignorant of God's righteousness, and going about to establish their own righteousness, have not submitted themselves unto the righteousness of God.*

It is not our righteousness that we should be offering to God to secure a place in heaven. We need something else.

Philippians 3:9 *And be found in him, not having mine own righteousness, which is of the law, but that which is through the faith of Christ, the righteousness which is of God by faith.*

It is God's righteousness we ought to seek because only with his righteousness can we be "good" enough.

Now, for my Mormon readers who may still doubt this, I will offer these Mormon scriptures to you.

Alma 24:10 *…he hath forgiven us of those our many sins…and taken away the guilt from our hearts, through the merits of his Son.*

Helaman 14:13 *And if ye believe on his name ye will repent of all your sins, that thereby ye may have a remission of them through his merits.*

Moroni 6:4 *And after they had been received unto baptism…and cleansed by the power of the Holy Ghost…relying alone upon the merits of Christ, who was the author and the finisher of their faith.*

This last verse is wonderfully powerful. Focus on the word "alone."

After repenting and being baptized and turning to the right life, even then we dare not present to God our own merits and say, "See how good I am" as Cain did. No. That would be a fool's defense. But rather, after all the good we imagine we've done, we turn to

God and plead our cause on the merits of Christ only, and offer no other defense. That's what the word "alone" means.

D&C 38:4 *...I am Christ, and in mine own name, by the virtue of the blood which I have spilt, have I pleaded before the Father for them.*

Even Christ knows that pleading our merits is hopeless. He won't do it. If Jesus said to God, "Look how good that person is," and he pointed to you, you'd lose. Jesus knows that, so he doesn't even try. Instead, he pleads for you and me with his own merits, and that persuades God.

[6] After All You Can Do

But what about this verse?

2 Nephi 25:23 *It is by grace that we are saved after all that we can do.*

So, we have to work really hard and be really good so that we can *earn* grace? That makes no sense and is self-contradictory. The problem is you *can't* do all that you can do. Is visiting your home teaching family once a month "all that you can do"? No? Maybe you should visit them twice a month. Is that "all that you can do"? How about every day, thirty days every month?

This verse can mean either of two things. It could mean you have to be really good (after all you can do) to earn grace, which makes no sense. Or it could mean after all you can do you finally realize you can't do all you can do, no amount of doing is good enough so now turn to grace.

1 Peter 1:10 *Of which salvation the prophets have enquired and searched diligently, who prophesied of that grace that should come to you.* ***:11***

> *Searching what, or what manner of time the Spirit of Christ which was in them did signify, when it was testified beforehand the sufferings of Christ, and the glory that should follow.* ***:12*** *Unto whom it was revealed, that not unto themselves, but unto us they did minister the things, which are now reported unto you by them that have preached the gospel unto you with the Holy Ghost sent down from heaven; which things the angels desire to look into.*

In other words, the prophets of old received revelation about the future Christ, his atonement, and the resulting grace, and *didn't understand their own prophecies* so that they had to study them like anyone else and never really understood them.

So, for Nephi to say "after all you can do," the truth is, he really didn't understand the full meaning of his own prophecies, nor the unattainableness of his "after all you can do."

Unless, that is, we allow those words to have its second natural meaning.

Words are very often ambiguous, having two or more possible meanings that are consistent with the context. In this verse another meaning is possible. And that's what I think Nephi's words mean. Try works. And when that fails, try grace.

[7] Conclusion

I know it's disconcerting to learn that you can never be good enough to earn heaven. We would prefer a connect-the-dots playbook: Do this, do that, and you're in. The problem is, not only does God tell us we fall short and will always fall short, but we know in our own hearts that we fall short. That's the dilemma, knowing we can never achieve what we must achieve: personal righteousness. It's like grabbing bubbles which burst the moment we touch them. That's why Peter said —

Acts 15:10 *...which neither our fathers nor we were able to bear.*

This has been the human condition from the very beginning. Cain and Abel both faced this dilemma and responded two different ways. The righteous Abel brought an offering to God that confessed his sins. But the wicked Cain brought an offering that extolled his virtues, "See my fruits? Aren't they great?" And it has been so ever since. The righteous never see themselves as righteous because they don't dare. And the wicked always see themselves as righteous. So, the righteous, as we call them, look for a different escape and find it in Christ. And the wicked are stuck in their self-aggrandizing delusion.

The message of Christianity is two-fold. First, Jesus died and resurrected. That event *is* Christianity. And second, all people have fallen short and have failed to achieve righteousness. We failed because it's our nature to fail. However, God has allowed Christ to substitute his righteousness for our own, and thus we become saved citizens of heaven after all.

Although at first it may seem disconcerting that we have fallen short and cannot achieve the goal we seek, it is not disconcerting at all. Actually, it is unburdening. Isn't it better to be allowed to return home because a loving parent wants you rather than because you've earned it as a reward, like paying rent? Speaking for myself, I'd much prefer God giving from his love rather than me earning and collecting on a debt. God owes me nothing yet gives me everything. Of that, I am sure.

Man's Divine Nature

John 10:34, Psalms 82:6

The Bible has so much to say about man's sin nature that we tend to forget that it also has a lot to say about man's divine nature. With all our foibles and follies, it is God's intent that we become like him.

> ***Genesis 3:22*** *And the* LORD *God said, Behold, the man is become as one of us, to know good and evil: and now, lest he put forth his hand, and take also of the tree of life, and eat, and live forever* ***:23*** *Therefore the* LORD *God sent him forth from the garden of Eden.*

This verse asserts that Adam and Eve's "fall" was in fact a promotion of sorts, that by presuming to eat the fruit, man gained the knowledge of good and evil and thus became as the Gods.

> ***Exodus 4:16*** *…thou shalt be to him instead of God.*
> ***Exodus 7:1*** *…I have made thee a god to Pharaoh…*

God made Moses a god to Pharaoh.

> ***Psalms 8:5*** *For thou hast made him a little lower than the angels…* ***:6*** *…thou hast put all things under his feet.*

Wrong. This faulty translation fails to make the Bible's real point. The Hebrew is Eloheim and should be translated: "a little lower than the gods."

And the next verse is far reaching in its scope. How much is "all"? How about the entire universe under our feet? How about even the ability to create universes? Do we have any limits? Thanks to modern science, the human race seems to be on a fast track to finding out what limits there really are, if there are any.

> **Psalms 17:15** *As for me, I will behold thy face in righteousness: I shall be satisfied, when I awake, with thy likeness.*

In our afterlife, when we awake from death, we will have the likeness of God. What exactly "likeness" means is not so clear. It may mean appearance or it may mean all of God's attributes: to be like.

> **Psalms 82:6** *I have said, Ye are gods; and all of you are children of the most High.* **:7** *But ye shall die like men…*

God clearly assigns to mortals the station of godhood. We are gods because we are his children. Like father like son. So, the Mormons are not heretics to draw attention to this Biblical fact. Those who are annoyed by this truth try to mitigate it with the "But ye shall die like men." That is a long stretch, and irrelevant. Yes, we fell and became mortal and sinful, but that is a complete aside from the fact of our initial and final destinies: to be and to become what our Father in Heaven is. On this issue, the Mormons have it exactly right. But then, there is this verse which upsets everything —

> **Isaiah 43:10** *…before me there was not God formed, neither shall there be after me.* **:11** *I, even I, am the LORD; and beside me there is no saviour.*

I would be dishonest to ignore contrary evidence and this verse certainly is that. If there is only one God, none before and none after, how can we be gods alongside of God?

This verse is not just problematic for divine man doctrine, it is also problematic for trinity doctrine. In other words, if there is only one God, how can there be a God the Father and a God the Son and a God the Holy Ghost? So, my claim is that any argument that untangles the trinity complication also untangles the divine man complication. For if there are three gods who are one God, then why not a million gods who are one God?

But then one might argue, "But the Bible presents trinity doctrine to us, so that has to be defended. It doesn't present divine man doctrine." I argue back, "Oh, but the Bible does present divine man doctrine to us ***(Psalms 82:6)***, and so it too must be defended."

So then, how do we defend trinity and divine man against ***Isaiah 43:10-11***?

My answer to that is to notice that "God" is "Eloheim", which is a plural.

So, who is Eloheim, this one God who is a plural? Answer: They are the godhead (or trinity), the Father, Son, and Holy Ghost. And we are, as Jesus said —

> ***John 17:21*** *That they all may be one; as thou, Father, art in me, and I in thee, that they may be one in us: that the world may believe that thou hast sent me.* ***:22*** *And the glory which thou gavest me I have given them; that they may be one, even as we are one:* ***:23*** *I in them, and thou in me, that they may be made perfect in one…*

But maybe the oneness of which Jesus speaks is only figurative. If that is the case, then that creates an impossible problem. For if us being one with God is figurative, then Jesus being one with God is also figurative, and that denies the trinity. Whatever oneness means for the Father and Son, it also means for the Father and Son *and us.* Jesus' words are emphatic, and the more so since he gives us his glory. What does that make us if not God? What he is, he is making us. It is impossible to escape that conclusion. To cast the idea in concrete —

Isaiah 44:6 *...I am the first, and I am the last; and beside me there is no God.*

Isaiah's God says: beside me there is no Savior ***(Isaiah 44:10)*** and no God ***(Isaiah 43:10)***. But Jesus identifies himself by the name "the first and the last".

Revelation 1:11 *...I am Alpha and Omega, the first and the last...* ***:17*** *...I am the first and the last.* ***:18*** *I am he that liveth, and was dead; and, behold, I am alive for ever more...*

Thus, Jesus is both God and Saviour. So, if beside Jesus there is no God, and beside God there is no Saviour, how can all that be true or even make sense?.

The more so since, all over the gospels, Jesus submits to his father. So, how can this be? How can Jesus, who submits to his father, be Isaiah's God beside whom there is no God and no Saviour?

All of that is so full of contradictions that the only way to resolve it is with my previous argument: Eloheim is a plural, and that allows *them* to be the one God. But it also allows *us* to be one with that one God who is a plural.

Luke 3:38 *Which was the son of Enos, which was the son of Seth, which was the son of Adam, which was the son of God.*

This pedigree of Christ identifies Adam as the son of God in exactly the same way as it identifies Seth as the son of Adam. God, after creating the world, did not "create" man but "pro-created" man. We really are his children. This is not figurative.

> ***Luke 15:31*** *And he said unto him, Son, thou art ever with me, and all that I have is thine.*

Yes, this is just a parable, The Prodigal Son. But how much of this parable did Jesus really mean? If Jesus really meant it, the father said to the faithful son, "All I have is thine." Now, if we are to understand the father as God, and the sons as ourselves, then God is saying to us, "All I have is thine," and "all" is a lot. But it's just a parable. But this next verse, however, is not just a parable, it is a clear assertion.

> ***John 10:34*** *Jesus answered them, Is it not written in your law, I said, Ye are gods?* ***:35*** *If he called them gods, unto whom the word of God came, and the scripture cannot be broken*

Jesus said, "I and my father are one." They said, "You are making yourself God, so we must kill you." His defense here is, "Yes, I said, 'I and my father are one,' but that is inescapably inferred from ***Psalms 82:6****… Ye are gods.*" What he said then is this: I am god is in the same sense that you are gods. So once again, to defend the notion of trinity or Christ's divinity is also to defend the notion of man's divinity. The two are conjoined. And we'll see even more of that.

> ***Acts 17:28*** *For in him we live, and move, and have our being; as certain also of your own poets have said, For we are also his offspring.*

We might haggle over the meaning of "children" of God, but how can we haggle over the meaning of "offspring" of God?

Offspring means biological progeny. God not only created us, he pro-created us. We are literally and not figuratively God's children. We are of the race of God.

Matthew 11:27 *All things are delivered unto me of my father…*

Hebrews 1:2 *Hath in these last days spoken unto us by his son, whom he hath appointed heir of all things, by whom also he made the worlds*

It would be pointless to say that we are co-inheritors with Christ until we know what Christ inherits. These two verses settle for us that Christ inherits everything. And that means really everything. "The worlds" meaning the universe which he created.

Romans 8:16 *…we are the children of God* ***:17*** *And if children, then heirs; heirs of God, and joint-heirs with Christ…*

Whether we were born to divinity or not is not the issue here. The issue here is that God makes us heirs of Christ's divinity, like adoption. So, while we might haggle over whether we were born to divinity or not, the end result is the same. What Jesus is is what we will become. If Jesus is God, then that is what we will become.

1 Corinthians 3:21 *…all things are yours;* ***:22*** *Whether…life, or death, or things present, or things to come; all are yours*

That's pretty inclusive. "All" is a lot. And "all" must include godhood, or it wouldn't be "all."

1 Corinthians 13:12 *…but then shall I know even as also I am known.*

Someday I will be omniscient. As much as God knows me, that's how much I will know. We will finally really understand ourselves.

Galatians 4:7 *Wherefore thou art no more a servant, but a son; and if a son, then an heir of God through Christ.*

This emphasizes the role of son-ship. We are not merely servants who receive gifts from an estate, we are sons who, by inheritance, step into the role of the father.

Revelation 21:7 *He that overcometh shall inherit all things; and I will be his God, and he shall be my son.*

This underscores once again our son-ship to God and connects it to universal inheritance, inheriting all things. And all things is big. In other words, there is nothing God has that we won't inherit. That's divinity. That is our destiny.

Now, this is conditional. Only "he that overcometh shall inherit all things." But clearly that is God's intent for all of us and the divine potential for each of us. And we humans, individually and collectively, should raise our sights higher and strive to become what God is. Actually, we do seem to have charted that course already, and that's good.

This discussion would not be complete without a frank discussion of Mormon theology, since Mormon theology hinges on this very issue. Here is what Mormon scripture says —

Doctrine and Covenants 132:20 *Then shall they be gods, because they have no end; therefore shall they be from everlasting to everlasting, because they continue; then shall they be above all, because all things are* *subject unto them. Then shall they be gods, because they have all power, and the angels are subject unto them.*

This Mormon doctrine, that man is intended to become gods, is deemed by all other Christian churches to be heretical. But, in light of the Bible verses I have discussed, it doesn't seem so heretical, does it? This Mormon verse just goes to the blunt conclusion.

***

Now, let's have some fun with this.

Jesus healed people. And from that we learn not only that Jesus is loving and powerful, but also that people can be healed — by people, doctors. Thus, the entire medical profession took its cue from Jesus. He was, as he said, "the way" — not just the way to a better afterlife in heaven, but also the way to a better here and now.

Here is his broad admonition to the whole human race —

John 14:12 *Verily, verily, I say unto you, He that believeth on me, the works that I do shall he do also; and greater works than these shall he do; because I go unto my Father.*

How many lepers did Jesus cure? Ten for sure, maybe dozens, maybe hundreds. Who knows. How many lepers has modern medicine cured? Thousands? Millions? Who knows. But one thing is for sure: Because one researcher (in this case, Doctor Gerhard Armauer Hansen) followed Jesus's lead and thought, "we can cure this evil disease," and he found a way. We can now cure leprosy which is today called Hansen's Disease.

How many blind people did Jesus cure? How many deaf people? Now the real question: How many dead people did Jesus raise? Three, plus himself made four, that we know of. Maybe more.

Here's my point: Whatever God did through the man Jesus, he was showing us "the way"; in other words, what Jesus did, we can do too, often through modern medicine, science, and engineering. We say to God, "Fix our problems." He answers, "*You* fix them. That's why I gave you dominion."

Well then, what else did Jesus do? I could make a list, but you can too. But to get directly to the point, Jesus created everything.

> ***John 1:3*** *all things were made by him*
> ***Colossians 1:16*** *by him were all things created*
> ***Hebrews 1:2*** *by whom* [Jesus]...*he* [God] *made the worlds.*

So, where does that put us? We, who are *joint heirs (**Romans 8:16-17**)* with Christ, have a big job ahead of us.

> ***Genesis 3:22*** *And the LORD God said, Behold, the man has become as one of us...*

> ***Genesis 11:6*** *...and this they have begun to do: and now nothing will be restrained from them, which they have imagined to do.*

We are on a collision course with our destiny. We cannot avoid it nor should we want to. So let's embrace it, and pursue it with all the will and passion that we, God's children, can muster.

Money

Proverbs

The Bible has a lot to say about money; and most of it is negative. You already know that you can't take it with you, but you should also know that how you deal with money may determine where you go after this life.

As you might expect, since Proverbs is a treasure trove of good advice about almost anything, it is also a treasure trove of good advice (do's and don'ts) about money.

[1] The Do's

1. **Work**

   Proverbs 14:23 *In labor there is profit but the talk of the lips tendeth only to penury.*

   Well, surprise, surprise. The Bible says work. I imagine some readers were hoping the Bible would instead advise us to run off to the hills, become spiritual hermits, and contemplate our navels. Nope. The Bible doesn't say that; it says work. In fact, the Bible is adamant.

   2 Thessalonians 3:10 *If any would not work, neither should he eat.*

   1 Timothy 5:8 *If any provide not for his own…he hath denied the faith…*

   Proverbs 6:10 *Yet a little sleep…so shall thy poverty come as one that travelleth…*

2. **Save**
   Proverbs 21:20 *There is treasure to be desired in the dwelling of the wise, but a foolish man spendeth it up.*
   Spend less than you earn so that you have a net positive balance. Saving and investing is not a bad thing but a good thing so that we can be self-sufficient, not a burden on others.

3. **Plan**
   Proverbs 24:3 *Through wisdom is a house built; and by understanding it is established;* ***:4*** *And by knowledge shall the chambers be filled with all precious and pleasant riches.*
   Want to live well in a nice home with nice things? Wisdom, understanding, and knowledge are pretty much requirements for achieving your goal. It's amazing how some people live any stupid way they want, squandering every opportunity, then are surprised when poverty catches up with them. Then they blame everyone else — parents, teachers, the "system" — for their own failure as though everyone else has a duty to feed them.

4. **Look**
   Proverbs 27:23 *Be thou diligent to know the state of thy flocks, and look well to thy herds.*
   The simple act of balancing a checkbook matters. You have to keep track of what you have so that you can know if you're heading in the right direction or wrong direction.

5. **Give**
   Proverbs 11:24 *There is that scattereth and yet increaseth and there is that withholdeth more than is meet but it tendeth to poverty.*
   A miracle of the universe (in the general scheme of things) that is not intuitively obvious is that generous people somehow do better in life than those who are stingy. "What goes around

comes around" is true. Good people draw goodness and bad people draw badness. I don't know why, it just is. The universe is a mirror that reflects back at you what you are. My granddaughter calls it karma.

Luke 6:36 *Give to every man that asketh of thee.*

Leviticus 25:35 *if thy brother be waxen poor…thou shalt relieve him…take thou no usury…* (Lend without interest to those in need.)

[2] THE DON'TS

1. **HASTY**

Proverbs 21:5 *The thoughts of the diligent tend only to plenteousness; but of everyone that is hasty only to want.*

Diligence is not just in the sense of work but also being careful how you spend your earnings. Haste is poor spending habits and foolish investments. Circumspection is in view here. This is the opposite of "He who hesitates is lost." More often, "He who hesitates is sometimes saved." Impulse buying leads to financial ruin. "I want what I want, and I want it *now!*" Well, okay, but don't be surprised when that thing you so desperately wanted is now a liability, broke you, and prevents you from getting the things you really should have wanted in the first place. Boat owners have a saying: "I had two happy days: the day I bought it and the day I sold it." Might this warning against haste apply as well to your love life? Certainly it does, but that would be a very long discussion for another time about lives screwed up from picking the wrong partner. Haste is always dangerous. It's sometimes necessary, but still dangerous.

2. **Lazy**

   Proverbs 20:13 *Love not sleep, lest thou come to poverty; open thine eyes and thou shalt be satisfied with bread.*

   Here's a definition of laziness: resting before you're tired. Some people just want to rest all the time. Want to have something? Then do something!

   Proverbs 6:6 *Go to the ant thou sluggard; consider her ways and be wise.* ***:9*** *How long wilt thou sleep, O sluggard? When wilt thou arise out of thy sleep?* ***:10*** *Yet a little sleep, a little sleep, a little folding of the hands to sleep.* ***:11*** *So shall thy poverty come as one that travelleth, and thy want as an armed man.*

3. **Indulgent**

   Proverbs 23:21 *For the drunkard and the glutton shall come to poverty…*

   Nothing makes a man more broke surely than overconsumption. People who can't control their lust for stuff are doomed to poverty. And credit cards tempt us to spend all we have *and more!* The first question should be: Do you really need all that stuff? If you restrict yourself to "needs" and eliminate the "wants" you'll do much better. Someone once said: "It is difficult to save money when your neighbors keep buying things you can't afford."

   Proverbs 18:9 *He also that is slothful in his work is brother to him that is a great waster.*

   Haggai 1:6 *Ye have sown much, and bring in little…put it into a bag with holes.*

4. **Stubborn**

   Proverbs 13:8 *…the poor heareth not rebuke.*

   After all the good advice that the Bible or any thoughtful friend might have to give, there are people who just will not listen.

Some people seem bound and determined to go broke, as though they want to be paupers. Hopefully, you aren't one of them. With common sense and some real ambition, you should do quite well. And that's really what God wants for you.

5. **Borrow**

Proverbs 22:7 *The borrower is servant to the lender.*

Lives are ruined by debt. Lifetime's of income are squandered by paying compound interest. If you buy a house for $300,000 you will discover at the end of 30 years that you have spent over a million dollars to pay off that loan. That mortgage debt then really did gut your lifetime of income and lifetime of work, and that's not fair. Okay, so you have a house. But it should have cost you only a third as much. You really would be better off, *much* better off, to get rid of that debt and all debts as quickly as possible so that the money you earn benefits you and your family rather than the bank.

Romans 13:8 *Owe no man anything.*

Proverbs 17:18 *A man void of understanding striketh hands and becometh surety*

Deuteronomy 15:6 *thou* [Israel] *shalt lend unto many nations but thou shalt not borrow…*

1 Corinthians 7:23 *Ye are bought with a price; be not ye the servants of men.*

[3] Who Owns the World's Wealth?

Ezekiel 16:17 *Thou hast also taken thy fair jewels of my gold and of my silver, which I had given thee, and madest to thyself images of men, and didst commit whoredom with them.*

Haggai 2:8 *The silver is mine, and the gold is mine, saith the* LORD *of hosts.*

[4] Priority

Luke 16:13 *No servant can serve two masters…Ye cannot serve God and mammon.*

This is a challenging verse, not because it is difficult to understand (it's clear enough), but because there are so many contrary examples: rich Abraham, rich Melchizedek, rich Joseph, rich Job, rich David, rich Solomon, rich Matthew, rich Zacchaeus, rich kings, rich popes, rich Christians of every bent dotting the pages of history. History is littered with Jewish and Christian wealth, and God doesn't seem anxious to punish his true believers who just happen to figure out how to get rich too. And further, because they are rich, they can better help others in need with help that actually matters, so they get to double down and buy heaven as well, which poor people cannot afford to do. Moneyed Christians seems a double unfairness that they really do get to have it both ways and in spades.

Given this reality of life, that there are many rich Christians, it's hard to understand Jesus saying "Ye cannot serve God and mammon" when there seems to be so many rich believers who do just that so very well, serve God *and* mammon.

We might argue that rich Christians don't serve mammon, that they are just blessed by God. But that argument is impossible to believe. You don't get rich without being aggressive and smart and attentive and taking full advantage of situations. Christians get rich like anyone else, by being good at taking care of business. In short, by "serving mammon" and serving him well.

So, in light of real world realities, how are we to take "Ye cannot serve God and mammon"? Certainly, Jesus means priority.

Jesus was not rich — (indeed he complained of it, ***Luke 9:58*** *...Foxes have holes, and birds of the air have nests; but the Son of man hath not where to lay his head.*) — but he hung around with rich people who were generous with him. So, it wasn't their wealth that Jesus was grousing about. It was something else.

Jesus could have been rich had he chosen to be. Can you imagine the monetary value of being able to cure any disease with a touch? — to walk into a hospital and empty all its wards by touching every patient? What could you sell that skill for?

That did not escape the attention of Simon the Sorcerer *(**Acts 8:19-20**)* or of Judas *(**John 12:4-6**)*. And it had even crossed Jesus' mind. That was the very thought that Satan suggested to him *(**Matthew 4:3-4**)*. It was a simple idea really, and very natural: Jesus, you have all this power. Use it to serve yourself. And Jesus said, no. I have something much better to do with it, like save the whole human race.

Now, when *that* man, who had that kind of power yet that kind of generosity says, "Ye cannot serve God and mammon," he knows what he is talking about, and we ought to pay attention.

Jesus had a priority, and that priority interfered with him serving himself; he just had so much to do that really mattered.

We have priorities as well. Jesus allows us to have priorities, to deal with more than one thing, and to arrange the multiple things in our lives in order of importance:

> ***Matthew 6:31*** *Therefore take no thought, saying, What shall we eat? Or, What shall we drink? Or, Wherewithal shall we be clothed?* ***:32*** *(For after all these things do the Gentiles seek:) for your Heavenly Father knoweth that ye have need of all these things.* ***:33*** *But seek ye first the*

kingdom of God, and his righteousness, and all these things shall be added unto you.

This puts it all together for us. Let's examine what he said.

First: "Take no thought" doesn't mean don't think about what you're doing, it means don't worry about it. Get on with life, get on with business, just don't be fretting about it.

Second: Of course, you need food and clothing and housing and a job and income and all the rest. And *God knows that!* God is not depriving you of the necessary things of life, and it is no sin to pursue those things.

Third: But there are some things that are even more important, like eternal life. And therefore, you should not sacrifice the more important for the less important. If you can have both, that's best. But if you must choose one over the other, then for heaven's sake, do not sacrifice that which can benefit you forever. Priority matters.

Fourth: God wants you to have both, everything. He wants to deprive you of nothing. But be aware of first things first. And when trade-offs are unavoidable, when it really is either/or, then make the right choices.

John 10:10 *...I am come that they might have life, and that they might have it more abundantly.*

God is not a cosmic killjoy. He is not trying to step on our fun. He is trying to maximize our joy. The problem is, when you grab one thing, you have to release something else. Here's the truth: You can have anything you want, but you can't have everything you want. You can have all the food you want, or you can be thin. Choose. You can buy a boat, or you can invest the money. Choose. You can have sex with many partners or you can be truly in love with one person. Choose. You can be a person with real integrity, or you can steal. Choose.

Now, if your highest priority is God, then that restricts many of your choices. You can be moving up the corporate ladder. You can be invested in stocks or real estate or whatever. But there will be certain things you must not do. What are they? You will know when you face them.

Here is the most important priorities verse in the Bible:

> ***Matthew 16:26*** *For what is a man profited, if he shall gain the whole world, and lose his own soul? Or what shall a man give in exchange for his soul?*

There is this saying, from whom, I don't know: "He is no fool who trades that which he cannot keep for that which he cannot lose." That's how to arrange priorities.

But here is the problem: Many Christians on the road to wealth fail to recognize a compromise when they see it. Some glaring examples are needed —

Not too many centuries ago, there were Christians who saw no conflict between their Christianity and owning slaves. No matter that slaves died on slave ships, somehow these "Christians" managed to keep their conscience free of guilt.

Not too many centuries before that, Christians saw no conflict between their Christianity and burning other Christians at the stake. Indeed, they saw it as their Christian duty. And somehow they too managed to keep their conscience free of guilt.

Today many Christians are still pro-choice, thinking it's okay to slice up living babies who die in agony. And they still manage to keep their conscience free of guilt.

My point: It's easy to compromise and not even know it. So, while you are on your road to wealth, and you're sure that God is your highest priority, I'm just saying you had better be *sure*, I mean *really* sure, that you are not compromising that highest priority somewhere along the way. Just keep Jesus' warning ringing in your ears: "Ye cannot serve God and mammon."

Well, maybe you can. Or maybe you can't. Are you sure?

[5] Money Is Good

Proverbs 22:4 *By humility and the fear of the LORD are riches…*

Isaiah 48:17 *…I am the LORD thy God which teacheth thee to profit…*

Deuteronomy 8:18 *But thou shalt remember the LORD thy God: for it is he that giveth thee the power to get wealth.*

1 Timothy 6:17 *…the living God who gives us all things richly to enjoy.*

If money is so bad, then why does God bless us with so much of it? God does not want us to be poor, he wants us to enjoy the best of his blessings, the riches of the earth. That's why he created the earth, to bless us. So, allow yourself to be blessed.

[6] Money Is Bad

But be cautious. Every good thing can be used in a wrong way. Just as water is a good thing, but it can drown you. And food is good, but it can make you fat. Money too is good, but it can destroy you, if you let it.

Proverbs 23:4 *Labour not to be rich…*

Trying hard to be rich can distract us from everything else that's important.

> ***Ezekiel 28:5*** *By thy great wisdom and by thy traffick* [commerce] *hast thou* [Tyre] *increased thy riches, and thine heart is lifted up because of thy riches*

Tyre's shipping trade made it a wealthy city. But when the Greeks came, all of Tyre's money didn't save it. Its walls were breached, and its citizens were killed or sold into slavery. Money has many benefits, but not every benefit. Even the rich drown, or die of cancer, or get their heads chopped off, sometimes *because* they are rich. Had Tyre been less rich, they might have handled the Greeks differently.

> ***1 Timothy 6:9*** *But they that will be rich fall into temptation and a snare, and into many foolish and hurtful lusts, which drown men in destruction and perdition.* ***:10*** *For the love of money is the root of all evil: which while some coveted after, they have erred from the faith, and pierced themselves through with many sorrows.*

For money, Delilah betrayed Sampson. For money, Balaam cursed Israel or tried to. For money, Judas sold Jesus. For money, Satan tried to buy Jesus but Jesus, fortunately for us, was not interested in the offer.

Money corrupts. It's said that every man has his price. Is that true? I hope not. It was not true of Jesus. The only way we'll know if that is true of us is if Satan ever makes an offer high enough to buy us. Then we'll know.

[7] What Money Can Buy

To keep a perspective about money, money can buy certain things, and spiritually-minded Christians ought not to discount the power of money.

> ***Proverbs 19:4*** *<u>Wealth maketh many friends</u>; but the poor is separated from his neighbour.* ***:7*** *All the brethren of the poor do hate him: how much more do his friends go far from him? He pursueth them with words, yet they are wanting to him.*

It's a sad reality of life if you're rich, everyone wants to be your friend, but when you're poor, you're shunned, even by your relations.

> ***Ecclesiastes 7:12*** *…money is a defence…*

Money certainly is a defense. Ask O.J. Simpson. Even a duel-murderer can escape justice by buying the best attorneys. It shouldn't be that way, but it is.

> ***Ecclesiastes 7:14*** *In the day of prosperity be joyful.*

Enjoy it while you can.

> ***Ecclesiastes 9:16*** *…the poor man's wisdom is despised.*

Nobody listens to poor people. What advice do they have that anybody wants to hear? But when a rich man talks, people listen. In other words, money buys influence.

> ***Ecclesiastes 10:19*** *…money answereth all things.*

A moment of truth. Money can buy a lot. If not quite anything, then pretty darned near anything. With money, Osama Bin Laden bought the deaths of 3,000 Americans followed by a decade of life and freedom when he should have been dead for his crime.

2 Thessalonians 3:10 *...if any would not work, neither should he eat.*

1 Timothy 5:8 *But if any provide not for his own...he...is worse than an infidel.*

Work produces money, money produces food, and food produces a good family life and essential joy. Money may be the root of evil, but it is also the root of a lot of good.

[8] What Money Can't Buy

Psalms 49:6 *They that trust in their wealth, and boast themselves in the multitude of their riches;* ***:7*** *None of them can by any means redeem his brother, nor give to God a ransom for me.*

If someone you love very much, your own brother in this case, is dying, all the money in the world isn't going to save him. The rich are just as powerless as the poor against cancer, or a car accident, or an assassin's bullet.

Proverbs 18:11 *The rich man's wealth is his strong city, and as an high wall in his own conceit.*

The word *conceit* implies that neither wealth nor a high wall do what they are expected to do. City walls are breached, and so is a rich man's wealth.

Jeremiah 48:7 *For because thou hast trusted in thy works and in thy treasures, thou shalt also be taken…*

When a city is captured, its rich are enslaved right along with its poor. The rich receive no special treatment.

Jeremiah 49:4 *Wherefore gloriest thou in the valleys, thy flowing valley, O backsliding daughter? That trusted in her treasures, saying, Who shall come unto me?*

Who shall come? It was the Babylonians who came and captured the city. And Jerusalem's money couldn't save it. Indeed, it was their money that drew the Babylonians.

Jeremiah 50:37 *A sword is upon their horses, and upon their chariots…a sword is upon her treasures; and they shall be robbed.*

Money won't protect you from robbery. The richer you are, the more the burglars want to get at you.

Ezekiel 7:19 *…their silver and their gold shall not be able to deliver them in the day of the wrath of the LORD: they shall not satisfy their souls, neither fill their bowels: because it is the stumblingblock of their iniquity.*

When God wants to take his vengeance on you, you won't be able to buy him off with a bribe, nor will you be able to eat your silver and gold. Your silver and gold were the root cause of your iniquity, but it won't help you in the end.

[9] Money is Temporary

In any case, money won't last. At best, it is temporary. It's a trite old saying but true: You can't take it with you, but that thought is all over Bible. When Howard Hughes died, someone asked, "I wonder how much he left." Someone else answered, "He left it all." Indeed, he did.

> ***Psalms 39:6*** *…he heapeth up riches, and knoweth not who shall gather them.*

> ***Psalms 49:16*** *Be not thou afraid when one is made rich, when the glory of his house is increased;* ***:17*** *For when he dieth he shall carry nothing away: his glory shall not descend* [into the grave] *with him.*

> ***Proverbs 27:24*** *For riches are not for ever: and doth the crown endure to every generation?*

Don't pay so much attention to celebrities and such. They'll die just like you. Death is the great equalizer. All their fame, wealth, advantage does not follow them into the grave.

> ***Proverbs 23:5*** *Wilt thou set thine eyes upon that which is not? For riches certainly make themselves wings; they fly away as an eagle toward heaven.*

> ***Ecclesiastes 5:14*** *But those riches perish by evil travail: and he begetteth a son, and there is nothing in his hand.* ***:15*** *As he came forth of his mother's womb, naked shall he return to go as he came, and shall take nothing of his labour, which he may carry away in his hand.*

Ecclesiastes 6:2 *A man to whom God hath given riches, wealth, and honour, so that he wanteth nothing for his soul of all that he desireth, yet God giveth him not power to eat thereof, but a stranger eateth it: this is vanity, and it is an evil disease.*

Jeremiah 51:13 *O thou that dwellest upon many waters, abundant in treasures, thine end is come, and the measure of thy covetousness.*

1 Timothy 6:7 *For we brought nothing into this world, and it is certain we can carry nothing out.*

[10] The Wicked Rich

Jeremiah 5:26 *For among my people are found wicked men: they lay wait, as he that setteth snares; they set a trap, they catch men.* ***:27*** *As a cage full of birds, so are their houses full of deceit: therefore they are become great, and waxen rich.*

Evil pays off. People who do evil things become rich. To deny that is to deny the obvious. Drug dealers, porn producers, lying businessmen, let's face it, they do well by doing bad.

Jeremiah 17:11 *As the partridge sitteth on eggs, and hatcheth them not; so he that getteth riches, and not by right, shall leave them in the midst of his days, and at his end shall be a fool.*

But no one takes it with them, do they? In a sense, the righteous man does take it with him because he spent his rightly earned wealth on right things which *are* his to keep.

Ezekiel 34:21 *Because ye have thrust with side and with shoulder, and pushed all the diseased with your horns, till ye have scattered them abroad*

Rich people have no care or concern for poor people. They'd just as soon be rid of them. No sympathy, no compassion.

Proverbs 3:31 *Envy thou not the oppressor…*

We just have to believe that evil people, however successful they are, will one day get their divine comeuppance. So don't envy them. They're in trouble with God.

[11] THE WICKED POOR

The politically correct thinking is that only rich people are wicked, that poor people can never be wicked because they are, after all, victims. Jesus' parable of Lazarus and the rich man is one of many texts that nudge us towards that idea.

But it is a wrong conclusion to believe that poor people are innocent simply because they are poor, and that rich people are guilty simply because they are rich.

In the parable of the talents, Jesus gives us quite the opposite view, and he does so, I believe, because far too many poor people have come to believe (because of political victimization) that because they are poor they are therefore not accountable.

Here then, for the balanced view, is the parable of the talents — the tail end of it anyway. I'll skip over the 5 and 2 talent servants and get right to the 1 talent servant.

Matthew 25:18 *But he that received one went and digged in the earth, and hid his lord's money.* ***:19*** *After a long time the lord of those servants cometh, and reckoneth with them.* ***:24*** *Then he which had received the one talent came and said, Lord, I knew thee that thou art a hard man, reaping where thou hast not sown, and gathering where thou hast not strawed.* ***:25*** *And I was afraid, and went and hid thy talent in the earth: lo, there thou* *hast that is thine.* ***:26*** *His lord answered and said unto him, Thou wicked and slothful servant, thou knewest that I reap where I sowed not, and gather where I have not strawed.* ***:27*** *Thou oughtest therefore to have put my money to the exchangers, and then at my coming I should have received mine own with usury.* ***:28*** *Take the talent from him, and give it unto him which hath ten talents.* ***:30*** *And cast ye the unprofitable servant into outer darkness: there shall be weeping and gnashing of teeth.*

I will paraphrase. The one talent servant returns the talent to the lord and offers an excuse: "I was afraid of you and afraid to lose your money, so I did the safest thing, I buried it, and here it is." He also, in a subtle way, accuses his lord of being too tough, too rigid, too mean so that he, the servant, was right to be afraid.

But the lord didn't buy into that. He got to the heart of the matter quickly: "So you think I'm too tough? Well, you're a liar and I'll prove it. If you were afraid of me as you say, then you would have deposited the money I gave you in the bank and would have at least made some interest for me. But you wouldn't even do that, wouldn't do the minimum. You're not afraid, you're just plain lazy and you deserve no trust at all. Buried it in the ground? Bah! Go to hell!"

This is a sad story. But sadder still is that many poor people have just that attitude, that somehow poverty justifies their indolence: "I'm poor, so why should I have to work?" In fact, the opposite is true. They should get off their butts and go to work, and maybe something good will happen. And if nothing good happens, at least they've accomplished something.

[12] Usury (Lending With Interest)

Is usury a good thing or a bad thing? It depends. The Bible has a lot to say about it, and you can pretty much make any case you want. But there is this interesting verse –

Jeremiah 15:10 *Woe is me, my mother, that thou hast borne me a man of strife and a man of contention to the whole earth! I have neither lent on usury, nor men have lent to me on usury; yet every one of them doth curse me.*

Jeremiah often feels sorry for himself, and who can blame him? This verse is one of those times, and here's the point he makes: Everyone is after me. But why? I don't loan money on interest or borrow, so why is everyone out to get me?

This makes the point that loaning on interest or borrowing makes enemies.

[13] Miscellaneous

And finally, a list of verses that just didn't seem to fit well in any of the other categories. Here then is a whirlwind tour of the Bible and money.

Exodus 20:15 *Thou shalt not steal.*

Don't take what doesn't belong to you. You must either earn what you have or accept it as a gift. That there is such a thing as stealing proves that there is such a thing as ownership. So, God dignifies the notion of private property by forbidding theft.

Proverbs 28:20 *A faithful man shall abound with blessings: but he that maketh haste to be rich shall not be innocent.* ***:22*** *He that hasteth to be rich hath an evil eye, and considereth not that poverty shall come upon him.*

As good as money is, there is a dark side to it. Because it is the measure of value, people discover they can cheat, they can increase their money without producing wealth or as it says here, "hasteneth to be rich", that is, take short cuts, basically, steal. The Bible condemns such as "not innocent" and points out that such greed, rather than leading to wealth, often leads to poverty. This is very practical advice; it's the greedy who blunder.

Proverbs 30:8 *...give me neither poverty nor riches...* ***:9*** *Lest I be full, and deny thee, and say, Who is the LORD? Or lest I be poor, and steal, and take the name of my God in vain.*

This verse extols the virtues of the productive middle-class. Being poor is a bad thing because it tempts one to steal and curse God. But being rich is a bad thing too because it tempts one to being smug and not be humble before God.

Ecclesiastes 3:6 *...a time to lose.*

No investor likes losing. But understand that it will happen. If you are unwilling to ever lose, then don't invest. Just keep your money in a CD and see if that does you any good.

There's an old war saying: "If you insist on winning every battle, you will lose the war." That is as true of investing as it is in warfare. Since you know that at times you must lose, you'd be wise to mitigate those loses and have a safe exit.

All successful investors lose sometimes. So will you. Don't let it scare you out of the game, or you really will lose.

Ecclesiastes 5:10 *He that loveth silver shall not be satisfied with silver; nor he that loveth abundance with increase: this is also vanity.*

Here is a paradox of money: it's never enough. Why do the rich continue to be so greedy that they always want more and more? Love of money can sap the joy out of life.

Ecclesiastes 5:11 *When goods increase, they are increased that eat them: and what good is there to the owners therefore, saving the beholding of them with their eyes?* ***:12*** *…the abundance of the rich will not suffer him to sleep.* ***:13*** *There is a sore evil which I have seen under the sun, namely, riches kept for the owners thereof to their hurt.*

Here is another paradox of money: When you have more money, you also have more responsibility, more debt, more dependants and employees, more bookkeeping, more taxes, and more and more stuff to constantly worry about and lose sleep over. "The more you own, the more you're owned," said my friend Roger Kasper.

Jeremiah 45:5 *And seekest thou great things for thyself? Seek them not: for, behold, I will bring evil upon all flesh, saith the* LORD*: but thy life will I give unto thee for a prey in all places whither thou goest.*

These words were spoken to Baruch, Jeremiah's lifelong friend and noble companion. Baruch is complaining about his own problems and God is saying to him, "What did you expect? With all the dying going on, I'm preserving you, isn't that enough? You want to be rich too?"

Proverbs 3:9 *Honour the* LORD *with thy substance* ***:10*** *So shall thy barns be filled with plenty.*

Generosity is a general principle. But this is saying more than be generous with people, it's saying be generous with God and he will be generous with you. But then, what does it mean to be generous with God? ***Matthew 25:40*** is a pretty good clue: *Verily I say unto you, Inasmuch as ye have done it unto one of the least of these my brethren, ye have done it unto me.*

> **Proverbs 14:4** *Where no oxen are, the crib is clean, but much increase is by the strength of the ox.*

Getting stuff done is messy. Don't complain about the dirt, the grease, the sweat, and particularly the ordinary people who are getting the real work done so society can continue.

> **Proverbs 30:8** *Give me neither poverty nor riches* ***:9*** *lest I be full and deny thee and say, Who is the LORD? Or be poor and steal and take the name of my God in vain.*

A final word: Poverty and wealth each have their own brand of temptation. Poor people and rich people each have their own difficulties dealing with God.

The Importance of Keeping an Oath

Deuteronomy 23:21-23, Hebrews 6:13-18

There is a big difference between saying you'll do something and promising on an oath to do it. Merely saying, "Okay, I'll go to the store and get some milk," offers no guarantees, only momentary intent and allows for any sort of distraction or inconvenience to derail that intent without loss of integrity. An intended trip to the store might have been waylaid and explained away by, "Sorry I couldn't make it to the store after all. My boss called me into a meeting." And that would be likely met with, "Don't worry about it, I'll go to the market after dinner."

But on the other hand, if there is a really good reason why that milk is needed *now* — the baby is hungry and crying — the mother might meet the father's offer with a doubting, "Are you sure?" And the father might meet that gentle request for a further commitment with, "I promise. I'll go now and come right home." That promise ratchets up the commitment to a reassuring, "This *will* get done, no matter what. Depend on it."

But there are situations where even a personal promise is not enough. Something even more binding is warranted, where a person is not merely inconvenienced by a missed trip to the store but might for instance be risking his life or someone else's to keep his word. Such situations might well call for an oath. For example, a new monarch might "swear to execute the duties of my office no matter what." Well and good. But what if that later means he has to execute his own son for treason, as Peter the Great of Russia had to do?

Taking an oath is serious business because it affirms that not only will you do a thing, but that you are staking your life, even your soul, on doing that thing. And worse, if you bring God into it — with words such as "I swear to God," which are often said by criminals in interrogation — then you are dragging God into your promise, essentially signing his name to your contract and thus making *him* the liar when you break your word. I imagine that God is not too pleased when his name is bantered about in such ways, securing other people's promises who have no intention of keeping them.

[1] Thomas Moore

In the play A *Man For All Seasons* by Richard Bolt, Sir Thomas Moore sits in prison on trial for his life. His crime? Treason, because he will not swear an oath agreeing to King Henry's divorce of his wife Catharine so that he can marry Anne Boleyn. Thomas would rather die than take an oath to affirm what is not true.

In the play, there are two dialogs that make the point. In the first, Thomas's wife Margaret visits him in prison and tries to persuade him to take the oath.

Thomas: You want me to swear to the act of succession?
Margaret: "God more regards the thoughts of the heart than the words of the mouth." Or so you've always told me.
Thomas: Yes.
Margaret: Then say the words of the oath and in your heart think otherwise.
Thomas: What is an oath but the words we say to God?
Margaret: That's very neat.

Thomas: Do you mean it isn't true?

Margaret: No, it's true.

Thomas: Then it's a poor argument to call it "neat," Meg. When a man takes an oath, Meg, he is holding his own self in his own hands. Like water. And if he opens his fingers then — he needn't hope to find himself again.

Anyone who believes that — that taking an oath is like holding your soul in your hands — would be terrified to ever take an oath. And Thomas was.

In the second dialog, Thomas finally did take an oath, not a lying oath, but a true oath, one for which he was willing to bet his soul. He was convicted on the perjured testimony of one man, Richard Rich. To rebut Richard's testimony, Thomas takes an oath.

Thomas: In good faith, Rich, I am sorrier for your perjury than my peril.

Norfolk: Do you deny this?

Thomas: Yes! My lords, if I were a man who heeded not the taking of an oath, you know well I need not to be here. Now I will take an oath! If what Master Rich has said is true, then I pray I may never see God in the face! Which I would not say were it otherwise for anything on earth.

Now *that* is an oath. The power of this oath is that it is impossible not to believe it. This man, Thomas Moore, who is terrified to take an oath, who would rather die than take a lying oath, and he proves it by putting his head on the chopping block, now he takes an oath offering up his soul as proof of its truth. You simply cannot not believe that oath.

But of course, they convicted him anyway because they were not interested in truth but only in getting a conviction.

To make one final point, why did Richard perjure himself?

Cormwell: Sir Richard, have you anything to add?
Richard: Nothing, Mr. Secretary.
Norfolk: Sir Thomas?
Thomas: To what purpose? I am a dead man. You have your desire of me…
Norfolk: Then the witness may withdraw.
Thomas: I have one question to ask the witness. That's a chain of office you are wearing. May I see it? The red dragon. What's this?
Cromwell: Sir Richard is appointed Attorney-General for Wales.
Thomas: For Wales? Why, Richard, it profits a man nothing to give his soul for the whole world… But for Wales!

"For Wales," indeed.

What would you trade your soul for? The world? For Wales? Maybe something less than Wales. Think on that the next time you are asked to take an oath. Are you willing to secure that promise with your soul?

Now to the Bible. What does the Bible have to say about taking oaths? Plenty. So, here we go.

[2] The Law

Deuteronomy 23:21 *When thou shalt vow a vow unto the* LORD *thy God, thou shalt not slack to pay it: for the* LORD *thy God will surely require it of thee; and it would be sin in thee.* ***:22*** *But if thou shalt forebear to vow, it shall be so sin in thee.* ***:23*** *That which is gone out of thy lips thou shalt keep and perform; even a freewill offering, according as thou hast vowed unto the* LORD *thy God, which thou hast promised with thy mouth.*

Here we have the basic law regarding oaths. Merely saying that you will do a thing allows for exceptions. But taking a vow, or what is also called a covenant ***(Ezekial 17:18)***, to do a thing and attaching God's name to it is binding. You *must* do what you took a vow to do. Why? Because your vow assures people that they can arrange their affairs with total confidence that you will follow through. In some situations, they might even trust their lives to your oath. That's why you made the vow, so that they *would* trust you. Therefore, you *must* perform, no matter what.

Here are some of the really important oaths or covenants in the Bible.

[3] JOSHUA AND THE GIBEONITES

> ***Joshua 9:15*** *Joshua made peace with them* [Gibeon, Hittites] *and made a league with them to let them live: and the princes of the congregation sware unto them.*

Joshua was tricked into taking a rash oath. The Gibeonites saw Israel coming and knew they (the Gibeonites) were soon to be on Israel's hit list and that they stood no chance against Israel's war machine. So, they came up with a plan. Their leaders came to Joshua wearing tattered clothes, looking as though they were concluding a long journey. They lied and said they had heard of Joshua's conquests in their far homeland and had come to congratulate him on his successes, and also to make an alliance.

Joshua liked that and made an alliance with them with an oath. He later discovered that these people were not from as far as they had claimed but were near, in fact so near that they were next on the hit-list.

Joshua had a problem. God had said, kill them. But Joshua had taken an oath not to. Which prevailed? The commandment or the oath? The oath did. The Gibeonites were not only not killed but were under Israel's protection. That's how important that oath was to Joshua.

You gotta hand it to the Gibeonites. They found a way out. This is much like Christians, isn't it? God has marked the whole world for damnation, but one group of people, Christians, have found an escape, the only escape: Jesus Christ, whose atonement binds God's judgment by an oath.

[4] SAUL AND THE GIBEONITES

2 Samuel 21:1 *Then there was a famine in the days of David three years, year after year; and David enquired of the LORD. And the LORD answered, It is for Saul, and for his bloody house, because he slew the Gibeonites.*

That oath that Joshua was tricked into making with the Gibeonites was binding not only on Joshua but also on God. God was so determined to honor Joshua's oath that when Saul broke it more than three hundred years later, God killed Saul's remaining descendants in retribution.

[5] JEPHTHAH AND HIS DAUGHTER

Judges 11:30 *And Jephthah vowed a vow unto the LORD, and said, If thou shalt without fail deliver the children of Ammon into mine hands* ***:31*** *Then it shall be, that whatsoever cometh forth of the doors of my house to meet me, when I return in peace from the children of Ammon, shall surely be the LORD's, and I will offer it up for a burnt offering.*

This rash vow cost Jephthah everything.

> ***Judges 11:34*** *And Jephthah came to Mizpeh unto his house, and, behold, his daughter came out to meet him with timbrels and with dances: and she was his only child; beside her he had neither son nor daughter.* ***:35*** *And it came to pass, when he saw her, that he rent his clothes, and said, Alas, my daughter! Thou hast brought me very low, and thou art one of them that trouble me: for I have opened my mouth unto the LORD, and I cannot go back.*

The question is — and everyone who has read this story has asked it — did Jephthah really sacrifice his daughter? Here's what it says.

> ***Judges 11:39*** *And it came to pass at the end of two months, that she returned unto her father, who did with her according to his vow which he had vowed…*

The text does not say he killed his daughter, it says he fulfilled his vow. So, did he kill her or not? There are a few things to note here.

First: What Jewish priest would ever agree to a human sacrifice when that's the very issue that separated Israel from its neighbors and God's very complaint against Israel that resulted in the Diaspora ***(Jeremiah 7:31*** *And they…burn their sons and their daughters…which I commanded them not)*, and the point of Abraham's sacrifice of Isaac which God prevented by accepting a substitute ram. If Israel sacrificed every child that was "the LORD's", that would be every firstborn as God slew the firstborn in Egypt.

Second: The Torah anticipates illegal sacrifices — (e.g. the taking of a human life for a sacrifice to God) — and provides for a legal escape from an illegal vow.

***Leviticus 27:2** …When a man shall make a singular vow, the persons shall be for the LORD by thy estimation. **:3** And thy estimation shall be of the male from twenty years old even unto sixty years old, even thy estimation shall be fifty shekels of silver, after the shekel of the sanctuary. **:4** And if it be a female, then thy estimation shall be thirty shekels. **:5** And if it be from five years old unto twenty years old… **:8** But if he be poorer than thy estimation, then he shall present himself before the priest, and the priest shall value him; according to his ability that vowed shall the priest value him.*

So, the Bible places a monetary value on a human life so his daughter gets a legal escape. But still the point is made, don't take rash oaths. (You can read more about this in Volume I: Old Testament.)

[6] SAUL AND JONATHAN

***1 Samuel 14:26** And when the people were come into the wood, behold, the honey dropped; but no man put his hand to his mouth: for the people feared the oath. **:43** Then Saul said to Jonathan, Tell me what thou hast done. And Jonathan told him, and said, I did but taste a little honey with the end of the rod that was in mine hand, and, lo, I must die. **:44** And Saul answered, God do so and more also: for thou shalt surely die, Jonathan. **:45** And the people said unto Saul, Shall Jonathan die, who hath wrought this great salvation in Israel? God forbid…So the people rescued Jonathan, that he died not.*

Saul's oath nearly cost Jonathan his life and would have except the people demanded that the king spare his son's life. Jonathan was a national hero, and should he die for such a trivial thing as eating honey not knowing about his father's rash oath?

But now the question is, did Saul then break his oath by not killing Jonathan? Maybe he did. But Saul had broken other oaths ***(2 Samuel 21:1)***, so he was not big on oath-keeping. Or maybe he used Jephthah's legal escape.

Should Saul have kept his oath and killed Jonathan on a triviality? The lesson is he shouldn't have made the oath!

[7] SOLOMON AND BATHSHEBA

> ***1 Kings 2:20*** *Then* [Bathsheba] *said, I desire one small petition of thee* [Solomon, her son the king]; *I pray thee, say me not nay. And the king said unto her, Ask on, my mother: for I will not say thee nay.*

By contrast, this hasty affirmation that Solomon will do whatever his mother asks is not an oath but common courtesy: "Of course, Mom, I'll do what you ask." As it happened, however, what she asked of him was extremely dangerous for the kingdom (though she naively didn't know that), and of course, he would not do it. Had he taken an oath, he would have been bound by it. But since he took no oath, he is free to use common sense. This is why Jesus says don't take oaths, just say yea or nay.

[8] SHIMEI

> ***1 Kings 2:43*** *Why then hast thou* [Shimei] *not kept the oath of the LORD, and the commandment that I* [Solomon] *have charged thee with?* ***:45*** *And king Solomon shall be blessed, and the throne of David shall be established before the LORD for ever* ***:46*** *So the king commanded Benaiah the son of Jehoiada; which went out, and fell upon him* [Shimei] *that he died. And the kingdom was established in the hand of Solomon.*

Shimei took an oath to Solomon to remain for the rest of his life at home in a self-imposed prison. He broke that oath by traveling to Gath to retrieve two runaway servants. He may have thought that he had good reason to break his oath, but one never has a good enough reason to break an oath. Now that the oath was broken, what was the king to do with him? Solomon had no choice — he had to execute him. Because if he did not, then Solomon's law would have meant nothing because an oath would have meant nothing. That's why Solomon specifically said, *the throne of David shall be established.* Solomon understood you can't just break an oath to the king and get away with it. If so, then what law would ever hold up? And so Shimei died. Oath-breaking was a capital crime.

[9] Elijah

1 Kings 18:15 *And Elijah said, As the LORD of hosts liveth, before whom I stand, I will surely shew myself unto him to day.*

Elijah tells Obadiah to tell Ahab to come meet Elijah. Obadiah is afraid that Elijah will disappear, again, and Ahab will kill Obadiah. So, Elijah takes this oath to assuage Obadiah's fear — he basically swears, "I'm not going anywhere. Tell the king I'm here. You know I will be because I've sworn it."

[10] Zedekiah

Ezekiel 17:16 *As I live, saith the Lord GOD, surely in the place where the king dwelleth that made him king, whose oath he despised, and whose covenant he brake, even with him in the midst of Babylon he shall die.* ***:18*** *Seeing he despised the oath by breaking the covenant, when, lo, he had given his hand, and hath done all these things, he shall not escape.*

Zedekiah broke his oath with the king of Babylon and paid a high price for it. Death would have been easy compared to what he suffered. He was forced to watch his sons killed, then his eyes were burned out so that the last thing he saw was the death of his family.

[11] Oaths in General

2 Chronicles 6:22 *If a man sin against his neighbour, and an oath be laid upon him to make him swear, and the oath come before thine altar in this house;* ***:23*** *Then hear thou from heaven, and do, and judge thy servants…*

This is why we take an oath in court, because to lie under oath draws not just the wrath of the court but also the wrath of God.

Psalms 15:4 *He that sweareth to his own hurt.*

In other words, keep your word even when (especially when) it harms you to do so. That's the point of an oath.

Ecclesiastes 5:4 *When thou vowest a vow unto God, defer not to pay it; for he hath no pleasure in fools; pay that which thou hast vowed.* ***:5*** *Better is it that thou shouldest not vow, than that thou shouldest vow and not pay.*

Breaking your word is bad, but breaking your vow/covenant is worse because, in a sense, you are breaking God's word because you basically signed God's name to your promise.

Ecclesiastes 9:2 *All things come alike to…he that sweareth, and he that feareth an oath.*

This is a stark contrast between those who take oaths easily and those who are afraid to take an oath, as was Thomas Moore: "If I were a man who heeded not the taking of an oath, you know well I need not to be here."

Zechariah 5:3 *…the curse…* ***:4*** *…shall enter into the house…of him that swareth falsely by my name…*

This points us to the 3rd commandment, ***Exodus 20:7*** *Thou shalt not take the name of the LORD thy God in vain.* We typically take this commandment to mean don't use any reference to God in an expletive. And that's not wrong. But the real point is, don't use God's name to make a false oath. That will bring a curse on you.

Zechariah 8:17 *…love no false oath.*

[12] JESUS ON OATH TAKING

Jesus gives of the best advice of all.

Matthew 5:34 *…Swear not at all…* ***:37*** *But let your communication be, Yea, yea; Nay, nay: for whatsoever is more than these cometh of evil.*

You're better off to just not take an oath at all, ever. Just say that you will or will not do a thing and let it go at that. If you have a reputation as an honest person who keeps his word, then your simple word, yes and no, is generally good enough. It's only people who habitually don't keep their word who find themselves having to make promises and take oaths to persuade people that *this* time they really mean it. If people often require you to promise, you should be asking yourself why. Probably because you're unreliable and people have come to expect that when you say you'll do a thing, you don't mean it.

[13] PETER

It appears that Peter took an oath, and broke it.

Matthew 26:74 *Then began he to curse and to sware, saying, I know not the man. And immediately, the cock crew.*

Peter denied Jesus three times. And the third time, since people were not believing his first two denials, he took an oath. What's really hurtful about this is that Jesus had just chided the scribes and pharisees about the recklessness of oath taking ***(Matthew 23:16-22)***, and now Peter was caught by a lie reinforced by an oath.

But Jesus, ever the forgiver, forgave Peter of even that, and from then on, Peter never doubted, never waivered, and when the time came, Peter went to his cross for Jesus and requested that he be crucified upside down because he wasn't worthy for his head to be equal to his Lord's. That's devotion. And it says a lot about how far Jesus' love can actually reach, even to the forgiving of a broken oath.

[14] GOD'S OATHS

But the most important oaths in the universe are those that God has made, for it is on those promises that we bet our eternity.

Isaiah 45:23 *I have sworn by myself, the word is gone out of my mouth in righteousness, and shall not return, That unto me every knee shall bow, every tongue shall swear.*

> ***Jeremiah 22:5*** *…I swear by myself, saith the* LORD*…*
> ***Jeremiah 44:26*** *…Behold, I have sworn by my great name…*
> ***Jeremiah 51:14*** *The* LORD *of hosts hath sworn by himself…*

> ***Ezekiel 16:59*** *For thus saith the Lord GOD; I will even deal with thee as thou hast done, which hast despised the oath in breaking the covenant.* ***:60*** *Nevertheless I will remember my covenant with thee in the days of thy youth, and I will establish unto thee an everlasting covenant.*

> ***Hebrews 6:13*** *For when God made promise to Abraham, because he could sware by no greater, he sware by himself,* ***:14*** *Saying, Surely blessing I will bless thee, and multiplying I will multiply thee.* ***:17*** *Wherein God, willing more abundantly to shew unto the heirs of promise the immutability of his counsel, confirmed it by an oath:* ***:18*** *That by two immutable things, in which it is impossible for God to lie, we might have a strong consolation, who have fled for refuge to lay hold upon the hope set before us.*

The reason we believe in and trust the salvation that God offers us is not merely because God offered it, and not merely because he promised it, but because he promised it with an oath so that he *cannot* break his promise. He swore by his own name. That is critically important, especially considering the number of times that God has changed his mind.

[15] Conclusion

We can't hide from oath-taking. Just showing up for jury duty often subjects us to taking some kind of an oath. What scares the willies out of me is that oath (which is fortunately not so common anymore) to "obey the rules of the court, so help me God!" It's the "so help me God" that scares me. What about law? What about facts of the case that the judge may order you to ignore? I am fearful that the "rules of the court" might require me to acquit a man I know is guilty or convict a man I know is innocent. That or break my oath. Now, I've never been cornered like that, and I don't know what I would do in that situation. But at the very least, I listen real carefully to what the court is asking of me while I have my hand raised.

Or better yet, whenever you're asked to make an oath just remember Jesus's advice:

Matthew 5:34 *...Swear not at all...*

Pessimism

Ecclesiastes

Give the devil his due. There really are two sides of just about everything. When you do what's right and smart, do you get what you deserve? Well, it depends on whether you are looking at it from the Proverbs point of view or the Ecclesiastes point of view. The difference between these two books is the difference between an optimist and a pessimist.

Question	Answer (Proverbs)	Answer (Ecclesiastes)
Is wisdom really such a good thing?	**Proverbs 1:5** *A wise man will hear and will increase learning.*	**Ecclesiastes 1:18** *In much wisdom is much grief and he that increaseth knowledge increaseth sorrow.*
Should I work hard?	**Proverbs 21:5** *The thoughts of the diligent tend only to plenteousness.*	**Ecclesiastes 2:22** *What hath man of all his labour?* **:23** *all his days are sorrow and grief.*
Should I plan and prepare?	**Proverbs 27:12** *A prudent man foreseeth the evil and hideth himself.*	**Ecclesiastes 9:11** *the race is not to the swift nor the battle to the strong but time and chance happeneth to them all.*

The basic message throughout Proverbs is if you live life right, everything will turn out right. But Ecclesiastes says it ain't necessarily so.

Which is true? The irony is, they both are true. That's why the Bible preaches both messages, giving equal time to the pessimist as the optimist.

Drive safely and you'll arrive safely. True, but not absolutely. What if you get whacked by a drunk driver? That can happen. But we try to drive safely anyway, in spite of the occasional drunk out there because we know that driving safely tilts the odds greatly in our favor. Work hard and you'll be successful. True, but not absolutely. There are many hard-working failures, and a few lottery winners who contribute nothing.

Eat right, exercise, don't smoke, and you'll live longer. True, but not absolutely. I've had right living friends who died prematurely, and then there was George Burns who smoked all his life and lived to a hundred, while his wife, Gracie Allen, who never smoked a day in her life, died of lung cancer. The scriptures are paradoxical because life is paradoxical.

The harder you work, the luckier you get. Time and chance do happen to all of us, but the "righter" you live, the better the odds that life will turn out right. That's the best we can do.

But there is one point on which the optimist and the pessimist can agree on completely:

How do I get back to God?	**Proverbs 19:16** *He that keepeth the commandment keepeth his own soul.*	**Ecclesiastes 12:13** *Fear God and keep his commandments for this is the whole duty of man.* **:14** *For God shall bring every work into judgment.*

So, whichever side you're inclined to be on at the moment, whether you think life is fair or futile, whether life's generosities have made you an optimist or life's cruelties have made you a pessimist, whether you are a happy person or a sad person, whether you are a Proverbs person or an Ecclesiastes person, remember this: There is room in heaven for both. God does not judge your disposition, he judges your obedience. In the long view, all that matters is whether or not you have given yourself to God, however he has blessed, or cursed, you in this life.

John 6:37 *He that cometh to me, I will in no wise cast out.*

Now that's an absolute you can bet on.

Pride

Proverbs

Here is a list of verses about pride, arrogance, bragging, and other forms of general snooty-ness.

Psalms 101:5 *Him that hath an high look and a proud heart will not I suffer.*

We can't stand arrogance, and neither can God. After all, what do you have to be arrogant about?

Proverbs 15:25 *The LORD will destroy the house of the proud…*

This can be literal. Pride destroys a man's ability to correctly assess his true peril thus bringing about his downfall.

Proverbs 16:5 *Every one that is proud in heart is an abomination to the LORD: though hand join in hand, he shall not be unpunished.*

"Hand join in hand" means although he tries to save himself with both hands; in other words, no matter what he does, God will punish him. And why should God punish him? Pride sets a man up for failure and disappointment two ways: First, pride blinds a man to the real dangers. And second, since no one likes a braggart, when bad things happen, no one is on his side, everyone is cheering his downfall.

Proverbs 16:18 *Pride goeth before destruction, and an haughty spirit before a fall.*

When a man is about to make a mistake, often it is pride that holds him to that destructive decision. He could consider alternatives, but his pride keeps him on course.

Proverbs 18:12 *Before destruction the heart of man is haughty, and before honour is humility.*

This makes perfect sense. A man who is sure of his course is often very wrong and is defeated. But a man who checks his course and checks again just to make doubly sure (because he knows he could be wrong) is far more likely to get it right. Like the old carpenter's saying: "Measure twice, cut once."

Proverbs 18:19 *A brother offended is harder to be won than a strong city: and their contentions are like the bars of a castle.*

In any argument, there are two wedges that drive people apart: First, the issue itself. But second, there is pride. The issue may have merits on both sides, and each wants to win because each has a valid point. But once pride takes over, all reasonableness is lost and each wants to win for ego's sake. And the issue, which originally made sense, is lost.

Proverbs 21:4 *An high look, and a proud heart, and the plowing of the wicked, is sin.*

"Plowing of the wicked" is more literally "lamp of the wicked"; in other words, everything looks good, a bright prosperity.

Proverbs 25:6 *Put not forth thyself in the presence of the king, and stand not in the place of great men.* ***:7*** *For better it is that it be said unto thee, Come up hither; than that thou shouldest be put lower in the presence of the prince whom thine eyes have seen.*

This speaks of humility versus arrogance. If you're doing good work, you don't have to promote yourself, your superior will promote you. If you promote yourself, brag, and your superior has to put you in your place, that's humiliating.

Proverbs 25:14 *Whoso boasteth himself of a false gift is like clouds and wind without rain.*

The subject here is bragging. It accomplishes nothing and is humiliating.

Proverbs 25:27 *It is not good to eat much honey: so for men to search their own glory is not glory.*

This is rich with meaning. You cannot get glory by seeking glory. If heroism is the objective then it is phony. Heroism is real when one acts heroically in a dangerous situation that one did not seek. It's like humility in that regard. Some virtues (perhaps all virtues) resist those who seek them because the seeking them almost always implies an ulterior motive, a reason *why* you want that virtue, which is different than having the virtue innately.

I am not speaking of hypocrisy, that's much too blunt. A hypocrite is a person who wants the *appearance* of a virtue. What I'm talking about is much more subtle than that, a *genuine* seeking of a virtue because you actually *want* the virtue. That is not hypocrisy by any means, but it still hints of double intent. A man says, "I want to be a kind person," and so he makes himself a kind person. That is laudable. But that motivated virtue is ever so slightly different than just being a kind person, not because he wishes to be kind, but because he is innately concerned for another person's well-being and has no expectation, or even awareness, of his own "virtue status." The virtue of kindness is not his objective. The other person's well-being is his objective. True virtue — well, that's not quite right, I'll rather say the "better" virtue. The better virtue is not inwardly directed to one's own desire for virtue but is outwardly directed to the needs of others.

Proverbs 26:12 *Seest thou a man wise in his own conceit? There is more hope of a fool than of him.*

This is very true. A genuine fool is not as foolish as a conceited person.

Proverbs 26:16 *The sluggard is wiser in his own conceit than seven men that can render a reason.*

The lazy man is not only lazy, but he is smug, so smug that he thinks he is smarter than everyone else, he has it all figured out, or so he thinks.

Proverbs 27:2 *Let another man praise thee, and not thine own mouth; a stranger, and not thine own lips.*

Nothing makes a man more ridiculous than touting his own greatness. A truly great man needs to say nothing of it — his greatness will be obvious to everyone.

Proverbs 27:21 *As the fining pot for silver, and the furnace for gold; so is a man to his praise.*

We talk about pride as though it's always a bad thing. It's not always. Sometimes what a person needs is a compliment, a little stroking of the ego to get him or her going again. Just a sense of achievement can be the difference between success and failure in life. Is that a bad thing? Of course not.

Proverbs 28:25 *He that is of a proud heart stirreth up strife: but he that putteth his trust in the* LORD *shall be made fat.*

The worst problem with pride is that it won't let go. A person engaged in a dispute might handle the tension okay and come away with no hurt feelings. But once pride takes over, that person must win at all cost, and that's where the damage is done.

Trusting the *LORD* basically is a silent "whatever" — to surrender an argument even though you are sure you are right. In other words, "You may be right. Let's just agree to disagree and move on" avoids arguments and saves friendships.

Proverbs 29:23 *A man's pride shall bring him low: but honour shall uphold the humble in spirit.*

Pride and honor are two different things. Honor is how you behave. Pride is what you say about how you behave. In other words, how you claim to behave. Honor is a virtue. Pride is a claim to virtue.

Ezekiel 16:23 *And it came to pass after all thy wickedness, (woe, woe unto thee! saith the* LORD GOD;) **:24** *That thou hast also built unto thee an eminent place, and hast made thee an high place in every street.* **:25** *Thou hast built thy high place at every head of the way…and multiplied thy whoredoms.*

Your whoredoms have given you celebrity status and you love it, so you increase your whoredoms. We have pride in many different things, but some people have pride in the evil they do, and ironically, their pride is encouraged by people who praise them for it. And so it becomes a vicious cycle: sin causes pride, and pride encourages more sin.

> **Daniel 4:30** *The king spake, and said, Is not this great Babylon, that I have built for the house of the kingdom by the might of my power, and for the honour of my majesty?* **:31** *While the word was in the king's mouth, there fell a voice from heaven, saying, O king Nebuchadnezzar, to thee it is spoken; The kingdom is departed from thee.*

Even the great Nebuchadnezzar lost his kingdom, apparently because he went insane for awhile. However great you are, whatever great things you have or have done, it's all temporary, and very fragile.

> **Daniel 5:20** *But when his heart was lifted up, and his mind hardened in pride, he was deposed from his kingly throne, and they took his glory from him.* **:22** *And thou his son, O Belshazzar, hast not humbled thine heart, though thou knewest all this;*

Belshazzar learned the same lesson as Nebuchadnezzar. Belshazzar lost his kingdom in a single night when the Persians breached the wall for an easy victory.

Sign-Seeking

Matthew 12:38-40, Isaiah 7:10

A lot is said in churches about sign-seeking. Don't seek for signs, we're told. If your faith requires signs, then your faith must be weak. And indeed, Jesus did say—

> ***Matthew 12:38*** *Then certain of the scribes and of the Pharisees answered, saying, Master, we would see a sign from thee.* ***:39*** *But he* [Jesus] *answered and said unto them, An evil and adulterous generation seeketh after a sign …*

But that invites this question: Should we reject signs and hope to never see a true miracle because, after all, we don't really need them? Many people read it that way: "I don't need signs because Jesus said it's wicked to seek them." Is that what He meant?

But if He did mean that, then what are we to do with this verse in Isaiah? God spoke to King Ahaz through the prophet Isaiah and demanded that Ahaz ask for a sign so that God could prove himself.

> ***Isaiah 7:10*** *Moreover the* LORD *spake again unto Ahaz, saying,* ***:11*** *Ask thee a sign of the* LORD *thy God; ask it either in the depth, or in the height above.* ***:12*** *But Ahaz said, I will not ask, neither will I tempt the* LORD. ***:13*** *And he* [Isaiah] *said, Hear ye now, O house of David; Is it a small thing for you to weary men, but will ye weary my God also?*

Jesus said it's wicked to seek for a sign. But Isaiah said it's a sin not to. What's the difference? Here's the difference:

The Pharisees who were speaking to Jesus demanded a sign *rhetorically*; that is, they were saying, "Show us a sign! Bet-cha can't."

Their request came not from belief but from disbelief. Kink Ahaz, on the other hand, believed. In fact, he believed so much that he didn't want to offend God by asking for a sign, so he declined God's offer, and, ironically, *that* made God mad.

That is exactly the opposite of what many Christians believe Jesus meant. But it wasn't their wanting a sign that annoyed Jesus; what annoyed Him was that He had shown them many signs, and they were never satisfied. That's what their wickedness was.

But there's an even better answer to those who are content not to have signs from God, and that is this: Jesus, after chiding the scribes and Pharisees a bit, *did* give them exactly what they asked for—He gave them a sign. And not just any sign, but *the* sign that proved He was exactly who He said he was.

> ***Matthew 12:39*** *… and there shall no sign be given to it, but the sign of the prophet Jonas.* ***:40*** *For as Jonas was three days and three nights in the whale's belly; so shall the Son of Man be three days and three nights in the heart of the earth.*

Jesus really reached out to them. He was basically saying, "Alright, you're not impressed that I changed water to wine, that I stilled the storm, that I gave sight to the blind and healed lepers, that I raised the dead—you've seen all that, and you still won't believe me. Okay, how about this? I will die. And I will lie dead in the earth for three days. And then I will rise from the dead by my own divine power. How's that for a sign? Will you believe me then?"

Those Christians who claim to be content without signs will say, "Well, yes, He did the miracles and rose from the dead, but no one believed him. So our faith should not be based on signs." To which I reply, nonsense! People *did* believe his signs, especially his resurrection. That is what the Christian message is all about and how the Christian religion was born, from those people who witnessed His miracles and His resurrection firsthand—and believed. So don't say the miracles don't convert; that's unbiblical and it's ludicrous.

I'll say it another way: If our faith is not based on the miracles (signs) that Jesus did, in particular, his resurrection, then what exactly *is* our faith based on? His preaching? His radical claims to be the son of God? For heaven's sake, no. Anyone can say anything, and Jesus knew that. That's why Jesus said—

> ***John 14:11*** *Believe me that I am in the Father, and the Father in me; or else believe me for the very works' sake.*

This is what He was saying to His disciples: I'm not asking you to believe my claims without proof. So, here's the proof: my miracles. And the biggest one of all will be my resurrection. When that happens, believe *that!*

Still, many Christians say, "But it's the Holy Spirit that makes us believe, not the miracles." Well, okay. But to believe *what* exactly? Does the Spirit convince us that Jesus is the Son of God because He said so? No. The Spirit causes us to believe that He did what the Bible claims He did, that is, the miracles and the resurrection, and therefore what Jesus said is true, and therefore He is the Son of God. If you leave signs and miracles out of that progression—"my faith doesn't need miracles"—then it all falls apart.

Faith, real faith, needs miracles, needs signs, needs proof. If your faith can do without miracles, then you don't need Jesus; you can just as well pray to a rock or some other false god. That's blind faith. True faith requires something rational.

That is exactly the point that Elijah made to the Baal worshipers when his altar was consumed by fire from heaven (***1 Kings 18:38***).

The priests of Baal chanted and prayed to their idol all day and couldn't even conjure up a spark, which was the point. The true God does miracles, false gods do not. Still, some Christians will grumble, "But no one believed." Oh? The crowd of witnesses believed, enough to turn on the false priests and kill them (***1 Kings 18:40***). "But they didn't continue believing." Oh? When Elijah thought he was the one true believer remaining, God told him not so; there are 7000 more (***1 Kings 19:18***).

Here's the point of all this: Without the miracles, there is nothing to believe *in.* Christianity needed miracles, and it needed people to believe them and tell the world. And that's just what happened. Consider Thomas:

> ***John 20:25*** ... *Except I see in his hands the print of the nails, and put my finger into the print of the nails, and thrust my hand into his side, I will not believe.*

If ever there was a sign seeker, it was Thomas. How did Jesus react to that demand? Did Jesus say, "Thomas, I'm going to cut you off because you won't believe without a sign"? No, that is not what Jesus said. What Jesus said was—

> ***John 20:27*** ...*Thomas, Reach hither thy finger, and behold my hands; and reach hither thy hand, and thrust it into my side: and be not faithless, but believing.* ***:28*** *And Thomas answered and said unto him, My LORD and my God.*

Thomas became a confirmed believer *because he saw and touched.* He would not have believed otherwise. But because he personally witnessed, he was faithful to the end of his life, which ended violently. And to what do we owe his unshakable devotion? To the fact that Jesus did miracles, especially the resurrection, and Thomas was a witness.

And the rest of us? We believe the witness's accounts that the miracles actually happened and conclude that Jesus was who He said He was. So it is still the miracles that convert us today.

It really annoys me when Christians undercut the importance of miracles by saying stupid things like, "I don't need miracles, because if I needed miracles, that would make me a sign seeker." What that is really saying is, "I don't want my faith to rely on miracles because, the truth is, I don't have enough faith to believe that God might actually do some. If I expect a miracle and don't get one (and I won't), that will hurt my faith, and I don't want that." That's the real truth behind the "I don't need miracles" attitude.

Here's the deal: If God gives you a sign, believe it. If God invites you to seek a sign, seek it. If God demands that you believe with only the signs already given, believe. Get as close to God as you can by whatever he makes available. What could be simpler?

And the sign seekers? They will always make their rhetorical demands.

> ***Jeremiah 17:15*** *Behold, they say unto me, Where is the word of the* LORD*? Let it come now.*

This is just their kind of thinking—a rhetorical demand from unbelief. They expect nothing will come of it, and that is why they make their demand, to demonstrate that nothing will happen. That's what a sign-seeker is, a confirmed non-believer demanding what he is sure can't happen.

But that does not describe true followers of Christ who seek a sign, and when it comes, they really believe and really commit. Would we accuse Paul of being a sign-seeker because it took a vision to convert him? Would we accuse Thomas or any of the prophets of sign-seeking because they saw and believed? Of course not. Wanting God to act is not sign-seeking. Wanting God to *not* act and demanding that He does, that is sign-seeking.

Yes, lots of folks see miracles and will not believe. But that's a far cry from "miracles don't convert." Miracles *do* convert *some* people, just not others.

So don't say that miracles don't convert. That's nonsense. God is a god of miracles, which is why we believe in Him. True believers believe *because* of the miracles. Of course, miracles convert; they converted you.

What is a true religious conversion? It is this: [1] You look at a miracle, whether a present one or a 2000-year-old one. It does not matter. [2] You realize that the miracle is undeniable. [3] You realize that the miracle is proof of a divine power that caused the miracle. And [4] you commit yourself to the will of that divine power. That's conversion.

Slavery

Jeremiah 34:8-24, Philemon

Slavery in ancient Israel was a very different thing than what we normally think of as slavery, as for instance, in the Roman empire where a slave owner could do whatever he wanted with his slaves, including crucify them on a whim.

Slavery in Israel was not that, not absolute ownership over another person. There were rules, and slavery was part of a legal system, the Torah, which outlined in detail certain punishments for certain crimes. Capital crimes, for instance, required capital punishment (execution) — simple enough. For crimes of personal injury, retribution was brutal ("an eye for an eye") but effective, and certainly more fair than other legal systems which required, for instance, a hand for a loaf of bread. Crimes which involved monetary damage, like theft, required monetary compensation.

But what about crimes that were none of those? Like for instance, you accidently killed your neighbor's cow, and you didn't have the money to pay for it because you were dirt poor? Or you borrowed money for an investment that went bad, and you couldn't repay the loan? How would the law deal with that?

England had its debtor's prisons, which they somehow thought was fair. But ancient Israel had no prisons other then the self-imposed cities of refuge. So how could a debtor pay off a debt? Temporary slavery was the answer, and it made sense.

Roman slavery, and also slavery in general, was not only unfair because one person had absolute right over another, but it was also unfair because it was life-long, there was no relief. In fact, it was longer than life-long because the child of a slave was also a slave, so the misery was passed on from generation to generation.

Hebrew slavery was not that. It was more like indentured servitude for the debtor to pay off his debt as best he could, then freedom, unless he chose to remain a slave.

We do similar things today. Are convicted prisoners slaves? We don't call it slavery (because the word is so unsavory), but we think it not unreasonable for prisoners, convicted felons, to be pressed into chain gangs to build railroads and other civil projects. Or make license plates. Or any other such productive work that makes their time in prison at least useful. And why not? They're in prison to "pay their debt to society," so why shouldn't they work and be productive rather than lay in their cells watching TV? Besides, most prisoners, I think, would rather be doing something than nothing.

Is that slavery? By any meaningful definition it is. But we don't call it that today.

And then there was indentured servitude in Colonial America, which was very much like biblical slavery. But again, we wouldn't call it slavery. It was a debt bondage by agreement. If someone wanted to immigrate from Europe to America and had no money for passage, then that person could sell himself, for some specified number of years, to a plantation owner to pay off his passage.

Is that slavery? Some would say yes. Others would say that demanding payment for a contracted debt is fair enough and is not slavery.

How about a contract that you can never get out of? Frank Sinatra, when he was young and not yet famous, signed such a life-long contract with Tommy Dorsey. Then when Frank got famous, he wanted out of that contract, but he couldn't get out of it. How did he get out of it? His good friend Lucky Luciano walked into Tommy's dressing room one day, put a pistol barrel in Tommy's mouth and said, "I'm buying Franky's contract from you for one dollar." Tommy sold it, and Lucky gave it to Frank. It was a friendship thing.

Contracts like that do amount to slavery, do they not? So, gangsters are good for some things; in Frank Sinatra's case, a little abolitionist violence was helpful.

What about American soldiers? A soldier enlists for four years, and during those four years if he's off base without proper leave he is AWOL and can go to the brig or face court marshal. And if he leaves during wartime, that's desertion and he can be shot! Well, in theory anyway. American deserters were not shot during World War II. But British, German, and Russian soldiers *were* shot for desertion. Stalin said, "It takes a brave man to be a coward in the Red Army." Indeed.

But you get the idea. A soldier is *not* free to leave as he chooses, and that makes him, if not actually, then at least something like a slave.

My point is that in modern America we have institutions that are like slavery but are not slavery. And why are they not? Because we very carefully define them not to be.

Slavery was outlawed in America by the 13th Amendment of our Constitution. Here are the words: "Neither slavery nor involuntary servitude, except as a punishment for crime whereof the party shall have been duly convicted, shall exist within the United States, or any place subject to their jurisdiction."

So, imprisoned criminals are not slaves. Why? Because the Constitution says so. Also, indentured servants are not slaves. Why? Because they indentured themselves voluntarily. Only *in*voluntary servitude is slavery. Why? Because the Constitution says so. So, a young and foolish person could, in theory, volunteer for a life-time of servitude without realizing the long term implications — as Frank Sinatra did. The Constitution allows it. Is that illegal today? I don't know; for that you'd have to talk to an attorney.

But my point is that any discussion about biblical slavery and its fairness or unfairness has to first deal with what exactly do we mean by slavery. Our Constitution insists that prisoners and voluntarily indentured servants are legally not slaves, although in fact they are.

Well, if those folks are not slaves, legally I mean, then what are we to make of the "slaves" of Hebrew law?

Here's what I'm saying, or at least what I think I'm saying. What Hebrew law calls slaves is not at all like what Romans (or other ancient peoples or American plantation owners) called slaves. What the Torah calls slaves is much more like what we call prisoners or what we call indentured servants. And with that clarification, biblical slavery is not the evil that we fought the Civil War to end.

With that very long introduction, let's get to it and find out what "slavery" in the Old Testament was all about. Here are the biblical rules of slavery.

[1] Duration

> ***Deuteronomy 15:12*** *And if thy brother, an Hebrew man, or an Hebrew woman, be sold unto thee, and serve thee six years; then in the seventh year thou shalt let him go free from thee.*

The maximum sentence for a man or a woman in slavery was six years, tops. That's it. The seventh years was the Jubilee year and all slaves (well, Israelite slaves, foreigners didn't get the same respect) were freed. It didn't matter the size of the debt.

[2] Kidnapping

One thing was absolutely forbidden: man stealing. Kidnapping someone to make him (or her we presume and infer from ***Jeremiah 34:9***) a slave was a capital crime.

Deuteronomy 24:7 *If a man be found stealing any of his brethren of the children of Israel, and maketh merchandise of him, or selleth him; then that thief shall die; and thou shalt put evil away from among you.*

You can't just kidnap someone and make him (or her) your slave. That is a capital crime. We have this very problem rampant in America today. We call it trafficking. In the Bible it's a capital crime and should be. Especially when children are the victims.

[3] ESCAPE

A slave has a legal right to try to escape, and you have a legal obligation to help him.

Deuteronomy 23:15 *Thou shalt not deliver unto his master the servant which is escaped from his master unto thee.*

Wow! So, the Underground Railroad was legal in Israel. This gives us permission and a commandment to be abolitionists. It appears that the Apostle Paul was in violation of this verse when he wrote Philemon, except that they lived under Roman law and not under Jewish law, and an escaped slave could easily end up on a cross, which is what happened to Spartacus and his 50,000 slave rebels. So Paul, I believe, was not defending slavery, he was probably protecting the life of this escaped slave who had come to him.

[4] JUST THE WAY THINGS WERE

2 Kings 5:2 *And the Syrians had gone out by companies, and had brought away captive out of the land of Israel a little maid; and she waited on Naaman's wife.* ***:3*** *And she said unto her mistress, Would God my* *lord were with the prophet that is in Samaria! for he would recover him* [Naaman] *of his leprosy.*

Unfortunately, 3000 years ago slavery was so taken for granted that the Bible doesn't even bat an eye at the injustice done to this girl. This young Jewish girl had been kidnapped into slavery — foreign, not Jewish — and had no hope of deliverance. She even seemed resigned to it and devoted herself to her masters. The rest of the story is important, but it was just the captive slavery that I wanted to show you.

Another dark aspect of slavery, beyond the forced servitude, is the cheapness of life, the complete lack of respect for another person's life.

Amos 8:6 *That we may buy the poor for silver, and the needy for a pair of shoes…*

Not only are people bought and sold, but they are bought and sold cheaply, and that's the final insult.

Albert Schweitzer, that noble doctor who devoted his life to serving the poor and the sick in Africa, talked about "reverence for life." Slavery is the exact opposite of that. Slavery has no reverence for life.

Not even Christianity changed this view of things. Even after Rome became Christianized, there was still slavery. The Spanish and the Portuguese took captured Indians as slaves, and even Christopher Columbus took slaves from the West Indies.

I'm only pointing out that slavery was so pernicious, and seems to always have been, that it just didn't occur to anyone, not even Bible authors, that it ought to end.

It took the Industrial Revolution to change things. Actually, it made things worse — (Eli Whitney's cotton gin grew the cotton industry and also the slave industry) — but eventually it became obvious that machines did the hard work, so who needed slaves?

To give the devil his due, maybe it was the other way around. Maybe people's growing dislike of slavery was the catalyst *for* the industrial revolution. If the "good life" thrived on the backs of slaves, then ending slavery meant ending that good life. So, what was the alternative? The answer: machines. So maybe abolition did us a second good thing. Not only did it end slavery, but perhaps it also gave us this new, technologically good life that is so much better and without the pain of conscience.

[5] Backlash

Conscience was not the only motivation to end slavery. Personal safety was another. Slavery was always hazardous, and the world's great abolitionists (Moses, Spartacus, and John Brown, for instance) worked hard to increase that hazard. Pharaoh did not want to free his Israelite slaves, and at Moses' word, Egypt paid a heavy price.

Here's a verse that shows how slaves felt about slavery.

> ***2 Kings 9:32*** *And he* [new king Jehu] *lifted up his face to the window, and said, Who is on my side? Who? And there looked out to him two or three eunuchs* ***:33*** *And he said, Throw her* [Jezebel] *down. So they threw her down: and some of her blood was sprinkled on the wall, and on the horses: and he trode her under foot.*

It's interesting that eunuchs, castrated male slaves, were the most willing to kill Queen Jezebel — "I think we can accommodate that request!"

The downside of slavery, from the master's point of view, is that the master is always surrounded by people who hate him, or her in Jezebel's case, and, given the chance, would gladly slit his throat, or in this case, toss her out of a window. Think about it. Who would hate a slave owner more than the slave owner's eunuchs?

[6] EQUALITY

Here is an excellent argument against slavery:

Job 31:13 *If I did despise the cause of my manservant or of my maidservant, when they contend with me* ***:14*** *What then shall I do when God riseth up? And when he visiteth, what shall I answer him?* ***:15*** *Did not he that made me in the womb make him? And did not one fashion us in the womb?*

The point is that servants in general and slaves in particular are on an equal footing with their masters before God. Thomas Jefferson was right, "all men are created equal." Well, that's what he wrote anyway. The slaves he owned probably had a different story, but at least the words were right. And in the end, it was the words that mattered.

[7] THE FLIP SIDE

Isaiah 49:24 *Shall the prey be taken from the mighty, or the lawful captive delivered?*

We don't believe in slavery. But there are "lawful captives", for instance prisoners pressed into road gangs, indentured servants who have exchanged a certain period of time of their lives for financial benefit, soldiers who have signed on for four years, long-term contracts where we obligate ourselves to perform some service. Slavery per se is wrong, but those obligations we create for ourselves we consider to be morally acceptable. The difference is willingness, or some willingness anyway at some point.

[8] The High Price of Slavery

> ***Jeremiah 34:8*** *...Zedekiah had made a covenant with all the people which were in Jerusalem, to proclaim liberty unto them.* ***:9*** *That every man should let his manservant, and every man his maidservant, being a Hebrew or a Hebrewess, go free; that none should serve him of them, to wit, of a Jew his brother.* ***:10*** *...then they obeyed and let them go.* ***:11*** *But afterwards they turned, and caused the servants and the handmaids, whom they had let go free, to return, and brought them into subjection for servants and for handmaids.*

So, the Jews had a momentary attack of good conscience and let all their slaves go free. But it didn't last long. They were soon overwhelmed with buyer's remorse (seller's remorse?) and snatched all their slaves back, I suppose when they realized that doing their own cooking and laundry etc. was harder than they thought.

But that's not the end of the story. God had something to say about it. When God had given the Torah, he had freedom and liberty in mind; that's why their laws regarding slavery were so circumscribed. And when the people said, "Free our slaves? Why?" they put themselves in the role of Pharaoh, and God took a dim view of that.

> ***Jeremiah 34:13*** *Thus saith the* LORD, *the God of Israel; I made a covenant with your fathers in the day that I brought them forth out of the land of Egypt, out of the house of bondmen, saying,* ***:14*** *At the end of seven years let ye go every man his brother an Hebrew, which hath been sold unto thee; and when he hath served thee six years, thou shalt let him go free from*

thee: but your fathers hearkened not unto me, neither inclined their ear. ***:15*** *And ye were not turned, and had done right in my sight, in proclaiming liberty every man to his neighbor; and ye had made a covenant before me in the house which is called by my name.* ***:16*** *But ye turned and polluted my name, and caused every man his servant, and every man his handmaid, whom he had set at liberty at their pleasure, to return, and brought them into subjection, to be unto you for servants and handmaids.*

So, God outlines their crime. Liberty should have been their passion, but instead, the good life on the back of slaves was their passion. They misunderstood the whole point of why they were a nation in the first place. It was always about freedom.

And now, the punishment.

Jeremiah 34:17 *Therefore thus saith the LORD; Ye have not harkened unto me, in proclaiming liberty…behold, I proclaim a liberty for you, saith the LORD, to the sword, to the pestilence, and to the famine; and I will make you to be removed into all the kingdoms of the earth.* ***:18*** *I will give the men that have transgressed my covenant…* ***:19*** *The princes of Judah…and all the people of the land, which passed between the parts of the calf,* ***:20*** *…into the hand of their enemies…and their dead bodies shall be for meat unto the fowls of the heaven, and to the beasts of the earth.* ***:21*** *And Zedekiah king of Judah and his princes will I give…into the the hand of the king of Babylon's army…* ***:22*** *…and I will make the cities of Judah a desolation without an inhabitant.*

And that is exactly what happened. God exacted a heavy price for enjoying the good life on the backs of slaves.

God had brought them out of Egypt and into freedom and gave them a law of justice and judges and rules for slavery that made sense. They rejected the judges and demanded a king, and rejected liberty in favor of slavery. And now, since that's what they wanted, that's what they would have. God sold them into slavery to the Babylonians.

[9] Paul

> ***Philemon 1:1*** *Paul, a prisoner* [slave] *of Jesus Christ, and Timothy our brother, unto Philemon our dearly beloved, and fellow laborer.* ***:10*** *I beseech thee for my son Onesimus, whom I have begotten in my bonds.* ***:11*** *Which in time past was to thee unprofitable, but now profitable you to thee and me.* ***:12*** *Whom I have sent again: thou therefore receive him.* ***:17*** *If thou count me therefore a partner, receive him as myself.* ***:18*** *If he hath wronged thee, or owed thee ought, put that on mine account.* ***:21*** *Having confidence in thy obedience I wrote thee, knowing that thou wilt also do more than I say.*

A chief criticism of the Bible (by people who want to criticize the Bible) is that Paul is pro-slavery. But that is an unfair characterization.

Onesimus was a slave and also a Christian, owned by Philemon, also a Christian. Onesimus, unhappy about his circumstance, ran away and came to Paul. What he was expecting Paul to do is not clear. Maybe he thought Paul might help him escape; after all, Christianity had a lot to say about freedom, and under Jewish law, Paul would even be obligated to help him ***(Deuteronomy 23:15***).

But they didn't live under Jewish law, they lived under Roman law, and for a slave to escape or for someone to even help him escape, were capital crimes.

Onesimus was risking his life and maybe even Paul's.

But isn't abolition the moral imperative? Not in the first century Roman empire. Slavery was just part of the sea of injustice that they all swam in. I expect that Paul and his fellow disciples thought about how wonderful the world would be if one day all men were free.

But at that time, it could be nothing but a fantasy. The last real freedom fighter was Spartacus, and he had died in battle, and 50,000 of his followers were crucified. Is that really what God expected of his fledgling church, to openly oppose this millennia-old unjust institution of slavery? Is that really the hill that Christianity wanted to die on?

A much better strategy was: Let's first give people a conscience, coming, as it must, from Jesus Christ and the Jewish God. Then we'll see just how far that conscience can take the human race into goodness.

In the meantime, Christianity would have to survive and coexist with slavery if it was to be any good to anyone at all.

So, what to do about Onesimus. To help him escape would only get him killed, and maybe Paul too. To kick him out would be mean, not the kind of thing that one Christian does to another. The only thing that made sense to do was to lecture the young Onesimus on what it meant to be a good slave (as unjust as it was) instead of a rebelling one (which might get him killed) and appeal to Philemon's sense of Christian mercy. And so, Paul wrote a letter of recommendation from his own hand filled with every gushy sentiment he could think of.

Notice how carefully Paul begins. I am a slave too, of Jesus Christ. And you and I are brothers in this labor, and you are beloved. And then Paul makes his plea.

Another thing that Paul does is recommend Onesimus. While as he was before "unprofitable" (good for nothing and lazy and a troublemaker), he is now "profitable" (I've lectured him and he now understands that he has to be a team player, putting your interest ahead of his own). And with that recommendation, Paul, risking his own reputation, sends Onesimus with the letter back to Philemon, crossing his fingers and praying that (1) Philemon will be forgiving, and (2) Onesimus will be a better, more loyal, more productive slave.

Unfair? Of course it was unfair, but that was the world they lived in, and that was the circumstance that Onesimus was born to. Sorry, but for real freedom, they would have to wait nearly 2000 more years. And when that happened, when slaves were finally freed, Christianity and the Christian conscience were largely responsibility.

So, give Paul a break. We enjoy our hindsight morality.

[10] Epilog

1 Corinthians 7:21 *Art thou called being a servant* [slave]*? Care not for it…*

We are all slaves of something: poverty, money, ugliness, fat, food, stupidity, work, laziness, passion, poor heath, drugs — the list is long of the things that exist, it sometimes seems, for the single purpose of enslaving us.

Paul here is advising slaves, actual slaves, don't fret about it. Enjoy life and live life rightly in spite of the many leashes that tug at you, and in every situation do the best that you can.

Well, if real slaves could get on with life and be happy, then surely we, who are so blessed, can do at least as well.

John 8:32 *And ye shall know the truth, and the truth shall make you free.*

Sorcery

Exodus 7:10-22, Acts 13:6

What does the Bible say about sorcery? Plenty. What conclusions you come to is up to you, but here, at least, you have a list of relevant verses to ponder and puzzle over. Make of it what you will. The authors just reported events; you decide what they mean.

[1] PHARAOH

> ***Exodus 7:10*** *And Aaron cast down his rod before Pharaoh and before his servants, and it became a serpent* ***:11*** *Then Pharaoh also called the wise men and the sorcerers: now the magicians of Egypt, they also did in like manner with their enchantments.* ***:12*** *For they cast down every man his rod, and they became serpents: but Aaron's rod swallowed up their rods.* ***:20*** *And Moses and Aaron do so…he lifted up his rod and smote the waters that were in the river…and the waters that were in the river turned to blood.* ***:22*** *And the magicians of Egypt did so with their enchantments …*

> ***Exodus 8:6*** *And Aaron stretched out his hand over the waters of Egypt and the frogs came up.* ***:7*** *And the magicians did so with their enchantments* ***:17*** *Aaron stretched out his hand with his rod and smote the dust of the earth and it became lice* ***:18*** *And the magicians did so with their enchantments to bring forth lice, but they could not…*

We are supposed to be impressed that Aaron's magic was greater than Pharaoh's magic — that Aaron's serpent ate the magicians' serpent, that while the magicians could repeat some of Aaron's tricks (turn water to blood and create frogs), they could not do others (turn dust to lice). But what's baffling is that the magicians could do them at all. If I saw a magician turn a stick into a snake, I would be impressed whether or not someone else's snake ate his snake. That God's magic is more powerful than Satan's magic is fine, what's troubling is that Satan has magic that works at all.

Did the magicians really do these things? The text says they did, and that's weird.

But there's another possibility regardless of the text.

Maybe the magicians were doing parlor tricks, you know, the rabbit from the hat kind of thing, and that was the basis of Egyptian religion. So, God challenged that by doing what they did *for real.* "You want to convince the people you can turn a stick into a snake? Okay, I'll *really* turn a stick into a snake." Now, that I can believe. Whether that's what happened or not, well, we can ask God when we get to heaven. It may be that Satan really can turn a stick into a snake.

[2] The Law

> ***Leviticus 19:26*** *Ye shall not…use enchantment, nor observe times.* ***:31*** *Regard not them that have familiar spirits, neither seek after wizards, to be defiled by them.*

> ***Leviticus 20:6*** *And the soul that turneth after such as have familiar spirits, and after wizards…I will…cut him off from among the people.* ***:27*** *A man also or a woman that hath a familiar spirit, or that is a wizard, shall surely be put to death: they shall stone them with stones…*

A familiar spirit is a demon obeying a witch.

The first penalty is not so bad, to be cut off from the people. But the second, put to death, that's pretty vicious stuff. But then again, people back then were pretty vicious about almost everything, so why should we be surprised and appalled by this?

> ***Deuteronomy 18:10*** *There shall not be found among you anyone that maketh his son or daughter to pass through the fire, or that useth divination, or an observer of times, or an enchanter, or a witch.* ***:11*** *Or a charmer, or a consulter with familiar spirits, or a wizard, or a necromancer.* ***:12*** *For all these things are an abomination to the* LORD*.* ***:14*** *For these nations, which thou shalt possess, hearkened unto observers of times, and unto diviners: but as for thee, the* LORD *thy God hath not suffered thee so to do.*

The first thing on this list of don't is don't murder your children in religious rituals (pass through the fire).

It seems that child sacrifice and idolatry are always somehow linked — the way to get rid of an unwanted child and do it legally and be guilt free is to offer him as a sacrifice. There is no guilt if "God" made me do it, or in contemporary times, if I kill my child under the guise of politically correct women's rights. So maybe God was not so harsh after all to make sorcery a capital crime.

[3] BALAAM

> ***Numbers 22:6*** *Come now therefore, I* [Balak] *pray thee, curse this people* [Israel]; *for they are too mighty for me…* ***23:23*** [Balaam said] *Surely there is no enchantment against Jacob, neither is there any divination against Israel: according to this time it shall be said of Jacob and of Israel, What hath God wrought.*

This story is long; I'll abridge it for you.

On the way to the Promised Land, Israel had to pass through the land of their cousins the Midionites. Balak was the Midionite king. Moses assured them, we'll cause you no harm, we're just passing through; the Canaanites are our enemies, not you.

But Balak didn't see it that way. To him, Israel was very threatening, and he wanted to be rid of them.

So, what did he do? He hired a prophet, Balaam, a true prophet of the true God, and paid him to pronounce a curse on Israel. And so for money, Balaam tried — a divine hit man, or a hit prophet, I suppose.

What happened, however, surprised Balaam and Balak. When Balaam attempted to utter a curse, out of his mouth came a blessing instead. This happened three times until finally Balaam gave up.

The reason this story means anything in this essay about sorcery is because it defines "enchantment" for us. An enchantment is a curse. And the reason you don't want to curse someone is because the curse might actually work, and you'll be accountable for what happens.

[4] King Saul

> ***1 Saumel 15:23*** *For rebellion is as the sin of witchcraft, and stubbornness is as iniquity and idolatry. Because thou* [Saul] *hast rejected the word of the LORD, he hath also rejected thee from being king.*

Rebellion is a pretty bad thing, and it must be very bad to compare it to witchcraft. But if that's so, then what's *really* bad is witchcraft in order to be able to make the comparison. When you say "this is as bad as that," it's the "that" that's awful.

> ***1 Samuel 28:7*** *Then said Saul unto his servants, Seek me a woman that hath a familiar spirit, that I may go to her, and inquire of her. And his servants said unto him, Behold, there is a woman that hath a familiar spirit at Endor.* ***:8*** *And Saul disguised himself, and...came to the woman by*

night. ***:11*** *Then said the woman, Whom shall I bring up unto thee? And he said, Bring up Samuel.* ***:12*** *And when the woman saw Samuel, she cried with a loud voice: and the woman spake unto Saul, saying, Why hast thou deceived me? For thou art Saul.* ***:13*** *And the king said unto her, Be not afraid: for what sawest thou? And the woman said unto Saul, I saw gods coming out of the earth.* ***:15*** *And Samuel said unto Saul…* ***:17*** *…the* LORD *hath rent the kingdom out of thine hand, and given it to thy neighbor, even to David.* ***:19*** *Moreover the LORD will also deliver Israel with thee into the hand of the Philistines: and tomorrow thou and thy sons be with me.*

This story of the Witch of Endor is stunning for many reasons. First, because this is the first mention in the Bible of an afterlife. Nowhere in the Torah did Moses speak of an afterlife, this is the first, the beginning of the Bible's declaration of an afterlife. And that it would come to us from the mouth of a witch, is, as I said, stunning.

And what's more stunning is that it actually happened. She really did encounter the departed spirit of the dead Samuel.

Some will disagree, saying that, no, she was just a charlatan, conducting just another fake séance to con someone out of their money. That's not possible. Or, indeed if she was a fake, the Bible goes to great lengths to convince us otherwise.

Consider: (1) She did not know this was king Saul asking this of her until Samuel (or some other dead person) told her so. Then she feared for her life. (2) She prophesied accurately, as only Samuel could, that tomorrow Israel would lose its battle with the Philistines. (3) She prophesied accurately that tomorrow Saul *and his sons* would die. The unlikely accuracy of that prediction has to impress. Finally, (4) there would be no successor to Saul's dynasty, and the kingdom would be given to one specific person: David. If nothing else impresses you, surely that must.

Therefore, we must conclude, if we are to believe the Bible at all, that this witch was the real deal. Which brings us to this nagging question: If sorcery works, why was God so determined to stamp it out? It appears that God's objection to sorcery is precisely because it *did* work — (that and they murdered children in ritual sacrifice). And it does appear (according to the Bible anyway) that there really are multiple and competing divine powers at work in the universe.

> ***1 Chronicles 10:13*** *So Saul died for his transgression which he had committed against the* LORD, *even against the word of the* LORD, *which he kept not, and also for asking counsel of one that had a familiar spirit, to enquire of it.* ***:14*** *And enquired not of the* LORD*: therefore he slew him, and turned the kingdom unto David the son of Jesse.*

[5] JEZEBEL

> ***2 Kings 9:22*** *And it came to pass, when Jorem saw Jehu, that he said, Is it peace, Jehu? And he answered, What peace, so long as the whoredoms of thy mother Jezebel and her witchcrafts are so many?*

So, along with all her other faults, Jezebel was a witch as well. You didn't know that, did you? Or maybe you did.

[6] CHILD SACRIFICE

> ***2 Kings 17:17*** *And they caused their sons and their daughters to pass through the fire, and used divinations and enchantments, and sold themselves to do evil in the sight of the* LORD, *to provoke him to anger.*

> ***2 Kings 21:3*** *And he* [king Manasseh] *made a grove, as did king Ahab in Israel; and worshipped all the host of heaven, and served them.* ***:6*** *And he made his son pass through the fire, and observed times, and used*

enchantments, and dealt with familiar spirits and wizards: he wrought much wickedness in the sight of the L*ORD* *to provoke him to anger.*

2 Kings 23:24 *Moreover the workers with familiar spirits, and the wizards, and the images, and the idols, and all the abominations that were spied in the land of Judah and in Jerusalem, did Josiah put away that he might perform the works of the law which were written in the book that Hilkiah found in the house of the* L*ORD*.

2 Chronicles 33:6 *And he caused his children to pass through the fire in the valley of the son of Hinnom: also he observed times, and used enchantments, and used witchcraft, and dealt with a familiar spirit, and with wizards: he wrought much evil in the sight of the* L*ORD* *to provoke him to anger.*

Always, it seems that murdering children and sorcery go together. False gods permit and even require people to do evil things. In this case, finally, one good king, Josiah, had had enough and "put away" the evil, which probably means he killed those child murdering priests of Baal and the rest of those monsters. They deserved it.

Hinnom, you should know, morphed into its Greek transliteration *Gehenna*, which is translated into the English word *Hell.*

When the Jews returned after the Diaspora, they were determined to never repeat any of that evil — no Jew would ever again bow to an idol. But they wondered, what should they do with the Hinnom valley, that evil place where children were burned alive? What they decided to do with it was (and it was fitting) they used it for a trash dump.

And so from then on, at night the Jews of Jerusalem could see off in the distance the glow of trash burning in the Hinnom valley which reminded them of evils long ago.

Then, 500 years later, a prophet named John came and said, "Who hath warned you to flee from the fires of hell (Gehenna, Hinnom)?"

You've always wondered why hell burns with fire? Well, now you know. Because children died there in excruciating agony, as children do today in abortion clinics.

Who deserves hell? Maybe those who kill children will be the first in line.

[7] Isaiah

Isaiah 2:6 *Therefore thou* [God] *hast forsaken thy people the house of Jacob, because they…are soothsayers like the Philistines …*

Isaiah 8:19 *And when they shall say unto you, Seek unto them that have familiar spirits, and unto wizards that peep, and that mutter: should not a people seek unto their God? For the living to the dead?*

Isaiah 19:3 *…I will destroy the counsel therefore: and they shall seek to the idols, and to the charmers, and to them that have familiar spirits, and to the wizards.* ***:12*** *Where are they? Where are thy wise men?* ***:13*** *…the princes of Noph* [Memphis, Egypt's religious center] *are deceived.*

Isaiah 29:4 *…thy voice shall be as one that hath a familiar spirit.*

Isaiah 44:25 *That frustrated the tokens of the liars, and maketh diviners mad; that turneth wise men backwards, and maketh their knowledge foolish.*

Isaiah 47:12 *Stand now with thine enchantments, and with the multitude of thy sorceries, wherein thou hast laboured from thy youth; if so be thou shalt be able to profit, if so be thou mayest prevail.* ***:13*** *Thou art wearied in the multitude of thy counsels. Let now the astrologers, the stargazers, the monthly prognosticators, stand up, and save thee from these things that shall come upon thee.*

[8] JEREMIAH

Jeremiah 10:2 *Thus saith the LORD, Learn not the way of the heathen, and be not dismayed at the signs of heaven; for the heathen are dismayed at them.*

Jeremiah 14:14 *Then the LORD said unto me, the prophets prophecy lies in my name: I sent them not, neither have I commanded them, neither spake unto them: they prophecy unto you a false vision and divination, and a thing of naught, and the deceit of their heart.*

Jeremiah 27:9 *Therefore hearken not ye to your prophets, nor to your diviners, nor to your enchanters, nor to your sorcerers, which speak unto you, saying, Ye shall not serve the king of Babylon.*

Jeremiah 29:8 *...Let not your prophets and your diviners...deceive you, neither hearken to your dreams which ye cause to be dreamed.* ***:9*** *For they prophecy falsely unto you in my name: I have not sent them, saith the LORD.*

[9] EZEKIEL

Ezekiel 12:24 *For there shall be no more any vain vision nor flattering divination within the house of Israel.*

That was true. When the Jews were taken captive into their Diaspora, they learned the bitter lesson that God had been trying to teach them. And when they finally returned home seventy years later, no Jew would ever again bow to an idol or practice sorcery.

> ***Ezekiel 13:6*** *They have used vanity and lying divinations…* ***:7*** *Have ye not seen a vain vision, have you not spoken a lying divination, whereas ye say, The* LORD *saith it; albeit I have not spoken?* ***:23*** *Therefore ye shall see no more lying vanity, nor divine divinations…*

> ***Ezekiel 21:21*** *For the king of Babylon stood at the parting of the way, at the head of the two ways, to use divination: he made his arrows bright, he consulted with images, he looked in the liver.*

> ***Ezekiel 22:28*** *…vanity and divining lies…*

[10] DANIEL

> ***Daniel 2:2*** *Then the king commanded to call the magicians, and the astrologers, and the sorcerers, and the Chaldeans, for to shew the king his dream.* ***:4*** *Then spake the Chaldeans to the king in Syriack, O king, live forever: tell thy servants the dream, and we will shew the interpretation.* ***:5*** *The king answered and said to the Chaldeans, The thing is gone from me, if you will not make known unto me the dream, with the interpretation therefore, ye shall be cut in pieces, and your houses shall be made a dunghill.*

The king had probably long suspected that his magicians were useless, that they feigned supernatural powers to get political power. He'd always tolerated them, but this dream of his had so disturbed him that he needed the truth: "What does my dream mean?" And the only way he could be sure he was getting a true interpretation is if they could tell him his dream. "The thing has gone from me" probably doesn't mean "I've forgotten it," it probably means, "Why should I tell you?"

> ***Daniel 2:10*** *The Chaldeans answered before the king, and said, There is not a man upon the earth that can shew the king's matter: therefore there is no king, lord, nor ruler, that asketh such things at any magician, or astrologer, or Chaldean.*

Now the truth comes out. They have no clue. They're a bunch of phonies and always have been. Now they have to admit it because their lives are on the line and they have to come clean to say, "But what you're asking of us cannot be done."

> ***Daniel 2:24*** *Therefore Daniel went…and said…Destroy not the wise men … I will shew unto the king the interpretation.* ***:27*** *…The secret which the king hath demanded cannot the wise men, the astrologiers, the magicians, the soothsayers, shew unto the king?* ***:28*** *But there is a God in heaven that revealeth secrets, and maketh known to the king Nebuchadnezzar. Thy dream, and the visions of thy head upon thy bed, are these…*

And so, Daniel, being the true prophet that he was, told the king his dream and the interpretation. And because Daniel told the dream, the king believed the interpretation.

Notice Daniel's magnanimity: "Destroy not the wise men." Daniel could have told the king to go ahead and kill all the wise men. But instead, Daniel saved their lives, and he became their boss.

> ***Daniel 2:48*** *Then the king made Daniel a great man, and gave him many great gifts, and made him ruler over the whole province of Babylon, and chief of the governors over all the wise men.*

There is no indication that the wise men were bitter or jealous of Daniel's sudden rise to power. Later there was a plot against him, but that was political (governors) not religious leaders. I believe that these wise men, these religious leaders of Babylon, were grateful, first of all to be alive, but also to finally have a religious leader who actually knew what he was talking about, who could actually do it, who could talk to God and get a real answer. I further think they were loyal to him and to all things Jewish, and that loyalty became a long running tradition which trailed through the years until five centuries later, a group of Persian Magi saw a new star and understood that to mean that it was time for the Jewish Messiah to be born. Then they caravanned to, of all places, a small po-dunk town in Israel called Bethlehem where they found the child king and gave him gifts.

> ***Daniel 5:7*** *The king* [Belshazzar, the final king] *cried aloud to bring in the astrologers, the Chaldeans, and the soothsayers,* ***:15*** *but they could not shew the interpretation of the thing.*

So here we go again. This time it's God's writing on the wall that the magicians could not read. But Daniel could, and so again the king (different king) rewarded him.

Of course, it didn't do Daniel any good because Babylon was conquered by the Persians that night. But soon after that, Daniel impressed the Persians as much or even more than he impressed the Babylonians.

But the point is, true prophets of the true God are useful, but magicians and sorcerers are useless.

[11] Minor Prophets

Micah 3:6 *…ye shall not have a vision; and it shall be dark unto you, that ye shall not divine.*

Micah 5:12 *And I will cut off witchcrafts out of thine hand; and thou shalt have no more soothsayers:*

Nahum 3:4 *Because of the multitude of the whoredoms of the wellfavored harlot, the mistress of witchcraft, that selleth nations through her whoredoms, and families through her witchcrafts.*

Zechariah 10:2 *For the idols have spoken vanity, and the diviners have seen a lie, and have told false dreams; they comfort in vain…*

Malachi 3:5 *…I will be a swift witness against the sorcerers, and against the adulterers, and against false swearers, and against those who oppress the hireling in his wages, the widow, and the fatherless, and that turn aside the stranger…*

[12] Gospels

Matthew 2:1 *Now when Jesus was born in Bethleham of Judaea in the days of Harod the king, behold, there came wise men from the east to Jerusalem.*

And now the most familiar story in the world: the Christmas story. Just who were those wise men, these Magi, from "the east," actually "far east," which can only be Persia? How did they know? What did they know? Why did they come? All Matthew tells us is that they came to worship him who was "born king of the Jews." And why should they take an interest in a Jewish monarch?

Those are mysterious questions, and the answers are just as mysterious, and too involved (and out of context) for this short essay on sorcery. But suffice it to say that the Magi had long religious traditions, and much of it trailed from Babylon and from a Jewish prophet named Daniel. That's what I believe. I know it's circumstantial, but nothing else makes sense.

> ***Matthew 24:24*** *For there shall arise false Christs, and false prophets, and they shall shew great signs and wonders; inasmuch that, if it were possible, they shall deceive the very elect.*

[13] Acts

> ***Acts 8:9*** *But there was a certain man, called Simon, which before time in the same city used sorcery, and bewitched the people of Samaria, giving out that he was some great one.* ***:13*** *Then Simon himself believed also: and when he was baptized, he continued with Philip, and wondered, beholding the miracles and signs which were done.* ***:18*** *And when Simon saw that through the laying on of the apostles' hands the Holy Ghost was given, he offered them money.* ***:19*** *Saying, give me also this power, that on whomsoever I lay hands, he may receive the Holy Ghost.* ***:20*** *But Peter said unto him, Thy money perish with thee, because thou hast thought that the gift of God may be purchased with money.*

This Simon the Sorcerer recognized power when he saw it. He was no fool. And he knew that such power could be very profitable. Can you imagine the money you could make if you walked through hospitals and cured everyone of everything with just a touch? That's what Simon wanted. Power. Profitable power. But what he got instead was a rebuke from Peter and a curse, "Your money perish with thee."

This was exactly the deal that Satan offered Jesus in the first temptation. "You have power. Use it — to serve yourself." Thank God that Jesus had a much different objective than Simon the Sorcerer.

> ***Acts 13:6*** *And when they had gone through the isle unto Paphos, they found a certain sorcerer, a false prophet, a Jew, whose name was Barjesus.* ***:9*** *Then Saul, (who also is called Paul,) filled with the Holy Ghost, set his eyes on him.* ***:10*** *And said, O full of all subtilty, and all mischief, thou child of the devil, thou enemy of all righteousness, wilt thou not cease to pervert the right ways of the Lord?* ***:11*** *And now, behold, the hand of the Lord is upon thee, and thou shalt be blind, not seeing the sun for a season. And immediately there fell on him a midst of darkness and he went about seeking some to lead him by the hand.*

Being a false prophet and pretending to have divine powers that you don't have can bring serious consequences, especially when you're face to face with someone who really does have such powers. Fortunately for Barjesus, his curse was only "for a season." Paul could have been much more brutal. But Paul was not vicious, probably because he had himself been stricken by that exact same curse (blindness) on the road to Damascus.

> ***Acts 16:16*** *And it came to pass, as we went to prayer, a certain damsel possessed with a spirit of divination met us, which brought her masters much gain by soothsaying.* ***:17*** *The same followed Paul and us, and cried, saying, These men are the servants of the most high God, which shew unto us the way of salvation.* ***:18*** *And this did she many days. But Paul, being grieved, turned and said to the spirit, I command thee in the name of Jesus Christ to come out of her. And he came out the same hour.*

This is a very peculiar story, all the more reason to believe it actually happened, that the author is just reporting facts without trying to explain them. If the author were making it up, he certainly would not have made up *this* odd story.

Question: Why would a demon testify for Christ? You'd think a demon would rather try to create problems. Maybe a demon can't lie, not about Jesus. Or maybe the demon was trying to curry favor, since he's damned. Or maybe he was trying to get in on the action. All of these seem outlandish, but I can think of no other explanations.

But I do think that the spirit world that surrounds us is more complex than we think, and God has good reason to forbid necromancy — because it is dangerous.

Another question: Why would the apostles not be glad for such testimony as it would only bring more people to Christ? Because regardless of any beneficial result from a demon's true testimony, demons are still the enemy seeking to destroy lives and souls. And besides, this poor girl deserved to be free of the demon that possessed her.

The story rings true because it is bizarre — it's not at all pat like fiction must be.

> **Acts 19:13** *Then certain of the vagabond Jews, exorcists, took upon them to call over them which had evil spirits the name of the Lord Jesus, saying, We adjure you by Jesus whom Paul preaches.* **:15** *And the evil spirit answered and said, Jesus I know, and Paul I know; but who are ye?* **:16** *And the man in whom the evil spirit was leaped on them, and overcame them, and prevailed against them, so that they fled out of the house naked and wounded.* **:19** *Many of them also which used curious arts brought their books together, and burned them…*

Demons are dangerous, as these would-be exorcists found out.

[14] Epistles

Galatians 5:19 *Now the works of the flesh are manifest, which are these…* ***:20*** *…witchcraft…* ***:21*** *…they which do such things shall not inherit the kingdom of God.*

2 Thessalonians 2:9 *Even him, whose coming is after the workings of Satan with all power and signs and lying wonders* ***:11*** *And for this cause God shall send them strong delusion, that they shall believe a lie.*

Revelation 9:21 *Neither repented they of their murders, nor of their sorceries, nor of their fornication, nor of their thefts.*

Revelation 18:23 *…for by thy sorceries were all nations deceived.*

Revelation 21:8 *But the… unbelieving…and sorcerers…shall have their part in the lake which burneth with fire and brimstone: which is the second death.*

Revelation 22:14 *For without* [outside the city of God] *are dogs, and sorcerers, and whoremongers, and murders, and idolaters, and whosoever loveth and maketh a lie.*

Thou Shalt Not Steal

Exodus 20:15, Matthew 12:1-2

> ***Exodus 20:15*** *Thou shalt not steal.*

God sanctioned the private ownership of property when he wrote, "Thou shalt not steal." Without ownership, stealing is a meaningless concept. You cannot steal what nobody owns. So, God allows ownership because he forbids stealing.

In addition to the general principle, the Bible says much about different kinds of stealing.

[1] Burglary

> ***Exodus 22:2*** *If a thief be found breaking up, and be smitten that he die, there shall no blood be shed for him.* ***:3*** *If the sun be risen upon him, there shall be blood shed for him; for he should make full restitution; if he have nothing, then he shall be sold for his theft.*

If you kill a night burglar, since at night you can't tell if the burglar means real malicious harm or not (maybe rape and murder), then you were in your right to kill him, and it was the burglar's bad luck; he shouldn't have been prowling around at night. There were no questions asked. The police had better things to do than to arrest a man for killing a night burglar in self-defense. That's why "there shall no blood be shed for him," which means the man who killed him should not be executed.

But a day burglar was a slightly different thing. Maybe a day burglar wasn't so dangerous and killing him was more an act of murder rather than self-defense and maybe killing that burglar is a capital crime. Or maybe not. In any case, it needed to be investigated. You can't just kill, for instance, a fleeing felon out of spite. After all, the law's job is to exact a proper restitution from the thief, so don't be a vigilante.

All of this is police action, requiring government — in Israel's case, judges — to oversee the protecting of private ownership by catching thieves and punishing them.

[2] Finders Keepers

The law also deals with such things as, what I call, friendly embezzlement, that is, helping yourself to your friend's stuff just because you can. But it also makes clear that you're not responsible for your friend's stuff just because he left it at your house.

> ***Exodus 22:7*** *If a man shall deliver unto his neighbor money or stuff to keep, and it be stolen out of the man's house; if the thief be found, let him pay double.* ***:8*** *If the thief be not found, then the master of the house shall be brought unto the judges, to see whether he have put his hand unto his neighbour's goods.*

[3] Man Stealing

Particularly serious — more serious than stealing stuff — is stealing people: kidnapping.

> ***Deuteronomy 24:7*** *If a man be found stealing any of his brethren…that thief shall die.*

We can imagine the motives that bad people might have for stealing people. And slavery was, unfortunately, legal throughout much of world history. Romans grabbed whomever they wanted, as did Greeks, Persians, and so on. But in the Torah, man stealing was a capital crime. If Bible-believing Europeans had understood that, perhaps the Atlantic slave trade might not have happened.

Then there's kidnapping for ransom, and kidnapping for political terrorism, and kidnapping for rape and sex trafficking. All of those, according to God's law, are capital crimes.

[4] Borrowing

Now, there are some subtle variations of stealing.

Psalms 37:21 *The wicked borroweth and payeth not again.*

Some people file bankruptcy, not because they need to but because it's profitable to — a legal loophole to cheat creditors. When abused, bankruptcy is stealing made legal.

That's not to say that there isn't a right time for bankruptcy. Of course, in modern law, which disavows slavery, bankruptcy is the means by which bankrupt people get to start over. And that's a good thing. It's "grace," in financial terms. I'm just saying that good laws intended to protect can be used by bad people to steal.

[5] Employers

Deuteronomy 24:15 *At his day thou shalt give him his hire, neither shall the sun go down upon it; for he is poor.*

There are so many ways that a rich man can take advantage of a poor man, and it's not fair. This verse speaks of a poor day worker. He mows your lawn today so that he can feed his family tonight. But then the boss-man says, "Sorry, I only pay on Fridays. Come back then for your check." And this he does for a few pennies interest he makes holding onto the poor man's money while the poor man's family goes hungry all week.

God says that's not right, and it is the law's job, the judge's job, to make sure that doesn't happen. If the poor man earned it today, pay him today. Don't use technicalities to cheat him.

The problem today is that rich people can afford good attorneys, but poor people cannot. So, people are not so equal under the law as we suppose.

[6] MERCHANTS

Proverbs 11:1 *A false balance is an abomination.*

A false balance is how merchants cheat customers, where a one-pound weight is really a pound and a smidgen, to exact an extra charge for goods or services not earned. How many false balances plague us today is impossible to count: undisclosed interest, hidden charges and fees, fine print, double taxes, inflation by banks and government — our economy is infested with false balances. What we need is a double dose of just plain honesty.

[7] JESUS

We need to know what stealing is, but we also need to know what stealing isn't. And we can get a handle of that by first asking this question: Did Jesus steal? I will of course try to persuade you that he did not, but there is a verse that seems on the edge that might give some anti-Jesus people a cause to accuse him. And that is what we should deal with now.

Matthew 12:1 *At that time Jesus went on the sabbath day through the corn; and his disciples were an hungered, and began to pluck the ears of corn, and to eat.*

Every now and then someone will try to use this verse to justify petty theft. "Well, Jesus and his disciples stole corn, so why can't I use company supplies for personal use?"

This question deserves an answer, particularly since we believe that Jesus was sinless.

1 John 3:5 *in him is no sin.*

So, what's going on here? Did Jesus and his disciples steal corn or not? They did not. First of all, if they had been guilty of theft, the Pharisees would have been the first to say so, looking for any occasion at all to accuse him. But they didn't accuse him of theft. What did they accuse him of?

Matthew 12:2 *Thy disciples do that which is not lawful to do upon the sabbath day.*

The Parisees accused them, not of stealing, but of harvesting on the Sabbath.

Exodus 34:21 *Six days thou shalt work, but on the seventh day thou shalt rest: in earing time and in harvest thou shalt rest.*

The pharisees exaggerated that commandment to mean you can't even pick an ear of corn on the Sabbath. But they didn't accuse Jesus of stealing. And why is that? Because the Jewish law was quite clear about what stealing was and what it wasn't.

Deuteronomy 23:24 *When thou comest into thy neighbour's vineyard, then thou mayest eat grapes thy fill at thine own pleasure; but thou shalt not put any in thy vessel* ***:25*** *When thou comest into the standing corn of thy neighbor, then thou mayest pluck the ears with thine hand; but thou shalt not move a sickle unto thy neighbor's standing corn.*

Back then, as now, travelers and poor people needed some things to be free. Today, as you travel, you can use a restroom at a gas station, or get a drink from a park fountain, or park safely for the night at a rest-stop. Using these free amenities is not stealing but sort of a social understanding.

Moses wrote just such an entitlement into the law. Farmers, according to the law, did have a social obligation to assist travelers and poor people. The rule was that anyone passing through a vineyard or field of standing corn was welcome to eat some grapes or pluck an ear or two for a quick meal. Fair enough. A few grapes, a few ears would not be missed and were a great benefit to travelers — there were no fast food restaurants for a quick Big Mac.

But there were some rules, some very important restrictions.

First: Only *standing* corn. If you helped yourself to the barn, to the corn that was already harvested, that would be stealing.

Second: You can eat only what you can pick with your hands (don't bring a "sickle") and eat there (don't fill a "vessel"). Like an all-you-can-eat, there's no take-out.

Sadly, generosity is so often met with greed that God needed to forbid taking advantage of generosity. But that's just the way things were, and are. So, while God provides an entitlement so travelers won't go hungry, he also limits that entitlement so farmers won't go hungry.

Perhaps we could better balance our entitlements today with a bit more fairness and restraint. We taxpayers, after all, are burdened with a lot. There do seem to be a lot of "sickles" and "vessels" in our cornfields. Jesus did not walk away with armloads of other people's corn. He was no thief. Today, people walk away with bunches of other people's stuff.

Success or Failure

Joshua 1:8, Matthew 6:33

We all have goals that we are trying to achieve. Love and family, business and financial, intellectual, spiritual; in every area of our lives there are objectives that we reach for.

Our goals often compete with each other for our time and attention, and we are constantly weighing and rebalancing priorities. Sometimes we discover that what is most important is not the most expedient, and things we thought we needed to do right now actually have to wait.

For each goal, we anticipate success. Without the expectation of success, there would be no point to having a goal.

The Bible has some good advice on how to achieve success. It's not all spiritual as in, for example, how to get to heaven. Much of it is very practical and very specific to our day-to-day problems of life — tactical, if you will. But this essay is not about that, it is more strategic, more about achieving success in a general sense.

Here then is some biblical advice on how to be successful, in a general way.

> ***Matthew 6:33*** *But seek ye first the kingdom of God, and his righteousness; and all these things shall be added unto you.*

First things first. This is God's directive to prioritize. Before you try to secure the things of this world you ought to first secure the things in the next. Then you're free to obtain the things of this world.

Jesus is not a party-poop. He knows that life is to be lived and "all these things" you should have. Just get yourself right with God first. That's all he's saying. Why? For one thing, today could be your last. But setting that fatalism aside, being right with God actually helps you achieve everything else, and guilt free.

Here is one of my favorite sayings: "He is no fool who gives up that which he cannot keep for that which he cannot lose." Once you are secure with God, then you can work down the list.

> ***Joshua 1:8*** *This book of the law shall not depart out of thy mouth; but thou shalt meditate therein day and night, that thou mayest observe to do according to all that is written therein: for then thou shalt make thy way prosperous, and then thou shalt have good success.*

The law, that is the Mosaic law, was the constitution of a new nation, namely, Israel. And Joshua's advice was to know that law and live by it, and you will be successful.

This was true spiritually (obey God and he will bless you), but it was also true practically. It helps to know the laws that you are dealing with. If you are starting a business, you need to understand the laws concerning your business: Maybe that's corporate law, or contract law, and if you hire people, there are piles of laws that you have to know and apply. And then there is ethics: how to treat people and just be fair.

Basically, when you're going to play a game, you need to first know the rules of the game. And it is so with all the games of life. Everything you might endeavor to do you will find yourself swimming in laws, rules, regulations, moral obligation, and just common sense. Ignore all that, and you do so at your own peril.

> ***2 Chronicles 27:6*** *So Jotham became mighty, because he prepared his ways before the LORD his God.*

2 Chronicles 28:5 *The* LORD *his God delivered him* [Ahaz] *into the hand of the king of Syria* ***:6*** *For Pekah the son of Remaliah slew in Judah an hundred and twenty thousand in one day, which were all valiant men; because they had forsaken the* LORD *God of their fathers.*

Whether you win or lose, is it really just a matter of being on God's side so that he'll be on your side and give you the victory? Well, yes, it is that. But in addition, it is also about stocking up passion among your followers, your teammates, your coworkers, your employees, all those people that have joined you in your cause.

Winning usually amounts to inspiring passion in those who are with you, and nothing inspires passion more than knowing that they are involved in the right cause, that God is on our side, so to speak. That's first. Give people the goal of making a difference. If you lead them to do good in the world, they'll follow you anywhere, and they will win.

Psalms 18:36 *Thou hast enlarged my steps under me, that my feet did not slip.*

If I believe that God is protecting me, I can be bold in taking a bigger step and not worry that I'll slip. So, be ambitious. Try to do something great. Don't be so timid. Someone said, "If you're going to dream anyway, dream big."

David the shepherd boy became David the king because he decided to take one gigantic step forward: he accepted Goliath's challenge. That's the kind of thing you need to do. Whether it be college or a new business or marriage, at some point you have to move past baby steps and start taking giant steps toward your great and noble goals.

Proverbs 16:3 *Commit thy works unto the* LORD, *and thy thoughts shall be established.*

When you finally decide to do things God's way and for him, then you succeed. And the reason you succeed is because if your objectives are in harmony with God's will, then they get traction. Things just start working out better because he's on your side. What is in your mind to do will actually work.

Proverbs 16:9 *A man's heart deviseth his way: but the* LORD *directeth his steps.*

This is very practical. You may know what you want to accomplish, but sometimes you need God to reveal to you how to do it. He will bring you to the success you seek by putting ideas into your head. We call that inspiration. If an idea is big, we call it revelation.

In any case, we often get a sense that such ideas come to us from outside ourselves, and that happens best when the goal is righteous because without righteousness, we're on our own, and we may or may not have the wherewithal to move from one step to the next. With God, the odds are much better.

Proverbs 29:25 *The fear of man bringeth a snare: but whoso putteth his trust in the* LORD *shall be safe.*

There are two fears that impede us: FOF and FOP — fear of failure and fear of people. Sometimes you need to just believe that good things can happen and push forward despite the risks. Overcoming fear gets inertia working for you instead of against you, and one way to overcome fear is to be confident that God is working with you and will lead you through the maze of necessary things.

Suicide

Matthew 27:4-5

This subject is disturbing, particularly to those family members who have lost a close loved one, a parent or a child or a sibling, to suicide. And the traditional Christian view, that suicides are damned as murderers, is not at all helpful. Their grief is painful enough, they don't need to hear that.

What is also not helpful is that the Bible says substantially nothing about the subject (other than the examples of Saul and Judas), so we are left to ourselves to grapple with it and understand it the best we can.

So, does the Bible say anything at all that might be of some comfort? There may be something helpful, and I'll get to that, but I must caution myself: I do not want to be so comforting that my comfort actually causes someone to proceed to that desperate act. Sometimes good intentions have bad consequences, and I am determined that no one will conclude from what I write here that suicide is ever acceptable.

[1] What Is Suicide?

To start, I'm not entirely sure just what suicide is. The reason being is that suicide is not the only motive for causing one's own death. "How can that be?" you might ask. Here is my answer.

Decades ago, a co-worker of mine accused Jesus Christ of committing suicide. He claimed that Jesus died because he chose to die, and if that's not suicide, what is?

I argued back this way: If a fireman rushes into a burning building, grabs a child, throws the child out the window into a safety net, but then he is himself unable to escape and perishes in the flames, is that an act of suicide? Using my co-worker's argument, it is, because the fireman took a direct action that brought about his own death.

While it is true that the fireman had assessed the likelihood of dying and rolled the dice with fate, so to speak, and lost, we would never call his heroic gamble a suicide. The same goes for Jesus dying for us.

Now let's ratchet up the argument. Suppose the fireman assessed the situation and *knew* he must die to save that child's life — he was in fact willing to exchange his life for hers. Is *that* an act of suicide? My co-worker's argument would still say, yes, because he *intentionally* brought about his own death.

I say, no. The fireman's act was not suicide, but was, in fact, an act of self-sacrificing heroism, and that is not suicide. Suicide requires the will to die, and the Bible says as much.

> ***John 15:13*** *Greater love hath no man than this, that he lay down his life for his friend.*

> **Romans 5:7** *For scarcely for a righteous man will one die: yet peradventure for a good man some would even dare to die.*

Neither the fireman nor Jesus was guilty of suicide. They must both be credited with heroic gallantry, and that is a far different thing from suicide.

By the way, I did convince my co-worker friend that Jesus' death was an act of heroism and not suicide. Whether he ever became a Christian or not, I don't know.

This situation is not rare but in fact happens all the time, where a person chooses to die to save another. I can think of people whom I would be willing to die for: off the top of my head there's my wife, any of my children, and any of my grandchildren for starters.

But what's the point? The point is that just because a person brings about his own death does not necessarily make it an act of suicide. Heroism is one alternate motive for bringing about one's own death, and heroism is not suicide.

So, there are two motives anyway that cause one to terminate his own life: suicide (the wish to die) and heroism (the wish that someone else live). Are there any other motivations for ending one's own life? Let me suggest a possible third.

[2] SELF-EXECUTION

Imagine, if you can, that you committed a murder. Not manslaughter, not any of those other variations of killing that are almost like murder but not quite, but actual murder: pre-meditated, full knowledge, sane, in-cold-blood murder. And imagine that you got away with it. Then imagine that years later your conscience got the best of you, that you could no longer live with the guilt, and you decided that justice finally had to be done — the death of your victim had to be avenged.

And so, you go to the police and confess your crime. You might say, "I committed a murder years ago. Law and justice demand that you arrest me, try me, convict me, and execute me." Now, there are two possibilities.

First: What if they believe you, convict you, and execute you? Is that suicide because you caused your own death? No, it is not. It is justice.

Second: What if they *don't* believe you? You take them to where you buried the body, but it's gone. They ask you, "Who did you kill?" You answer, "I don't know. Just some bum in an alleyway." Finally, it becomes clear to you that no matter what you do, you're not going to persuade the law that you had, in fact, committed the murder. In short, you are never going to get justice for your victim. What do you do then?

If you are really convinced that justice must be done, you take the only option available to you: you get a rope and hang yourself, and maybe leave a note explaining.

Now, is that self-hanging an act of suicide or something else? Is it self-execution?

Suicide is wishing to die and acting on that wish. But this person, this self-executioner, does not wish to die, what he wishes for is justice. In fact, if he wished to die (to escape guilt, for instance) that would defeat justice. Justice can only be served if he wished to live and was forced to die. *That* is justice.

My mind was drawn to this subject today because I saw a movie that ended with something like this. In the television series *Foyle's War* (about a British murder detective during WWII), in the 7th episode called "War Games", the story ends with the bad guy killing himself. It was certainly an act of suicide and nothing heroic about it. But it got me thinking about Judas Iscariot.

Now, I'm not asking you to agree with the argument I'm about to offer. But I am suggesting that there may be other motives besides suicide for ending one's own life. Heroism certainly is one such motive. Perhaps self-execution is another. And if you think about it, isn't that exactly the situation that Judas found himself in? Let's explore that example.

[3] JUDAS

Judas Iscariot is arguably the most despicable and tragic person in the Bible, perhaps in all history. For money, thirty pieces of silver, he betrayed his best friend and brought about his death. Then, overwhelmed with guilt and self-loathing, he committed suicide by hanging. So that's two deaths he caused.

Just for the challenge and the fun of it, I want to play the role of Judas' defense attorney, to play "angel's advocate" (certainly not devil's advocate). If there is an indefensible person, that person is Judas, and that's why I want to defend him. I think I can surprise you. You be the judge, the jury, and certainly the prosecuting attorney, and let's give Judas his day in court.

Here is my case:

Judas does not plead innocent, he does in fact plead guilty to the first charge. For money he betrayed his best friend Jesus, and in fact murdered him, and he confesses to that crime freely and without conditions.

> ***Matthew 27:4*** *Saying, I have sinned in that I have betrayed the innocent blood. And they said, What is that to us? See thou to that.* ***:5*** *And he cast down the pieces of silver in the temple, and departed, and went and hanged himself.*

Judas, understanding the enormity of his murder, submitted himself to the law and confessed and demanded justice. In other words, when Judas said to the Sanhedrin, "I have betrayed the innocent blood," what he was saying was, "I am guilty of murder, arrest me, convict me, execute me. Put *me* on a cross because that's what I deserve."

But they wouldn't arrest him. They said, "What is that to us?" And the reason they wouldn't arrest him is because if they did, they would be implicating themselves in the murder of an innocent man. If Judas was guilty of murder, then so were they.

So, what happened next? Judas did exactly what they advised him to do. They said to him, "See thou to it," which means, "*you* deal with it.," and he did exactly that. He "went and hanged himself." In other words, he obeyed their direct instruction.

The point I am making to the court is that when Judas hanged himself, that was not an act of suicide, to relieve himself of pain and guilt, but an act of self-execution, an act of justice. The law wouldn't execute him, so he took matters into his own hands: He executed himself *as he was instructed.* He had no alternative. Justice demanded he do it.

This interpretation is significant for two reasons:

First: Although Judas is guilty of murdering Christ and has already confessed to that, he is not guilty of murdering himself. His self-inflicted death was not a murder but was in fact an execution that needed to happen. No one else would do it so he did it himself. That is not suicide.

Second: Since Judas was in fact executed for his murder of Jesus, he did in fact pay the legal price: He was executed for murder. Now, whatever post-mortem penalties God wishes to inflict on Judas (hell or whatever), at least it cannot be said of Judas that he "got away with it." He didn't get away with it. He paid the full price for his crime.

And that's important because in American law there is the notion of double jeopardy.

> ***U.S. Constitution, Fifth Amendment:*** *Nor shall any person be subject for the same offense to be twice put in jeopardy of life or limb.*

Now if that legal notion has any meaning to the heavenly court, it must be applied here. And whatever penalty heaven inflicts on murderers who got away with it, heaven ought not to inflict that penalty on Judas because he *didn't* get away with it.

And regarding his own death, Judas should receive no penalty for that at all. He did not commit suicide, he was executing a murderer.

> ***Genesis 9:6*** *Whoso sheddeth man's blood, by man shall his blood be shed…*

Judas was simply being obedient to the express commandment of God. He was acting as executioner just as God, via the Sanhedrin, demanded.

My point: Causing one's own death is not always an act of suicide; there are other reasons why one might do that. Therefore, there is hope, and hope is what this is about.

[4] ALTERNATIVES

Quick review: The Bible says almost nothing about suicide, so that leaves us in a quandary. What I'm trying to do is to give families some hope that God has not slammed the door on their suicide loved ones — especially a child — and that maybe God has grace enough even for them, if for no other reason than as a show of grace to a believing and bereaving parent.

Now, what about suffering? There is cancer, and Parkinson's disease, and whole hosts of cruel and evil ways to die. Should a really sick person be allowed to terminate his own life to avoid such suffering? The Christian answer is I'd rather not because assisting a suicide even for a righteous motive might actually be a sin. And besides, euthanasia is unnecessary. How so? Because of…

> ***Proverbs 31:6*** *Give strong drink unto him that is ready to perish…*

In other words, give your dying friend whatever kills the pain. Back then that would generally be alcohol. Today that could mean morphine or any substantial narcotic to a person who is dying of cancer or any other painful disease. In other words, suicide and euthanasia are not the options that God permits. So don't think it for yourself and don't suggest it to another. And certainly don't help anyone terminate his or her own life.

Now let me separate this into two ideas. To help someone die can mean two different things. First, it can mean to help someone commit suicide, to cause themselves to die. That is morally questionable. Is it a sin or not? I accept that I don't know. But second, there is helping someone die when *death has already chosen them and there is no escape*. Your friend is not choosing death, that is already determined, but your friend is exercising a right to determine how and when to die when death is already certain. That cannot possibly be a sin. How can I know that? Well, what would Jesus do? Better is, what *did* Jesus do? After six hours of hanging on the cross, he said, "Father, into thy hands I commend my spirit," then, "It is finished." He allowed, actually caused, himself to die. Do we not have the right to do what Jesus did?

By what means might you help someone die? Well, there's the verse above. God *does* permit (per the verse above) the dying to get drunk and stay drunk to avoid pain, or in modern vernacular, stoned on whatever medication is strong enough to do the job. Doctors call that "snowing." In other words, passive euthanasia, allowing one to die with pain relief, is acceptable.

And how about this possibility? Why not a self-induced coma? Why should the dying have to suffer agony when we have the drugs to prevent it?

But illness is not the only reason people commit suicide. People sometimes choose to end their lives rather than to face overwhelming problems of life, for instance, bullying at school, bullying on the internet, abuse at home, financial disaster, guilt, psychological trauma, and more. To anyone who is so troubled that suicide seems the right answer, I have three pieces of advice.

First: There is an escape. You can simply refuse to go to school. You can shut down the internet, after all no one *needs* the internet, it's not oxygen. You can call child protective services. You can file bankruptcy. You can divorce an abusive spouse. Anything is better than dying, and especially dying by one's own hand.

Second: If there is no escape (like a molesting parent) there is still an escape. No problem is so bad that you can't just leave. I said that to a church class one time, and I drew lots of fire. They thought I was advocating divorce. I wasn't. I was advocating not committing suicide. Anything is better than suicide, including divorce, including running away, including just vanishing and going to some place of safety.

Third: If there *really* is no escape, remember, even this shall pass away. Time really does heal all, well at least most, wounds. True, some wounds cannot be healed, but they can improve with medical or psychiatric treatment. However bad your life is right now, in five years, I guarantee that it will be different. Jeffrey Holland (a Mormon apostle) said it like this: "Sometimes the only way out is through." Amen to that. And all you need to do to get out is to survive long enough to get through. Surely you can do that. Just survive and you'll be okay. And in the very worst case, death will eventually happen anyway, and not by your hand. There is this comforting saying (well, I think it's comforting anyway): "If the whole universe collapsed, it would only kill you once."

I don't mean to trivialize your current problems, I just mean to say, any decision you make is better than suicide.

Deuteronomy 30:19 *...choose life...*

[5] Defense

Now to the real issue. To those who have committed suicide, I offer a possible legal defense. And to their families, hope that God will not be so harsh. Here it is:

> ***1 Timothy 1:13*** *I obtained mercy: because I did it ignorantly in unbelief.*

If Paul got forgiveness for killing Christians (***Acts 22:4*** *unto the death*) and torturing them (***Acts 26:11*** *compelled them*) and escaped judgment simply because he was ignorant, why can't a suicide plead the same defense before God? "My life was so painful that I killed myself. But I did not know I was violating your commandment, so please God, forgive me." Isn't that what we all ask anyway? Forgiveness?

Now let me warn anyone who might be thinking, "I'll commit suicide then ask God for forgiveness based on ignorance." It doesn't work that way. That's not ignorance, that presumption. And God does not forgive presumptuous sins.

> ***Numbers 15:30*** *But the soul that doeth ought presumptuously…shall be cut off from among his people.*

So, if you are planning suicide, ignorance will not work as a defense before God, if for no other reason then you have just read this article and you now know better. If you're looking for a justification for a planned suicide, you haven't found it here. There is no forgiveness for presumptuous sins.

But what some of you *may* have found here, if you are a parent or a child of a suicide is hope. Hope that you might have a persuasive argument to bring to God's court to defend that person you love. Forgiveness is available, *if* the sins were ignorant.

Numbers 15:27 *And if any soul shall sin though ignorance…* ***:28*** *the priest shall make an atonement for the soul…and it shall be forgiven him.*

Was the suicide of your loved one done in ignorance? Well, you don't know that, do you? But it's fair to believe it. Also, there is the influence of chronic depression and mental illness which too often leads to self-harm or suicide. If that's not ignorance, it is at least not in the proper frame of mind. That is the plea you can make before God in your child's defense. There is hope. Remember that Jesus did say —

Luke 23:34 *Father, forgive them; for they know not what they do.*

If God can forgive those who killed his only begotten son, then why would God not forgive your loved one?

[6] Final Thought

For those who have lost a child though suicide, you now have a double reason to live right before God.

1 Corinthians 7:14 *For the unbelieving husband is sanctified by the wife, and the unbelieving wife is sanctified by the husband: else were your children unclean; but now are they holy.*

There is such a thing as divine nepotism. If God loves you, and if he loves you a lot, you might want to ask God, "Whatever divine favor you intend to grant to me, please grant it to my child instead."

Fair enough. After all, isn't that what atonement is all about, Jesus redirecting divine proxy favor from himself to us? And Jesus did say —

Matthew 21:22 *And all things, whatsoever ye shall ask in prayer, believing, ye shall receive.*

So, if you are a grieving parent of a child or have lost a family member to suicide, you should live your life in God's love as best you can, and ask God for comfort and mercy. Asking can't hurt. And why not? My bet is that one day you will be reunited with your unhappy child and share a happiness not known in this mortal life.

Thoughts

Proverbs 23:7, Romans 1:32

A fellow Christian once told me that good intentions will not save you, but bad intentions will damn you. I suppose that's true. And what are intentions but the thoughts of the heart, our deep down, core desires? It could well be that the whole purpose of life is to drill down to that core us and expose what we truly are to the universe.

The Bible has a lot to say about what we ought to do and ought not to do. But it also has plenty to say about what we ought to think and ought not to think. Here then is some thought advice from the Bible.

[1] Wrong Thoughts Make You Wrong With Yourself

> ***Proverbs 23:7*** *For as he thinketh in his heart, so is he.*
> ***Proverbs 4:23*** *Keep thy heart with all diligence; for out of it are the issues of life.*
> ***Matthew 15:8*** *But those things which proceed out of the mouth come forth from the heart; and they defile the man.*

What is this "thinketh in his heart"? We think with our brain, don't we? That's basic biology. Of course. Then what is heart-thinking all about?

Thoughts come into your mind like junk mail comes into your mailbox. There, you can consider it, read it, evaluate it, then keep it or toss it. But thoughts also come into your heart. And once a thought arrives there, it is joined to your soul; it becomes you.

Those "thoughts in your heart," if they are wrong thoughts, can make you someone that God doesn't want you to be.

It's not that bad thoughts are sin if they arrive in your brain and bounce off. But they become sin if they penetrate down to your heart. It's not what a man "thinketh in his brain" that does the damage but what he "thinketh in his heart." Those thoughts are what you are.

[2] Wrong Thoughts Make You Wrong With God

Proverbs 24:9 *The thought of the foolish is sin.*

Proverbs 15:26 *The thoughts of the wicked are an abomination to the LORD.*

Matthew 9:4 *And Jesus knowing their thoughts said, Wherefore think ye evil in your hearts?*

God can read our minds. Those "thoughts in your heart" do not go unnoticed by God. He's aware of who you really are, that inner-you that you think you have hidden. But God will find you out and use that to judge you.

Not just our deeds condemn us, but also the evil intent of our hearts, even though the intended sins are never actually executed. There might be many reasons why an evil person backs away from doing an evil thing: cowardice (the fear of getting caught) is one, lack of opportunity is another. Of course, not doing the bad thing for whatever reason is good. But still, the intent and the longing lingers.

[3] Are Wrong Thoughts Damning?

Doing bad things is sinful, that's clear enough. But what about thinking bad things? Is it really so bad to think something bad now and then? If the essence of sin is injury, what harm can a bad thought possibly do? Yielding to temptation is a sin, but is being tempted also a sin?

Thoughts flit in and out of your mind all the time. The question about bad thoughts is, are they really a part of you? Have they invaded your soul? Are they in your heart? A thought that you think in your heart is there to stay; you have allowed it to fuse with you, and it will be the devil (pun intended) to get rid of it.

But that soul-penetrating evil thought is not the kind of thought that most Christians fret about. Some Pharisee types will insist that if you think a naughty thought at all, even though you get rid of it quickly, that thought is evidence that you are not right with God because people who are right with God never think anything amiss.

If that is true, then we are all damned. So I will give you strong evidence that that is not true. That evidence is that Jesus was tempted — first with food, second with vanity, and third with power.

> ***Matthew 4:3*** *And when the tempter came to him, he said, if thou be the Son of God, command that these be made of bread.* ***:5*** *Then the devil taketh him up into the holy city, and setteth him on a pinnacle of the temple,* ***:6*** *And saith unto him, If thou be the Son of God, cast thyself down:* ***:8*** *Again, the devil taketh him up into an exceeding high mountain, and sheweth him all the kingdoms of the world, and the glory of them;* ***:9*** *And saith unto him, All these things will I give thee, if thou will fall down and worship me.*

How could Jesus reject a sin if he hadn't at least listened to the devil's offer to understand what the sin was so that he could say no?

Jesus did not sin, yet he heard the devil's offers before rejecting them. Therefore, sinful thoughts, *some* sinful thoughts, are not sin per se but are just the unavoidable wafting in and out of our brains of our daily "what ifs" that are an unavoidable part of being human.

We believe that Jesus was sinless, so that conversation that he had with the devil, those thoughts he was evaluating, cannot have been sinful even though he really did think about them.

Being tempted is not a sin. If the mere temptation is a sin, then Jesus is a sinner, and we believe he was not. So, how can there be sin in thought?

> ***Proverbs 19:21*** *There are many devices in a man's heart; nevertheless the counsel of the* LORD, *that shall stand.*

All kinds of things flow through our minds all the time, "many devices." But that doesn't mean that we are condemned for every mis-thought. What does matter is that we act on the counsel of the Lord and that it is always our intent to do so. However bad your thoughts are, do what God tells you to do and don't let the worst of your thoughts drill into your heart.

[4] So Thoughts Are Not Harmful Afterall?

Not so fast. The message so far is that it's okay to have a conversation with the devil now and then, but it's not okay to open a negotiation with him.

There is a whole class of thoughts that are sinful in and of themselves.

Romans 1:32 *Who knowing the judgment of God, that they which commit such things are worthy of death, not only do the same, but have pleasure in them that do.*

There is nothing surprising in the "they which commit such things." Doing sin is sin. Obviously. The surprise is in the "have pleasure in them that do." Here we find guilt by osmosis. The idea is, "I don't want to sin, but I do enjoy watching someone else sin." Well, guess what. That is sin. You are a participant by proxy. You are actually taking someone else's sin into your heart, and that's a risky thing to do.

And that's what this issue is really all about. Did that naughty thought flit through your mind and from there into your mental trash bin, or did it settle into your heart where it joined with your soul?

I saw a wonderful cartoon decades ago (I wish I'd kept it). Two guys were in hell surrounded by demons and fire. And one said to the other, "When I think of the sins I could have committed…"

That's the idea. Those sins were always in his heart. That he did not directly participate did not make him not a participant. It was the thoughts in his heart that got him in trouble because it was those thoughts that defined him.

People indulge in such thought-sins today through TV shows, movies, music, social media, or books full of violence, profanity, and lewd sexuality—entertaining themselves by watching, or listening to, or reading about other peoples' sins. Like the ancient Romans who were entertained by watching gladiators hack each other to death, if you think you're not held accountable for inviting those sins into your minds and hearts, think again. Jesus did say this:

Matthew 5:28 *…whosoever looketh on a woman to lust after her hath committed adultery with her already in his heart.*

[5] HOW DO YOU CLEAN UP YOUR THOUGHTS?

So, there is the challenge, namely, to keep the worst of our thoughts as far from our hearts as possible and to get them out of our minds as quickly as possible. To do that we probably need help. After all, even the apostle Paul had his continual struggles.

> ***Roman 7:14*** *For we know that the law is spiritual: but I am carnal, sold under sin.* ***:15*** *For that which I do I allow not: for that which I would, that do I not; but what I hate, that do I.* ***:17*** *No then it is no more I that do it, but sin that dwelleth in me.* ***:19*** *For the good that I would I do not: but the evil which I would not, that I do.* ***:24*** *O wretched man that I am! Who shall deliver me from the body of this death?*

Who indeed. This problem that Paul struggled with is the problem we all struggle with. And if doing right is a constant challenge, then thinking right is much more of a challenge.

This sort of sounds like that typical guilt transference trick, "the devil made me do it." An "I can't help it" excuse. If this were a lesser man, that might be true. But this is Paul. And while others are his equal (Peter, etc.) no one has given more (except Christ) for the truth than Paul. So, we ought not to doubt him. Sin *does* dwell in us and competes for our attention almost constantly and without relief.

What's the solution? Here are some Bible thoughts.

[5.1] TRUST GRACE

> ***Romans 8:1*** *There is therefore now no condemnation to them which are in Christ Jesus, who walk not after the flesh, but after the spirit.*

Always remember that it is a holy walk we are on and not a holy arrival. What we walk toward, what we seek after is the spirit and not the flesh. That does give us liberties, not to turn and walk in the wrong direction, but to accept that we are not yet where we want to be. But we are on the way.

[5.2] Pray

Psalms 51:10 *Create in me a clean heart, O God…*

Want a clean heart? Ask for it. God really does intervene, but only on request. If we think it is entirely up to us, then it is a hopeless battle that we fight.

[5.3] Commit

Job 31:3 *I made a covenant with mine eyes; why then should I think upon a maid?*

Who's in charge anyway? You or your eyes? The age-old excuse, "I couldn't help it," is utter nonsense. You do what you choose to do. Your eyes are not like a ring in your nose dragging you to where you don't want to go. It really does come down to free choice. Make yourself a promise and keep it.

A device that helps some people is to make a daily vow, or a weekly vow (I won't smoke *this week*). A monthly vow would be great but might not be keepable. Then just make another vow and so on for the rest of your life if necessary.

[5.4] STUDY THE SCRIPTURES

Psalms 119:9 *Wherewithal shall a young man cleanse his way? By taking heed thereto according to thy word.*

What God says matters. You can't make it up as you go along. What is right and wrong might not be what you think it is. But it is certainly what God says it is.

[5.5] RESIST

James 4:7 *Resist the devil and he will flee from you.*
2 Timothy 2:16 *Shun profane and vain babblings; for they will increase unto more ungodliness.*

Simply resisting goes a long way to reducing the devil's influence over you. As the mantra says, "just say no," and the temptation really does subside. Like a burglar who is looking for an open window, the devil will only spend so much time with a resisting target, then will move on to an easier mark.

[5.6] LOVE GOD MORE

Matthew 6:21 *Where your treasure is, there will your heart be also.*

If you want to be less attracted to evil, be more attracted to good. Your attention will be pointed to somewhere; if you don't like the direction you're facing, then turn. Point another way. Focus on what you want to be focused on, and you'll have less time to dwell on things you shouldn't be thinking about.

Tolerance

Every believer believes he or she is right in his or her own theology and that those who have a different opinion are by definition wrong.

Of course you believe you are right. If you don't believe you are right, you'd change your mind and believe something else. That goes without saying. It's tautological.

That of itself ("I'm right, you're wrong") is not a problem; that's just the nature of believing. The problem is when we believe that our rightness is so right that we are obliged to require others by some means (shouting? force? intimidation?) to believe as we do. That we call intolerance, or unbridled anger, and at its worst has caused Christians to burn other Christians at the stake or to die by other horrific means.

This natural impulse is, of course, not peculiar to religion. It crosses all human thought. People have killed each other over differing politics far more than they ever have over religion. But religion is where we ought to expect better behavior because it is, after all, supposed to be centered around love.

It's alright to disagree. It's alright to argue and debate. That's how truth emerges. It's even alright to get angry, as Jesus did when he cleansed the temple. But it is not alright to harm each other or to require by any means that others change their minds to accommodate our beliefs.

Our nation's founding fathers built into our Constitution protections against just such hostilities. Our first amendment guarantees (well, so long as our government allows it to guarantee) freedom of religion and freedom of speech, and those guarantees have made this a wonderful country — so far anyway. We'll have to wait and see what's ahead.

But doesn't the Bible require people to be Jewish? That's intolerance. Actually, no. It does not. The Torah defines many crimes to be capital crimes (with a death penalty): murder, kidnapping, sexual misbehavior, and others. But nowhere does the Torah define unbelief to be a capital crime or a crime at all. Sin is a crime. Not believing is *not* a crime, not anywhere in the Bible, and that is one of the reasons why the Bible is superior to other holy books — it does not require you to believe it, and that makes it a book worth believing because unforced belief is the only belief that matters.

What does the Bible say about tolerance? Anything? Well, some things. Here then is my short list of tolerance verses.

[1] THE HOUSE OF RIMMON

> ***2 Kings 5:18*** *In this thing the LORD pardon thy servant* [Naaman], *that when my master goeth into the house of Rimmon to worship there, and he leaneth on my hand, and I bow myself in the house of Rimmon: when I bow down myself in the house of Rimmon, the LORD pardon thy servant in this thing.* ***:19*** *And he* [Elisha] *said unto him* [Naaman], *Go in peace.*

Are we absolutely forbidden to participate in a false religion? Some Christians won't even go into the place of worship of another Christian church because they feel that other churches are apostate. What happened in this story of Naaman nudges us to a more tolerant view.

Naaman is now a believer in the true God, but his employer is the aging king of Syria. What Naaman is concerned about is that when he helps his boss go to church (so to speak) and helps his boss bow to a false god in a false house of worship, he himself,

Naaman, is required to bow with him. Naaman is asking the prophet Elisha, am I offending God when I do that? And Elisha's answer is no, you're fine, "Go in peace."

[2] The Magicians of Babylon

> ***Daniel 2:24*** *Therefore Daniel went in unto Arioch, whom the king had ordained to destroy the wise men of Babylon: he went and said thus unto him; Destroy not the wise men of Babylon:*

This is a vital point. Daniel used his privileged knowledge to save the lives of false prophets. He could have used this opportunity to kill all of them and install Jewish religion everywhere, but he didn't. This is a foundational verse for religious tolerance.

The Mormon church has a list of Articles of Faith which summarizes their core beliefs. One of them I call the article of tolerance. It reads thus —

> ***Article of Faith 11:*** *We claim the right to worship almighty God according to the dictates of our own conscience and allow all men the same privilege. Let them worship how, where, or what they may.*

This article guarantees that there will never be a Mormon inquisition.

That sentiment is today (finally) pretty much an axiom of most of Christianity. It will be nice when it is also an axiom of all religions and political leanings worldwide. That will be a day to bless.

A further thought on Daniel —

> ***Daniel 2:30*** *But as for me, this secret is not revealed to me for any wisdom that I have more than any living, but for their sakes that shall make known*

the interpretation to the king, and that thou mightiest know the thought of their hearts.

The reason that God revealed the king's dream to Daniel was for their sakes. In other words, God did it to save the lives of the magicians. That goes beyond tolerance. If even God is tolerant of and merciful to those who do not believe in him, then perhaps we should be as well.

[3] ISRAEL AND EVERYONE ELSE

Yes, it is true that Israel was (is) an elect nation (***Isaiah 45:4***), the apple of God's eye (***Deuteronomy 32:10***). But God never intended for Israel to have an "us only" relationship with him. What God had always intended was —

> ***Genesis 12:3*** *…and in thee* [Abraham] *shall all the families of the earth be blessed.*

[4] YOUR CALLING

You may believe that you belong to God's only true church. Many Christians believe that, and I won't challenge that — I'm sure there is merit in your claim. But do remember that whatever dispensation, or revelation, or commission you believe you and your people have received from God, God gave that truth to you to bless others, not to pick a fight.

Further, I ask you to consider at least the possibility that others have also received a directive which, while different from his directive to you, is from God anyway. Just consider that maybe that's true, and therefore, we should treat all Christians as fellow servants working toward a common goal.

Luke 9:49 *And John answered and said, Master, we saw one casting out devils in thy name; and we forbade him, because he followeth not with us.* ***:50*** *And Jesus said unto him, Forbid him not: for he that is not against us is for us.*

Numbers 11:27 *And there ran a young man, and told Moses, and said, Eldad and Medad do prophecy in the camp.* ***:28*** *And Joshua the son of Nun, the servant of Moses, one of his young men, answered and said, My lord Moses, forbid them.* ***:29*** *And Moses said unto him, would God that all the* LORD*'s people were prophets, and that the* LORD *would put his spirit upon them.*

John 21:21 *Peter seeing him* [John] *saith to Jesus, Lord, and what shall this man do?* ***:22*** *Jesus saith unto him, If I will that he tarry till I come, what is that to thee? Follow thou me.* [Don't worry about John's business, you just take care of your own.]

God has asked you to do something. Good. Do that. But maybe God has asked someone else to do something else. Don't be so concerned about what God has asked others to do and how they're faring, unless of course you want to be helpful now and then, and that would be good.

Here's a brief story to illustrate this whole thing: The first Catholic church built in Salt Lake City was built on a plot of land that was given to the Catholic church by Brigham Young as a gift. The message was clear: "Welcome."

Why Do People War?

James 4:1

James 4:1 *From whence come wars and fighting among you? Come they not hence, even of your lusts that war in your members?*

Wars, before they become an external act of violence executed by our hands, are first an internal act of lust felt by our hearts. Lust causes war. Within our bodies are the desires that lead to violence. Our nature is to fulfill our desires, and when we feel our desires strongly enough and there is no way to get what we want except by violence, and if we do not have the moral wherewithal to check that desire, then the desire turns to sin, and the sin to violence.

James 1:4 *But every man is tempted, when he is drawn away of his own lust and enticed.* ***:15*** *Then when lust hath conceived, it brings forth sin.*

One might here jump to a conclusion that all desire, all "lusts," are sinful. That couldn't possibly be true. For if that were true, then what God would be urging us to do would result in the extinction of the human race. We need our desires, our lusts, our wants, our coveting to keep us alive. Man is nothing if not a package of wants. So, lust per se cannot be the sin in view here. Well, if not lust per se, then what is the sin in view here?

To answer that, let's take a careful look at the 10th Commandment, the commandment against coveting. After nine commandments of do's and don'ts regulating real behaviors, God's list concludes with a final commandment that regulates not behavior but thinking. God is interested not in just what we do but also in what we think.

> ***Exodus 20:17*** *Thou shalt not covet thy neighbor's house...wife...servant*...etc.

So, God is here policing our thoughts. But to what degree? We see that desire is not the issue here, but rather, very specifically, desire for those things which already belong to our neighbor. Those are the things that God does not want us to want. Why? Because they are out of reach. The only way we can possess those things that belong to our neighbor, assuming our neighbor will not sell, is to take what we want by harming our neighbor. And that is exactly what the other nine commandments specifically (and the law generally) are all about: preventing us from harming each other. God has no problem with us wanting and taking whatever our heart desires, so long as what we want does not already belong to someone else.

What the 10th commandment is telling us is this: Not only don't take things that belong to someone else, don't even want them. Thus, we nip the problem in the bud, overriding the natural impulse to get things by any means, including violence.

This is really important because, sadly, there is that impulse to violence in all of us.

> ***Romans 3:9*** *Are we better than they? No, in no wise.* ***:10*** *There is none righteous, no, not one.* ***:15*** *Their feet are swift to shed blood.* ***:16*** *Destruction and misery are in their way.* ***:17*** *And the way of peace have they not known.*

This is God's opinion of the whole human race. Violence is natural. Civility we have to struggle for. Society does not corrupt men, men corrupt society. The impulse towards sin and violence does not come from without, it comes from within.

> ***Mark 7:23*** *All these evil things come from within…*

Don't blame society, don't blame the devil, don't blame your parents or your teacher or the kids next door — evil is already in us, born in the human heart.

So, how can we possibly escape ourselves? There is a way, only one way.

> ***2 Corinthians 5:15*** *he died for all that they…should not live unto themselves but unto him…* ***:17*** *Therefore if any man be in Christ he is a new creature: old things are passed away; behold, all things are become new.*

How then do we defeat the natural impulse to grab what we want away from our neighbor, creating conflict and war? The answer is to refocus our wanting away from things and towards the one object that God wants us to want: Jesus Christ.

Thank you for reading

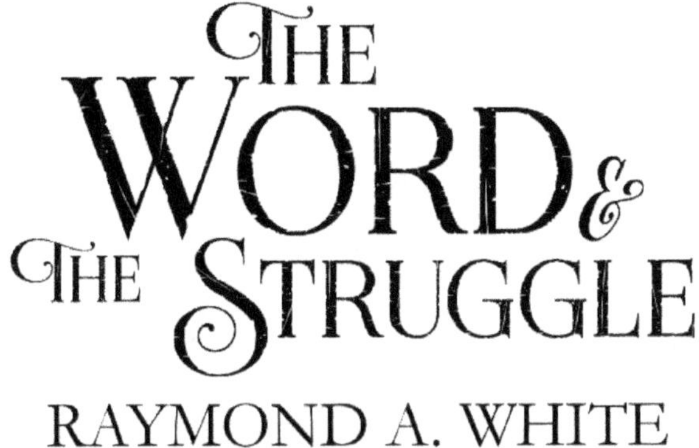

VOLUME III: THE CHARACTER OF MAN

Please post a review on your favorite online retailer.

To receive updates about the release of the next book in this series,

VOLUME IV: JESUS CHRIST

please join Skyrocket Press's email list here:
www.subscribepage.com/skyrocketpress

About the Author

Raymond A. White is a retired computer programmer who spent the bulk of his career at Jet Propulsion Laboratory working in the field of deep space exploration. He is also a lifelong student of scripture, having dedicated more than forty years of his life to studying ancient history and the Bible. In addition, Mr. White and his late wife of fifty-three years, are the parents of three adult children and grandparents to fifteen grandkids and four great-grandkids.

Learn more at:
http://www.skyrocketpress.com/

Read an excerpt from…

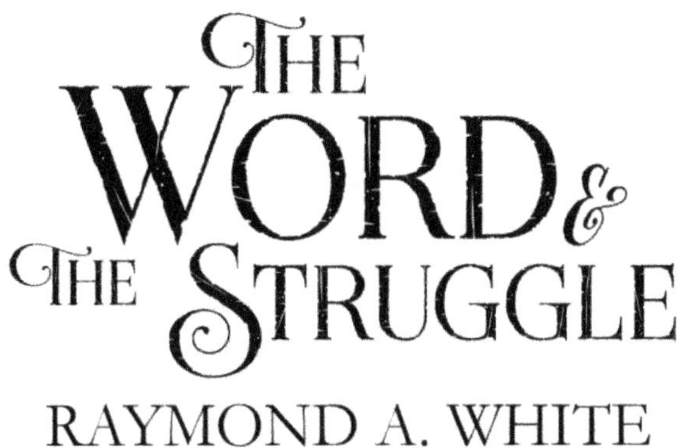

RAYMOND A. WHITE

VOLUME II: THE NATURE OF GOD

Contradictions in the Bible

Any Bible study would be less than honest without a fair acknowledgement of the many contradictions that appear in the divine text. What one does with them is another matter, but that they exist is undeniable.

Here are a few that I have noticed. I offer them, not to claim that the Bible is false, but rather that the Bible is true. By that I mean it is an actual account of man's dealings with God and an accurate reflection of the contradictory nature of man's existence. Contradictions exist in the Bible because contradictions exist in the reality that we live in. Mathematicians will, of course, point out that if a postulate contains even one contradiction, then the postulate must be false, and that certainly is reasonable. But that fails as an absolute when faced with Kurt Gödel's Incompleteness Theorem which proves that every mathematical system can be shown to have contradictions, and if they're *all* false, then we have nothing left. So, contradictions or not, math works.

Decades ago, when my daughter was in high school, she came home one day troubled by a teacher's assertion: "How can you believe in God when the notion of God is fraught with so many contradictions?" Presumably, the teacher had in mind things like the contradiction of predestination versus free will — stuff like that.

I recommended to my daughter to answer the challenge with this question: "How can you believe in science when it is fraught with so many contradictions?" Of course, I expected her teacher to reply to that with: "What contradictions do you have in mind?" So, I gave my daughter a short list:

- If nothing can escape a black hole, then how did the Big Bang happen?
- Is light waves or particles? Answer: Yes!
- Relativity says that black holes are singularities. Quantum mechanics says no.
- If nothing travels faster than light, how do entangled particles communicate?
- How can a quark spin in both directions at the same time? They do.
- Given Kurt Gödel's Incompleteness Theorem, how are we sure of anything?

So, don't tell me that theological contradictions are proof that God doesn't exist, because if that is so, then scientific contradictions are proof that the universe doesn't exist, and that is absurd. I never did hear back from her teacher.

What about contradictions and the Bible? They mean the same thing that contradictions in science mean, that reality is not so well behaved as we think it ought to be, and our brains are so far incapable of wrapping around it all.

One of my college physics teachers explained Heisenberg's Uncertainty Principle this way: First, he said if you know the electron's location, you can't know its velocity, and vice-verse. Second, he said that, therefore, the best we can ever know is the *probability* of its location and velocity, and he showed us a picture of a "probability cloud" which looked pretty cloudy. Then third, when a student asked, "Yes, but where is it really? What is the truth?" the teacher answered, "The *cloud* is the truth."

That, in my opinion, is the way to think of contradictions in the Bible and in science: The contradiction is the truth.

Before we begin, I ask one thing: When faced with a contradiction, do not pick one side to be your truth and reject the opposite side. That's the very sort of thing that caused Christians to burn each other at the stake in the Dark Ages, and that is exactly the kind of thing I want to avoid. And it can be avoided, simply by allowing the Bible to have its contradictions, and allowing *that* to be the truth. The cloud is the truth.

Now, let's begin.

[1] Sins of the Parents

Deuteronomy 24:16 *The fathers shall not be put to death for the children, neither shall the children be put to death for the fathers: every man shall be put to death for his own sin.*

Exodus 20:5 *...I the LORD thy God am a jealous God, visiting the iniquity of the fathers upon the children unto the third and fourth generation of them that hate me.*

Psalms 109:10 *Let his children be continually vagabonds, and beg: let them seek their bread also out of their desolate places.*

These verses contradict each other. Of course, we can point out that the first refers to law and the second to the tough life that some children have to endure in the real world, but that does not resolve the contradiction, not in the sense that both law and life's difficulties come to us from the mind and will of God. If God thought it unfair that children suffer because of their parents, he could have done something about it. He didn't, and laws, though well intended, can't change that. Legally, children shouldn't suffer for the sins of the parent. But actually, they do anyway. That's contradictory.

Mormons take a stab at resolving it by appealing to their 2nd Article of Faith: "Men will be punished for their own sins and not for Adam's transgression." If we just get rid of the notion of original sin, then we might get rid of the contradiction.

Well, not really. Original sin is just a Christian explanation of why children suffer, and Mormons reject it. But getting rid of the notion does not get rid of the problem that children do in fact suffer. We just try to do our best and look for another explanation of why.

Law helps, of course. It's illegal to abuse a child, and that's good. But it still happens. Also, you can't arrest the child of a murderer for being the child of a murderer. Such laws are good. But in terms of actual inheritance, the law has little impact. Innocent babies inherit syphilis from mommy's sexual misdeeds, brain damage from mommy's drug habit, stupidity, ugliness, poverty, and a host of other unjust ills, including abortion and sex trafficking, all from adults' decisions that children had no say in.

Don't tell me that children aren't punished for their parents' sins. That's a noble claim, but it's wishful thinking. Children always pay the price for their parents' misdeeds. That's why we parents must be so vigilant about *everything* — (our words, our deeds, our careers, our neighborhood, our whatever) — that can harm our children in the subtlest of ways. Yes, God wants us to keep our children safe, but it's easy to say, harder to do.

[2] Rahab's House

Joshua 2:15 *her house* [Rahab's] *was upon the town wall.*

Joshua 6:20 *the wall fell down flat.*

Joshua 6:22 *Go into the harlot's house, and bring out thence the woman.*

How can the Israelites go into Rahab's house when her house is on the wall and the wall is fallen down flat? Is this a trivial contradiction? Of course it's trivial, but it's a contradiction just the same.

[3] ISRAEL'S FORGIVENESS

Joshua 24:39 *He will not forgive your transgressions nor your sins.*

Isaiah 1:18 *...though your sins be as scarlet, they shall be white as snow...*

This is the essential tension of the Bible: Does God forgive or does he not? The answer is: It depends. Depends on what? On which verses you are willing to believe. Under certain circumstances, God will forgive, and under other circumstances, God won't. And knowing the difference is critical for your eternal good.

[4] GOD REPENTS, OR NOT

Genesis 6:6 *And it repented the LORD that he had made man on the earth.*

1 Samuel 15:11 *It repenteth me* [the LORD] *that I have set up Saul to be king:*

1 Samuel 15:29 [God] *is not a man, that he should repent.*

1 Samuel 15:35 *and the LORD repented that he had made Saul king over Israel.*

2 Kings 20:1 *...thou* [Hezekiah] *shalt die and not live...* ***:6*** *I will add unto thy days fifteen years.*

Ecclesiastes 3:14 *I know that, whatever God doeth, it shall be for ever: nothing can be put to it, nor any thing taken from it: and God doeth it, that men should fear before him.*

Jonah 3:4 *And Jonah began to enter into the city...and said, Yet forty days, and Nineveh shall be overthrown.* ***:10*** *And God saw their works, that they turned from their evil way; and God repented of the evil, that he had said that he would do unto them; and he did it not.*

Are we talking about the same God? God regrets making man, regrets making Saul king, says Hezekiah will die but then he will live, decrees Ninevah's destruction and then changes his mind. In 1 Samuel, God is adamant that he never changes his mind. But then he does change his mind, and then again insists that he doesn't change his mind. God seems to change his mind about changing his mind. If that's not a contradiction, I don't know what is.

[5] Who Blesses Who?

2 Chronicles 31:8 *they bless the* LORD.

Nehemiah 8:6 *And Ezra blessed the* LORD.

Nehemiah 9:5 *bless the* LORD *your God...and blessed be thy glorious name.*

Hebrews 7:7 *And without all contradiction the less is blessed of the better.*

The author of Hebrews bases his argument on logic, that if A blesses B, then A must be better than B.

That's reasonable thinking. The problem is that it doesn't hold up under biblical scrutiny. Ezra blessed the Lord. Does that mean that Ezra is better than the Lord?

The Hebrews text says, "Without all contradiction." Well, that's not true, is it? There is a serious contradiction here, and just saying "without all contradiction" doesn't make it so. And the author understood the seriousness of contradictions, that's why he insisted there isn't any — even though there is.

[6] CONVERTS ALLOWED OR NOT

> ***Nehemiah 13:1*** *On that day they read in the book of Moses…that the Ammonite and the Moabite should not come into the congregation of God for ever.* ***:3*** *Now it came to pass, when they had heard the law, that they separated from Israel all the mixed multitude.*

> ***Ruth 1:4*** *And they took them wives of the women of Moab; the name of the one was Orpah; and the name of the other was Ruth…*

Well, this is perplexing. Nehemiah and the neo-Jews decided to be hard-nosed, taking the law literally, and excluded all their neighbors from participating in Jewish religious observance. This "us-only attitude" resulted in massive divorce of Jews from their non-Jewish spouses ***(Ezra 10:18-44)*** and encircled the Jews with enemies who should have been their friends.

The monkey wrench in their "us-only" view was Ruth, the great-grandmother of David. She was a Moabite. So, would Nehemiah and Ezra have us excommunicate her posthumously? And also her posterity? Including King David and Jesus Christ?

Now, I understand their need to be apart. Before the Diaspora, their willingness to blend with and accommodate other religions got them in serious trouble sacrificing children which brought on the Diaspora. They didn't want to make that mistake again.

But what the law meant, I think, was, yes, only Jews could participate, but anyone could *become* a Jew, like Ruth did, like Rahab did. Why Nehemiah and Ezra were so hard-nosed about it, to the point where they did not allow converts, I can't say. But they were wrong, in my opinion. And remember, Nehemiah and Ezra were not prophets, they were scribes just struggling to figure out what God wanted them to do. This mass divorce seems to me to have been an over-kill, but at the time and under their circumstances (trying to restore their country and their religion) it seemed like the right thing to do.

[7] The Perfect Sinner

Job 1:1 *There was a man in the land of Uz, whose name was Job; and that man was perfect…* ***:3*** *And the* L*ORD said unto Satan, Hast thou considered my servant Job, that there is none like him in the earth, a perfect and upright man.* ***:4*** *And Satan answered the* L*ORD…* ***:5*** *But put forth thine hand now, and touch his bone and his flesh, and he will curse thee to thy face.*

Job 7:20 [Job says] *I have sinned…* ***:21*** *And why dost thou not pardon my transgression, and take away my iniquity?*

God says Job is perfect, but Job says he is a sinner. So, who's right?

This is the exact opposite of what usually happens. Most people say they're okay, and God says no they're not. So, again, who's right? This is very much like the righteous Able confessing his sins while the wicked Cain insists that he's okay. In the end, it doesn't much matter what you think about you, it only matters what God thinks about you. But this disagreement between God and Job is at least interesting because God saying Job is perfect while Job says he is a sinner is a clear contradiction.

[8] Being Good and Getting Rewarded

But even more interesting (still in Job) is the issue that Satan brings up to God: God says Job is perfect, and Satan counters with (to paraphrase): "Well of *course* he's perfect. He has everything he wants. Where is the so-called uprightness in that? Uprightness is only measured by what a man sacrifices to be upright. Job sacrifices nothing, so there's nothing extraordinary about his life to brag about. Now, separate him from his 'stuff', *then* we'll see just how upright, how perfect he really is."

Good point, so good that God pays attention and acquiesces. "You know," (to paraphrase), "you're right. Let's put him to the test and see if his uprightness is real."

So, where is the contradiction? Well, there is this —

James 1:13 *Let no man say when he is tempted, I am tempted of God: for God cannot be tempted with evil, neither tempteth he any man.*

But isn't that exactly what God is doing? Tempting Job? Well, we could say that God didn't do the actual tempting, Satan did. But in criminal law, if someone hires someone else to commit a crime, aren't the two equally guilty?

[9] Giving

Luke 6:30 *Give to every man that asketh of thee…*

2 Thessalonians 3:10 *…if any would not work, neither should he eat.*

Here's politics at work in the Bible. Jesus appears to be a Democrat and Paul appears to be a Republican. The problem of giving to *everyone* who has a hand out is that it is a formula for bankruptcy. This is the whole entitlement rift that separates our two political parties. Too much generosity may yet sink our country simply because beggars cannot resist taking. Everyone appreciates generosity. But for the want of a meal, does it make sense to kill the golden goose? Basically, the Bible authors faced the same tensions that everyone else faces, in this case, the tensions of being overly generous.

Let's dig a little deeper.

Deuteronomy 23:24 *When thou comest into thy neighbour's vineyard, then thou mayest eat grapes thy fill at thine own pleasure; but thou shalt not put any in thy vessel.* ***:25*** *When thou comest into the standing corn of thy neighbour, then thou mayest pluck the ears with thine hand; but thou shalt not move a sickle unto thy neighbour's standing corn.*

There are two messages in these verses. *First:* People who are traveling are welcome to help themselves to the crops of the local farmers. There was no McDonald's in those days but with food everywhere, who needs McDonald's? Just take some, it's not theft. Jesus and his disciples did just that.

Luke 6:1 *…he* [Jesus] *went through the corn fields, and his disciples plucked the ears of corn, and did eat…*

Second: Yes, you may take, but you may not *take-out.* Vessels and sickles are not permitted, only what you pick with your own hands is permitted. Also, you may help yourself only to standing corn; you may not help yourself to the harvest, the barns, the silos, the wagons, etc. So, yes, farmers are to be generous, but only to a point, certainly not to the point of impoverishing the farmer and his family. To give everything would destroy civilization. So, the contradiction of giving or not giving is resolved with a little common sense.

The Mormons have a verse that speaks to this issue:

> ***Doctrine and Covenants 56:16*** *Woe unto you rich men, that will not give your substance to the poor, for our riches will canker your souls; and this shall be your lamentation in the day of visitation, and of judgment, and of indignation: The harvest is past, the summer is ended, and my soul is not saved!* ***:17*** *Wo unto you poor men, whose hearts are not broken, whose spirits are not contrite, and whose bellies are not satisfied, and whose hands are not stayed from laying hold upon other men's goods, whose eyes are full of greediness, and who will not labor with your own hands!*

That sort of says it all. Woe to the rich who will not share, and woe to the poor who will not work but demand that everything be given to them. This sounds like the ongoing battle between Republicans and Democrats, the Democrats saying give everything to everybody, and Republicans saying not so fast, let's try to not bankrupt the country so that nobody has anything. Both sides have a point. Where do you draw the line? We can hope that's what politics — and common sense — is about.

[10] FORGIVE TO BE FORGIVEN

> ***Matthew 18:35*** *So likewise shall my Heavenly Father do likewise unto you, if ye from your hearts forgive not every one his brother their trespasses.*

Luke 15:28 And he [brother of the Prodigal] *was angry, and would not go in: therefore came his father out, and intreated him.* ***15:31*** *And he said unto him, Son, thou art ever with me, and all that I have is thine.*

There is a slight contradiction between these two parables of Jesus. In the Unforgiving Servant, Jesus asserts that if you don't forgive, God won't forgive you. But in the Prodigal Son, the father does forgive the faithful son for not forgiving his brother — "thou art ever with me, and all that I have is thine."

I think there is a difference between an unforgiving *attitude* and an unforgiving *act.* The Prodigal Son story comforts us by telling us that God is not so petty that he would condemn us just because we are wrestling with forgiveness.

But more importantly, there is the matter of *practical* forgiveness. We haven't disbanded our courts, nor should we *(**Romans 13:1-5**)*. And Paul, the most forgiven man on the planet, excommunicated people for sexual transgression *(**1 Corinthians 5:5**)*.

Also, Jesus tells me to forgive someone who sins against *me,* but is that telling me to forgive someone who sins against *you?* That would be presumptuous, and unjust.

So, there is a real tension in the Bible, and in criminal law, about the subject of forgiveness. How much forgiveness is too much forgiveness?

[11] Always Tell the Truth

Proverbs 12:22 *Lying lips are abomination to the* L*ORD: but they that deal truly are his delight.* ***:23*** *A prudent man concealeth knowledge…*

These two verses are immediately contradictory. If honesty is always God's delight, why are some truths good to conceal? There seems to be a spirit of the law that differs slightly from the letter of the law. Yes, God wants honesty, but if I am hiding a Jew in my attic, and a Nazi asks me if there is a Jew in my attic, I will certainly lie to the Nazi and worry later about defending my lie to God.

There is just such a story in the Bible.

> ***1 Samuel 19:14*** *And when Saul sent messengers to take David, she* [David's wife, Michal] *said, He is sick.* [David wasn't sick; Michal lied to save his life.]

> ***1 Samuel 20:28*** *And Jonathan answered Saul, David earnestly asked leave of me to go to Bethlehem.* [David didn't go to Bethlehem; Jonathan lied to save his life.]

Both Michal and Jonathan were willing to lie straight-faced to the king in order to save David's life. Does that make them dishonest people? You tangle with that.

[12] GLUTTONY

> ***Proverbs 23:21*** *The glutton shall come to poverty.*

> ***Proverbs 24:13*** *Eat thou honey because it is good.*

There's a fine line, I guess, between enjoying good food and gluttony. People get fat because they either don't know the difference or just have no restraint or just don't care. Remember Winnie the Pooh looking at Rabbit's honey store and pleading, "I don't want to eat it, I just what to taste it." Maybe it's true: You can't eat just one.

[13] FOOLS

Proverbs 26:4 *Answer not a fool according to his folly, lest thou be like unto him.*

Proverbs 26:5 *Answer a fool according to his folly, lest he be wise in his own conceit.*

These two back-to-back verses contradict each other. So, which is it? Engage a fool's stupidity or don't bother? I suppose it matters just how stupid his stupidity is. And someone (I don't know who) once said, "Some ideas are so stupid that only intellectuals could believe them."

[14] GOOD PEOPLE PROTECTED

Ecclesiastes 8:13 *But it shall not be well with the wicked, neither shall he prolong his days…*

Ecclesiastes 8:14 *…there be just men, unto whom it happeneth according to the work of the wicked; again, there be wicked men unto whom it happeneth according to the work of the righteous…*

These two verses not only contradict each other, but amusingly, they are back-to-back. Did the author not know what he was writing? Of course, he knew. He is just expressing the realities of life.

More —

Proverbs 10:3 *The LORD does not suffer the soul of the righteous to famish: but he casteth away the substance of the wicked.*

Ecclesiastes 7:15 *All things have I seen in the days of my vanity: there is a just man that perisheth in his righteousness, and there is a wicked man that prolongeth his life in his wickedness.*

This rare splash of pessimistic truth in Ecclesiastes contradicts almost the whole of Proverbs which says exactly the opposite, promising happiness and long life to the righteous, and an early death to the wicked.

Actually, both are true. Proverbs is simply pointing out the probabilities, the trend. It is true that a smoker is *far more likely* to die of cancer, but it is by no means certain. And when the opposite happens — like when comedian George Burns lived to a ripe old age in spite of his smoking while his wife Gracie died young of lung cancer from *his* cigar smoke — that seems a great injustice. And it is. But sometimes the unlikely gets you.

The good life that we expect from good living (as Jesus calls the "abundant life") is a matter of playing the odds, isn't it? And that's a good bet to make, especially when eternal life is at stake.

Contradictions abound, but I'll still bet my soul on the Bible. Jesus, was once aggravated with the crowd that had just abandoned him, and he asked his disciples if they wanted to leave him too. Peter replied, ***(John 6:68)*** *Lord, to whom shall we go?* Wise words. And another time, when the disciples were in a boat about to sink in a storm, and they saw Jesus walking on the water, Peter jumped from the boat to get to Jesus ***(Matthew 4:28).*** The point being that in a storm, it's safer to be near Jesus than in a sinking boat. Here's a saying that I like: "He is no fool who trades that which he cannot keep for that which he cannot lose."

[15] Be Righteous

Ecclesiastes 7:16 *Be not righteous over much; neither make thyself over wise: why shouldest thou destroy thyself?*

Matthew 5:48 *Be ye therefore perfect…*

This is for those who struggle so hard to be perfect. I know Jesus said, "Be perfect," and that's a right demand for God to make. But Jesus realized we are never going to be perfect and can never be, and so went to the cross for us.

And in our quest for righteousness, there does seem to be an over-righteousness. Some people become *so* righteous that they are impossible to live with. And in spite of Jesus calling us to perfection, there has to be moderation even in that. Jesus even calls some people out on that: ***Matthew 23:5*** *But all their works they do for to be seen of men.*

So, how do we balance the two? Trying to be perfect only to realize that we're trying too hard. Maybe that's the point where we turn to grace and have a little more confidence in God's love for us — and get over this "I'll never be good enough" existential panic.

[16] Work Hard, or Don't Bother

Proverbs 12:24 *The hand of the diligent shall bear rule.*

Proverbs 13:4 *the soul of the diligent shall be made fat.*

Proverbs 14:23 *In all labour there is profit.*

Proverbs 21:5 *The thoughts of the diligent tend only to plenteousness.*

Ecclesiastes 9:11 *...the race is not to the swift, nor the battle to the strong, neither yet riches to men of understanding, nor yet favour to men of skill; but time and chance happeneth to them all.*

Proverbs is wonderfully optimistic, and Ecclesiastes is wonderfully pessimistic. Does that make the Bible wrong? No. It makes the Bible true. The Bible's contradictions reflect the contradictions of real life. The optimist and the pessimist are both correct. The contradictions are the truth! The Bible authors simply reported events, and they reported them correctly.

Don't like contradictions? Too bad. Life is made of them.

Ecclesiastes 11:6 *In the morning sow thy seed, and in the evening withhold not thine hand: for thou knowest not whether shall prosper, either this or that, or whether they both shall be alike good.*

This verse resolves the contradiction between ***Ecclesiastes 9:11*** and all those optimistic Proverbs verses. This is saying work does have its rewards, but due to luck's flakiness, you'd better work harder and longer because you don't know exactly which effort will pay off. This is a really good verse.

The good life that we expect from good living is a matter of playing the odds. And that is *usually* a good bet, especially when eternal life is at stake.

[17] WORDS AND BOOKS

Ecclesiastes 12:10 *The preacher sought to find out acceptable words: and that which was written was upright, and words of truth.*

Ecclesiastes 12:12 *And further, by these, my son, be admonished: of making many books there is no end; and much study is a weariness of the flesh.*

My note to the author of Ecclesiastes: Make up your mind! Is the preacher wise because he thinks through these philosophical tangles, or is he a fool for wasting his time with so much *weariness of the flesh?* I guess it just depends on if he's having a good day or a bad day.

[18] Lamentation

Jeremiah 16:6 *…neither shall men lament for them…*

How can we take this verse seriously when Jeremiah writes an entire book that he calls Lamentations? *He* lamented for them. This verse contradicts an entire book!

[19] Escape

Jeremiah 44:27 *…all the men of Judah that are in the land of Egypt shall be consumed by the sword and by the famine, until there be an end of them.*

Jeremiah 44:28 *Yet a small number that escape the sword shall return out of the land of Egypt into the land of Judah…*

Sounds contradictory to me. In one breath God says, "You're all going to die." In the next breath God says, "Well, I didn't mean all of you." If you didn't mean all, God, then why did you say all? "Until there be an end of them" sounds quite literal, not an exaggeration.

[20] The Anti-Christ and His God

Daniel 11:37 *...nor regard any god...* ***:38*** *...shall he honour the God of forces: and a god whom his father knew not...*

Which is it? Will the anti-Christ worship no gods or gods of his own creating?

[21] The Holy Ghost

Matthew 12:28 *...if I cast out devils by the spirit of God...*

John 14:26 *But the comforter, which is the Holy Ghost, whom the Father will send in my name...*

Mark 6:7 *...and gave them power over unclean spirits.*

This is a three-way contradiction. [1] Jesus casts out devils by the spirit, [2] the Holy Ghost hasn't come yet but will, and [3] Jesus gives his disciples power over devils which means he gave them the spirit which hasn't come yet.

[22] Violence

Luke 3:14 [John the Baptist to soldiers] *Do violence to no man...*

Romans 13:4 *...he beareth not the sword in vain...*

The words of John the Baptist in Luke are certainly an exaggeration. If you strip the police of their ability to use lethal force against criminals, then you permit crime to grow unabated. Paul knows that; John seems not to.

[23] THE RICH

Luke 6:24 *…woe to the rich…*

Luke 7:9 *I have not found so great faith, no, not in Israel.*

Here is one rich man, a Centurion and a gentile, rich enough to have built a synagogue as a gift to the Jews. That impressed Jesus, enough to heal the Centurion's servant.

What happened to "woe to the rich"? Well, I guess it depends on what kind of rich, doesn't it? There was Zacchaeus ***(Luke 19:2)*** and Lazarus and Barnabas and a few other rich people that Jesus liked to hang with, so "woe to the rich" is not an absolute.

[24] CONVERTED BY THE DEAD

Luke 16:31 *And he* [Jesus] *said unto him, If they hear not Moses and the prophets, neither will they be persuaded, though one rose from the dead.*

Acts 9:6 *And he* [Paul] *trembling and astonished said, Lord, what will thou have me do?*

I understand Jesus' point, that many won't believe even if a dead person returned to them. Yet isn't that exactly what Saul of Tarsus did? Didn't he believe and become a Christian because "one rose from the dead (Christ)" and spoke to him? Isn't that the principal message of Acts? I saw him and believed?

[25] CHRIST THE SON OF DAVID

Luke 20:44 *David therefore calleth him Lord, how is he then his son?*

Jesus points to a biblical contradiction and says to some scribes (paraphrase), "That contradiction is the truth. Explain it." They can't, but it's still the truth, which is the point I've been making throughout this whole collection. The contradictions are the truth. We call them contradictions because our minds can't deal with them, but God still requires that we believe them.

[26] Not My Will

John 5:30 *...I seek not mine own will...but the will of the Father...*

These words are immediately self-contradictory. It is impossible to not seek your own will. It was Jesus' will to seek his father's will.

The problem lies in that we have wills in conflict ("cognitive dissonance," to make it sound technical). A fireman who rushes into a burning building to save a child does not wish to die, he wishes to live. But he wishes even more for the child to live, thus his two wills are conflicted, and the stronger will takes precedence. That's what "I seek not mine own will" means, as we see even more forcefully in the Garden of Gethsemane. Jesus does not wish to die, but he wishes to obey his Father more than to save his own life.

[27] A Good Man

Matthew 19:16 *...only God is good...*

Acts 11:24 *For he* [Barnabas] *was a good man...*

So, which is it? Is no one good or is Barnabas good? Of course, this is pointless. Then why am I pointing it out? To show it's pointless and should not hurt your faith.

There are big contradictions that are not pointless, like faith versus works, like predestination versus agency, like God's omnipotent love versus the existence of evil. They are inescapable, but none of them should keep you from believing. They're just perspectives on life and have nothing to do with how God really deals with us. Don't let the contradictions wear out your faith. A respected pastor, John McArthur, once said, "If you find a contradiction in the Bible, you can throw it away." Nope. Sorry, John. I disagree. I find contradictions all over the Bible, but I'm keeping it anyway.

[28] SIN AND DEATH

Romans 6:23 *For the wages of sin is death…*

Romans 7:8 *…without the law sin was dead.*

Sorry, Paul, you can't have it both ways. Either sin kills regardless of law, or sin kills only when triggered by law. Which is it? Can't be both. Paul, you're tripping over yourself. You're not reading your own words. Paul finally explains it my way:

Romans 7:13 *…sin by the commandment might become exceeding sinful.*

In other words, law makes sin twice as sinful. Sin is always sin, but broken law is its own sin. Therefore, sin plus law is twice as sinful. If that's what he means in ***7:8*** then I'm okay with that, but I think he exaggerates his point in ***7:8*** to absurdity. Even without law, sin is harmful. That's why it's sin. So, without law sin is dead? I don't think so.

[29] Faith and Works Versus Faith Alone

Romans 3:28 *Therefore we conclude that a man is justified by faith without the deeds of the law.*

Romans 8:1 *There is therefore now no condemnation to them which are in Christ Jesus, who walk not after the flesh, but after the Spirit.*

We can't escape this contradiction. ***3:28*** says no works at all, but ***8:1*** demands works (*walk after the spirit*). We can't be both ways, can we? Maybe we can. Clearly, ***8:1*** mitigates ***3:28***. Let's allow for the "holy walk" *(walk not after the flesh)* to not be a "holy arrival." Paul is not insisting that we live a perfect life but only that we reach *for* that perfect life by seeking the Spirit. So, if our works are inescapably flawed, then we'd better be trusting in our faith for our salvation rather than our flawed works. But those flawed works, flawed as they might be, are necessary, otherwise, where's the holy walk? It's the *striving* that God wants from us.

What's also interesting here is that both ideas are in the same book. I don't have to appeal to ***James 1:22, 2:20*** — as I have often done in the past — to highlight this contradiction. Paul contradicts himself. So, which do I believe? Uh, both.

[30] Continue

Romans 5:10 *For if, when we were enemies, we were reconciled to God by the death of his son, much more, being reconciled we shall be saved by his life.*

Romans 11:22 *Behold therefore the goodness and severity of God: on them which fell, severity; but towards thee, goodness, if thou continue in his goodness: otherwise thou shalt be cut off.*

These two verses say exactly the opposite. ***5:10*** says that because you are now reconciled and because Christ's life is stronger than his death, he is able to keep you. So don't worry. But ***11:22*** says that's true but only if you continue. So, which is it? Does Christ keep us (sovereignty), or do we keep ourselves (free choice)?

[31] Judge

Romans 12:17 *Recompense to no man evil for evil…*

1 Corinthians 5:3 *For I…have judged already…*

To judge or not to judge. The Bible is full of things like "judge not lest ye be judged," yet here is Paul, a man with a terrifying history of his own sins, judging a man whose sin seems minor compared to Paul's former life. Paul could beg off and say, "I'm not one to judge," but he knew better. God had called him to judge, and judge he must.

When you are called to jury duty, you must judge. If you beg off, or acquit the guilty on the pretext of "well, Jesus said 'judge not'," then you make yourself guilty.

"Recompense to no man evil for evil" means don't be a vigilante. It does not mean ending the justice of the law.

[32] Eating With Sinners

1 Corinthians 5:11 *…with such an one no not to eat.*

Paul tells us don't hang around with or even eat with bad people. But Jesus did just that, didn't he? Yes, he did.

Matthew 9:10 *And it came to pass, as Jesus sat at meat in the house, behold, many publicans and sinners came and sat down with him and his disciples.*

I suppose our understanding this contradiction has more to do with how susceptible we might be to the influence of bad people. Jesus was not susceptible to evil influence at all, so he could rightly go to people who needed him the most. There was one time, however, that he did avoid a hot spot.

Matthew 16:13 *When Jesus came into the coasts of Caesarea Phillippi, he asked his disciples…*

By "coasts" the Bible means "suburbs." This was not a beach town, but it was a party town like the Las Vegas strip. So apparently, Jesus did not venture into the city proper but was content to just visit its suburbs. You have discretion where to go and not.

[33] DIVORCE

Matthew 19:9 *…whoso marrieth her which is put away doth commit adultery.*

1 Corinthians 7:15 *But if the unbelieving depart, let him depart. A brother or a sister is not under bondage in such cases…*

The word *depart* can mean divorced and is translated that way in some versions (Contemporary English Version, New English Translation), but it has a much broader meaning and can also mean to separate, go away, abandon, leave, or walk out, all of which mean that a marriage is dissolved or is dissolving. Jesus is saying (or seems to be saying) that a woman who is divorced, even if it's not her fault, cannot remarry. That's a very harsh interpretation (I have a softer interpretation in my article on divorce in another book or on my website). Taking it at face value, Paul says the opposite, that an abandoned woman (my choice of words) is *not under bondage.* In other words, she can remarry. So, which is the truth? For this one, read my article, "Divorce".

[34] Silent Women

1 Corinthians 11:5 *But every woman that prayeth or prophesieth with her head uncovered dishonoureth her head…*

1 Corinthians 14:34 *Let your women keep silence in the churches: for it is not permitted unto them to speak; but they are commanded to be under obedience as also saith the law.*

Paul, how is a woman going to pray and prophesy if she isn't allowed to speak in church? Didn't think of that little detail, did you? And why the harshness against women? I assume it's just the characteristic of the age he was living in. Things have changed for the better, and Christianity was the main mover that changed them.

Another view some scholars believe is that Paul said no such thing but that additions to the text were added later by an anonymous author. I believe that.

[35] The "All Things" Paradox

1 Corinthians 15:27 *For he hath put all things under his feet.*

Creates an immediate self-contradiction, as Russell's Paradox. God cannot put himself under his own feet as the word "all" implies, and Paul knows it. That's why he continues by explaining a necessary inference:

> ***1 Corinthians 15:27*** *But when he saith all things are put under him, it is manifest* [obvious] *that he is excepted, which did put all things under him.*

So, this time anyway, Paul notices and corrects his own contradiction. Well, good.

This sort of paradox occurs in many places, such as in ***John 1:3*** *All things were made by him…* God certainly didn't make himself. Even though it doesn't say so, it's inferred. Clearly, we must allow such over-statements in scripture. If we hold scripture to its precise wording everywhere, we get nonsense. We have to allow people, even prophets, even the Holy Spirit, to talk as people talk, and that is: imprecisely. That relieves much of the contradictory tensions in the Bible.

[36] Not Imputing

> ***2 Corinthians 5:10*** *…everyone may receive things done in the body.*

> ***2 Corinthians 5:19*** *…not imputing their trespasses unto them…*

How can everyone receive the things done in the body if those things done in the body are not imputed, not kept a record of? I suppose that's Paul's point. But he doesn't resolve the contradiction. You are judged or you are forgiven. Can't be both, can it?

Maybe the contradiction is resolved if we allow "things done in the body" to include accepting God's forgiveness, so that "not imputing their trespasses" does not run afoul of judgement. Yes, I like that.

[37] Corinthian Saints: Are or Are Not

1 Corinthians 1:2 *...to them that are sanctified in Christ Jesus...*

2 Corinthians 5:20 *...be ye reconciled to God.*

Are these sanctified saints not reconciled, not atoned, not saved? How can that be? How can a sanctified saint become reconciled? Isn't he already?

[38] You Work or God Works

Philippians 2:12 *...work out your own salvation with fear and trembling.*

Philippians 2:13 *For it is God which worketh in you...*

These two verses are back-to-back which makes the obvious contradiction intentional. Is it you who is working in you or God who is working in you? Or both? I think both.

[39] Ignorance

1 Timothy 1:13 *...I obtained mercy, because I did it ignorantly in unbelief.*

1 Timothy 2:14 *And Adam was not deceived, but the woman being deceived was in the transgression.*

Paul received mercy because of his ignorance, but then turns around and blames Eve *because* she was ignorant. That makes no sense. Clearly (to me anyway), Adam was the transgressor because he was "not deceived." If you know better and do it anyway, doesn't that make you twice guilty? If either of them had an excuse, it was Eve. She, at least, could plead ignorance, as does Paul. I think ***2:14*** is just plain wrong, and Paul is just a little too eager to blame a woman. Let me remind you, Paul, of what else you wrote

Romans 7:13...*sin by the commandment might become exceeding sinful.*

It's the commandment that makes sin more sinful. So, how can Eve be held to a harsher account because she was ignorant? It's wrong, Paul, and it does seem that you are picking on her just because she is a woman.

[40] The Cretian Paradox

Titus 1:12 *One of themselves, even a prophet of their own, said, The Cretians are alway liars...*

How wonderful this verse is. It is Russell's Paradox right here in the Bible. Let me unravel it for you with this question: Is this Cretian lying or is he telling the truth? If he is telling the truth, then he must be lying because he said, "Cretians are always liars." But if he is lying, then he is wrong and Cretians are not always liars, and therefore, being a prophet, he is surely telling the truth. But if he is telling the truth ... and so forth. It's a reductio ad absurdum.

Does Paul know what he just wrote?

[41] Paul Versus James

Romans 4:2 *For if Abraham were justified by works, he hath whereof to glory; but not before God.* ***:3*** *For what saith the scripture? Abraham believed God, and it was counted unto him for righteousness.*

James 2:21 *Was not Abraham our father justified by works, when he had offered Isaac his son upon the altar?* ***:22*** *Seest thou how faith wrought with his works, and by works was faith made perfect?*

I am certain that James and Paul argued about this theological point, hopefully in private. Why am I certain? Because what James is saying no one would say just because it is obvious, *unless* he was saying it against someone else's assertion. Clearly that someone else is Paul. James' statement is an intentional poke in Paul's eye. What James is really saying is: "Paul, you've stretched your point beyond the limits of common sense, causing people to stumble. Now I have to reign you in a bit." James' words are too direct to not mean that.

Now let me ask you this: Is either one so right that the other must be damned for believing false doctrine? Of course not! These are the apostles, for heaven's sake. This difference of opinion will not get either of them damned, and I believe that in heaven, they are arguing about it still.

If that level of theological precision is not essential to their salvation, then why should we engage in such heated debates as we do over this very issue? We should learn to leave it be. Gratefully, we have long ago stopped burning each other at the stake.

[42] Conclusion

So, why did I put you through all this? (By the way, I hope you think it was fun and not tedious). I put you through this, not so you would disbelieve the Bible on account of its contradictions, but so that you *would* believe the Bible because of them. The Bible, like all the rest of us, has to struggle for consistency in a contradictory world. I also drug you through this so that you wouldn't take your own interpretations so seriously that you feel a need to take umbrage with your fellow Christians. You can discuss and compare, but don't argue. Arguing is pointless. It is all right for Christianity to be divided because:

[1] Our divisions have their roots in the Bible, in spite of Paul's admonition: ***1 Corinthians 1:10*** [Let] *there be no divisions among you.* Indeed, Paul likely caused more divisions than anyone else.

[2] The many divisions of Christianity actually make Christianity stronger. Just like an economy, it is innovation and competition that give the whole an immense power. Just like a nation, it is the separation of powers that guarantees freedom and motivates each participant to contribute fully. Christianity enjoys all of that and will yet move the entire world for good — if we don't kill each other.

[3] Who's to say that all those other churches have not received their revelation (their commission) from God as well as ours has? I know what I and my church have received, but I have no idea about you and your church. That's between you and God. It is as Jesus said to Peter: ***John 21:22*** *Jesus saith unto him, If I will that he tarry till I come, what is that to thee? Follow thou me.* In other words, Peter, don't worry about John, you just do what I asked *you* to do. And that applies to Christianity today: Don't worry about what other churches are doing, you just do what God has called you to do.

Contradictions in the Bible? Yes, there are many. And that's a good thing. Why? Because they not only keep me on my toes, but they also allow me, indeed require me, to live with and work with and get along with other Christians who have opinions different than my own. And that makes my Christian experience not only wonderful, but also interesting.

www.ingramcontent.com/pod-product-compliance
Lightning Source LLC
Chambersburg PA
CBHW070117100426
42744CB00010B/1850